THE THOUGHT OF CICERO

THE THOUGHT OF CICERO

PHILOSOPHICAL SELECTIONS

CHOSEN AND EDITED BY

S.J. WILSON, BA
FORMERLY SENIOR CLASSICAL MASTER,
METHODIST COLLEGE, BELFAST

PUBLISHED BY BRISTOL CLASSICAL PRESS
GENERAL EDITOR: JOHN H. BETTS
(BY ARRANGEMENT WITH BELL & HYMAN LTD)

This impression 2002
This edition reprinted, with permission, in 1986 by
Bristol Classical Press
an imprint of
Gerald Duckworth & Co. Ltd.
61 Frith Street, London W1D 3JL
Tel: 020 7434 4242
Fax: 020 7434 4420
inquiries@duckworth-publishers.co.uk
www.ducknet.co.uk

First published in 1964 by G. Bell & Sons Ltd
under the editorship of R.C. Carrington MA, D. Phil.
in the Alpha Classics Series

© 1964 by Bell & Hyman Ltd

A catalogue record for this book is available
from the British Library

ISBN 0 86292 192 9

Printed in Great Britain by
Antony Rowe Ltd, Eastbourne

GENERAL EDITOR'S NOTE

HITHERTO the Alpha Classics have been intended for pupils of the standard of the 'Ordinary' Level of the G.C.E. and equivalent examinations. The present volume inaugurates a series of advanced texts—the Alpha Classics designed for those who have reached, or are approaching, the Advanced Level. It is hoped that, with other volumes that are to follow, it may widen the scope of reading in the Sixth Form.

R. C. C.

PREFACE

THESE selections are offered in the hope that they may supply a need. It seems a pity that the reading of Cicero should be largely confined to his speeches and letters, and that pupils should often finish their study of Latin knowing little of the philosophical works, through which so many of the fundamental ideas of our own civilisation have come down to us. Yet they contain many interesting passages, not too difficult for Senior pupils.

An attempt has been made to choose passages coherent in themselves, and to group them so as to illustrate the Ciceronian point of view in ethics, politics, and religion. No alterations in the original text have been made, except for omissions and changes of punctuation. A few extracts from speeches have been added.

To give the essential background, an outline of Greek philosophy, severely compressed, has been included in the Introduction.

The intention of the Notes is to make rapid reading possible, while, to avoid repetition, some common Ciceronian idioms are given in a separate section.

The use of a dictionary is not precluded; but most words of less frequent occurrence are explained in the Notes, and a select Vocabulary contains a number of common philosophical terms.

For the text the Editor has made use of no single source, and acknowledges his debt to a variety of editions too numerous to mention in detail.

In addition to various editions of individual works, acknowledgement is due to the following: the *Oxford Companion to Classical Literature;* the *Oxford Classical Dictionary;* E. V. Arnold's *Roman Stoicism;* and Warde Fowler's *Social Life at Rome in the Age of Cicero.*

Finally, I wish to thank Prof. M. J. Boyd, M.A., of Queen's University, Belfast, for valuable advice; my colleague, Mr. J. A. Harrison, M.A., for his criticism and suggestions and for reading the manuscript; and Mr. P. A. M. Paice, B.A., to whom I am indebted for the line drawings.

S. J. W.

Belfast

January, 1964

CONTENTS

PLATES

OTHER ILLUSTRATIONS

I CICERO. This portrait dates from the first century A.D., and is probably a
copy of a contemporary original.

II THE SCHOOL OF PLATO. This mosaic from Pompeii (second cent. B.C.) shows Plato with his pupils in the gardens of the Academy, outside Athens, where he lectured from about 388 B.C. Cicero was much indebted to Plato, especially to his *Republic* and *Laws*, which he imitated. Quintilian even calls him *aemulus Platonis*, 'Plato's Roman rival.'

III ARISTOTLE (384–322 B.C.) ranks with Plato as the greatest of Greek philosophers. The Peripatetic School, which he founded, had lost much of its influence in Cicero's time, but, in the Middle Ages, Aristotle supplied the basis for philosophy and theology. Dante calls him 'the master of those who know'.

IV POSIDONIUS, of Apamea, later of Rhodes (135–50 B.C.), the most learned
Greek of his time, was equally famous as a philosopher, scientist and historian.
Cicero, as a young man, attended his lectures, and, although Posidonius'
works have been almost completely lost, it is clear that Cicero derived a great
deal from him.   Posidonius was also a friend of Pompey.

V ST. JEROME, by Albrecht Dürer (1471–1528). Jerome was a Christian scholar of the fourth century A.D. He is famous for his letters and his Latin version of the Bible, the Vulgate. At first he was repelled by the uncultivated style of the Scriptures, and used to delight in the classical writers. Then, one day, seized by a fever, he had a vision of judgement, and heard the voice of the judge condemning him in the words, *Ciceronianus es, non Christianus*: 'You are a disciple of Cicero, not of Christ'. The lion at the saint's feet is a symbol of passions subdued.

VI THE HOUSE OF LEARNING. This allegorical picture from the end of the fifteenth century shows the Seven Liberal Arts (see I 9 Note) inherited by the Middle Ages from ancient philosophy. Nicostrate, or Carmentis, prophetess and teacher of the ancient Italians, offers a pupil the alphabet. On the ground-floor is the school of Grammar and Literature, taught by the ancient grammarians, Donatus and Priscian. In the centre, above, is Cicero (Tullius), the master of Rhetoric. Logic, Arithmetic and Music, Geometry, and Astronomy are represented by Aristotle, Pythagoras, Euclid and Ptolemy. Metaphysics and Theology crown the edifice.

Diuisions 4 Aprilis die Mercurij

1. Omnis honestas rerum e quatuor partibus quarum una sit cognitionis altera communitatis tertia est magnanimitatis et clauoris ... quarta moderationis.

2. Defecta alia sunt magna quae facile apparent alia sunt parum quae plerumque sunt abdita.

3. Duplex est virtus una quae posita est in actione altera vero consistit in cogitatione.

4. Alij studiunt quo modo possint eloqui alij copiose prudenterq, alij cogitant optime fore eloquentia.

5. Rogamus et inquirimus non solum quid quisque se loquatur sed etiam quid quisq sentiat et quid de aliis sit in quis sentiunt.

DEFINITIONES

1. Prudentia est scientia rerum expetendarum et fugiendarum.
2. Sapientia est scientia rerum diuinarum et humanarum.
3. Iustitia est societas ac communitas universi generis humani.
4. Eloquentia eos complectitur quibuscum immunis amore.
5. Cogitatio vertitur in se ipsa.
6. Temperantia est omnium rerum moderatio.

Finis. Recitationis primi libri.

VII THE CICERONIAN TRADITION IN SIXTEENTH CENTURY EDUCATION.
This page from a Latin exercise book of King Edward VI (1546–1553), in the Bodleian Library at Oxford, shows philosophical precepts in Ciceronian language, written by the boy king, who came to the throne at the age of ten and died at sixteen. *Definitio 2* is the same as the definition of *sapientia* in XXXIX 36 f.

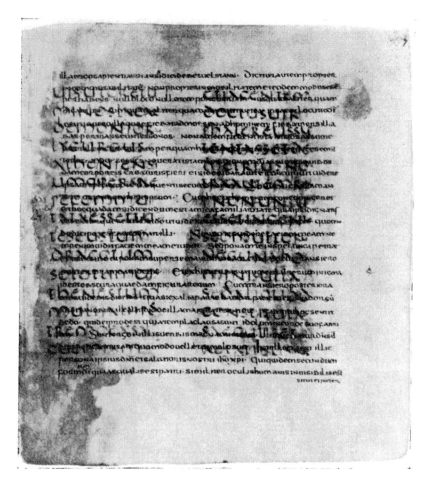

VIII   A Page of the Vatican Palimpsest of 'De Re Publica'.   The large
capital letters, known as uncials, date from the fourth century A.D., and are those
of the original Ciceronian text.   About 614 A.D. the manuscript was in the
Monastery of Bobbio in Northern Italy, where a scribe, either an ignoramus or
'*Ciceronis contemptor*', washed off the old text, and wrote over it a commentary on
the Psalms by St. Augustine.   In 1618, the monks presented it to Pope Paul V.
It lay in the Vatican Library until discovered in 1819 by Cardinal Mai, who
treated it with chemicals and succeeded in restoring a great part of the text of
Books I–III.   Our page begins at *suis, ut Cretam Minos* . . . and ends . . . *saeculis
et aetatibus. Nam,* which corresponds to XIII 13–20.

INTRODUCTION

I CICERO AND PHILOSOPHY

Cicero's reputation as a writer rests largely on his speeches. It is the fashion to ignore his philosophical works, and many who admire him as an orator would deny him the name of thinker. Yet these works contain some of his most brilliant writing, and it may even be claimed that they constitute his most valuable legacy. 'If we were required,' says a modern writer (Strachan-Davidson: *Cicero* p. 369), 'to decide what ancient writings have most directly influenced the modern world, the award must probably go in favour of Plutarch's *Lives* and the philosophical writings of Cicero,' while an ancient authority (Plutarch: *Life of Cicero* XXXII 5) records that Cicero often asked his friends to call him not an orator, but a philosopher, since philosophy was his real vocation, oratory only a means to an end.

II GREEK PHILOSOPHY

What philosophy meant in Cicero's time cannot be properly understood without some knowledge of its Greek background, since the Romans derived their philosophy, like their literature, from the Greeks.

1. Western thought began when the first Greek looked at the world as a whole and asked the question, 'What is it made of?' This was *Thales* of Miletus, who lived about the beginning of the sixth century B.C., and was reckoned by the Greeks as one of the Seven Wise Men. The answer

he gave, that the basic substance is water, may seem to us naive. But it is not the answer so much as the question which is important. It is the parent of both philosophy and science. To ask, 'What is the basic material substance of which all things are composed?' is scientific. To ask, 'What is the ultimate cause of all things, whether material or not?' is philosophic. The philosopher is more profound than the scientist, since he is seeking a complete explanation of the nature and origin of everything that is, while the scientist is satisfied with a physical explanation of what he observes. But, strange as this may seem in an age of specialisation like ours, neither Thales nor the Greek thinkers in general made a rigid distinction between the philosopher and the scientist. The same individual might be both.

Thales had many successors, who all made the same attempt to find a basic substance. Their answers were various. *Empedocles* of Agrigentum in Sicily (circ. 500 B.C.) imagined four basic elements, earth, air, fire, and water continually combining and separating under the influence of love and strife. *Anaxagoras* of Clazomenae, born about 500 B.C., thought of the world as originally a spherical mass, put into motion by a force, which he called *Nous* (intelligence), the ruler of all things. *Heracleitus* of Ephesus (circ. 500 B.C.), however, had already introduced scepticism with his idea that 'all things are in flux' (πάντα ρεῖ). He illustrated this by the saying that it is never possible to step into the same river twice. The conclusion of this would be that nothing is knowable, because there is nothing permanent that can be known.

2. Meanwhile, a new movement had been arising in Magna Graecia, as the Greek cities of Southern Italy were called. *Pythagoras* of Samos (born about 580 B.C.), settled here, fleeing from political tyranny at home, and founded a new society or brotherhood on monastic lines, whose members submitted to strict ascetic discipline, and to the

authority of their founder, whose *ipse dixit* was law. Thus a new attitude to philosophy was introduced: it became a way of life and a training for the soul (see XXXVII and XXXVIII). The main ideas of Pythagoras, much developed by his disciples, were:

(i) The doctrine of the soul, which, it was supposed, could pass from man to beast and vice versa (transmigration of souls).

(ii) The theory that number is the basis of the universe. Pythagoras arrived at this from his study of mathematics and astronomy, and of the relationship between the pitch of a musical note and the length of the string. He is said to have celebrated the discovery of his famous theorem about the right-angled triangle by sacrificing a hecatomb, or special offering of a hundred oxen.

(iii) Cicero (see II) repeats the tradition that he was the inventor of the name 'philosophy', the love of wisdom for its own sake.

The last great attempt to find a physical explanation for the universe, the atomic theory, is associated with the name of *Democritus* of Abdera (born about 460 B.C.) from whom it was taken over and developed by the Epicureans.

3. A new stage is marked by the appearance of *Socrates* (469–399 B.C.). He was not interested so much in physical speculation as in human behaviour (see II 34, where Cicero says that he 'brought down philosophy from the heavens to earth'). He held that virtue is knowledge and that nothing is so important for right living as knowledge of the truth. Indeed, he died a martyr for its sake. He went about asking questions like 'What is virtue?' 'What is temperance?' 'What is courage?' and sought to obtain true definitions of these by a method of question and answer. This was an admission, in the first instance, that neither he nor his listeners really knew anything. This ignorance was the starting-point of real knowledge. According to Plato, he was a strong believer in the immortality of the soul.

But he was regarded by his contemporaries as a dangerous innovator, who corrupted the youth and taught them to disbelieve in the national gods. On this charge he was condemned to death by drinking hemlock. In the *Apology* his disciple Plato gives us his account of his defence at his trial, and in the dialogue *Phaedo* his discourse with his friends about immortality on the last day of his life and a famous description of his death.

4. Socrates' disciple, *Plato* (427–347 B.C.), taught in the Academy at Athens and has left us a great number of brilliant dialogues. Since Plato was one of the world's profoundest thinkers, it is impossible to summarise his philosophy in a paragraph, but the following ideas may be emphasised:

(i) The soul is immortal, and knows truth before it enters the body. The physical world is ever-changing and not fully real. The soul can only know when it escapes from the deception of the senses and recollects the reality it once knew before birth. This Platonic doctrine that knowledge is recollection and that the body is the prison of the soul, finds notable expression in English in Wordsworth's famous 'Ode on the Intimations of Immortality', and in Shelley's 'Adonais':

> The One remains, the many change and pass:
> Heaven's light for ever shines, Earth's shadows fly;
> Life, like a dome of many-coloured glass,
> Stains the white radiance of Eternity.

(ii) The supreme object of learning is to raise the soul above time and sense to the contemplation of the eternal world, which alone is real (*cp.* Cicero's account of the progress of the soul in XXXVI).

(iii) The supreme good of society is justice, which is not, as popularly supposed, the interest of the stronger but the harmonious relation of all the elements in the state. This can only be attained when the state is governed by those whose souls have been trained in the principles of reason *i.e.* by philosophers. Plato's ideal state is described in the *Republic*.

5. *Aristotle* (384–322 B.C.), a pupil of Plato, taught in the Lyceum at Athens, and his school became known as the Peripatetic, from his habit of walking about while lecturing.

(i) He was a pupil of Plato and developed all that was true in his master's doctrine without what he considered some of his errors, *e.g.* undue scorn for the evidence of the senses.

(ii) He aspired to universal learning and his systematic treatises cover the whole field of knowledge.

(iii) He provided philosophy with a terminology and a classification which, in its Latin form, has come down to our own day.

Important works of Aristotle are:

(*a*) His treatises on *Logic*, which he founded and practically completed. His formulation of the laws of thought has remained valid since his time.

(*b*) *Ethics*, in which he discusses man's chief good or end (τέλος, *summum bonum*). This is attained when all the faculties reach their full and harmonious development without over-emphasis on either reason or the passions. Thus virtue is a mean between excess and defect (see IX 36).

(*c*) *Physics*. Here Aristotle was limited by the astronomy of his time, but treated in a profound manner the problems of time, space, and motion, of cause and effect.

In his treatises on *Biology* he shows extraordinary powers of observation.

(*d*) *Metaphysics*, or First Philosophy, which investigates the first and ultimate causes of all things, and is thus superior to the individual sciences, because it deals with the fundamental principles which lie at the basis of them.

So comprehensive was Aristotle's system and so illuminating his division of philosophy into distinct branches, that he was regarded in the Middle Ages as '*the* philosopher.' Dante calls him 'the master of those who know.'

6. After the conquest of the Greek world by Alexander, there was a decline in thought and nothing essentially fresh was added to the great systems of Plato and Aristotle. On the other hand, there was a renewed demand that philosophy should be the guide of life, and this produced two doctrines, which endured for centuries and had a profound influence on the Romans. These were Epicureanism and Stoicism.

Epicurus (341–270 B.C.) taught in the 'Garden' at Athens and formulated his philosophy about 300 B.C. His main tenets were:

(i) Wisdom is the conduct of life without superstition and the fear which it brings.

(ii) The *summum bonum* is pleasure, which he defined as the absence of pain. But Epicurus did not mean to encourage immorality, as his critics often accused him of doing: in fact, he lived a simple life, and thought that virtue was desirable, but only so far as its results were pleasurable and not for its own sake.

' (iii) The physical world is explained by the atomic theory. According to this, nothing can arise out of nothing or pass away into nothing. Only matter and space exist. Matter consists of indivisible particles, or atoms (from Greek ἄτομος), which are pictured as falling in a straight line through an infinite void. By a deviation from the straight (*clinamen*), collisions between the atoms take place and worlds come into existence (XXXII 60). Thus the universe, according to Epicurus, appears to have originated in an accident.

(iv) The gods exist, but do not care for mankind. (*Cp.* Tennyson, *Lotus-eaters*, 'on the hills like gods together, careless of mankind.')

(v) The soul, like the body, consists of atoms. It is mortal and is dissolved at death. No punishment need be feared in Hades.

Lucretius, a contemporary of Cicero, expounded Epicureanism in his poem *de Rerum Natura*.

7. *Stoicism* was founded at Athens in 315 B.C. by Zeno, who taught in the Stoa Poikile (Painted Portico). The Stoics, in contrast with the Epicureans, held that:

(i) The universe (*natura*) is governed by a single divine intelligence (*deus*), thought of as a fiery essence pervading all parts of it. Thus, God, Reason, and Nature are almost equivalents. (This identification of God with Nature is known as Pantheism.) The Universe passes through a series of cycles, each ending in a general conflagration, after which the whole process begins afresh.

(ii) The scale of nature, rising from the inanimate to the animate, reaches its highest point in man, who is distinguished from other living things by having an upward look (XXXIV 5). The wonderful organisation of his body is a mark of divine favour. His highest gift is reason (III), which enables him to contemplate the heavens (XXXV).

(iii) The soul is an immortal spark, embodied in matter, and destined to be re-united with the divine spirit at death. This conception appears in Cicero combined with the Platonic idea of immortality (XXV and XXVIII).

(iv) The *summum bonum* is virtue, which is to be pursued for its own sake. To be virtuous is to live according to nature (*secundum naturam*), that is, the will of God. The virtuous man possesses every possible perfection. He alone is wise, happy and free, he is even a king. These extreme assertions were known as the Stoic Paradoxes (VIII and IX). Stoicism is akin to Puritanism in its detachment from the world.

(v) Mankind is **a** universal brotherhood, for whose

benefit the world was made (XXXV 20), inhabiting a world community (*cosmopolis*), and recognising a universal law (XX and XXI).

Zeno was succeeded as head of the school by *Cleanthes* (330–231 B.C.), the 'theologian of Stoicism', whose 'Hymn to Zeus' is a noble expression of the Stoic idea of God (XXX 4). He also formulated four arguments for the existence of God. His successor, *Chrysippus* (280–206 B.C.), was the great systematiser of Stoicism.

8. The connecting link between Stoicism and Rome was *Panaetius* of Rhodes (180–110 B.C.). He was a friend of the younger Scipio and of the historian Polybius. Cicero made much use of him in his *De Officiis*, and he is said to have originated the idea that the Roman constitution was a mixture of monarchy, aristocracy and democracy (XIII Introductory Note).

A contemporary of Cicero was *Posidonius* (135–51 B.C.), a Syrian Greek of Apamea, settled in Rhodes, where Cicero became his pupil. He was a man of versatile mind and the author of numerous historical, philosophical, and scientific works, which have perished. He was responsible, according to Cicero (XXXI 10), for a sphere representing the movements of the heavenly bodies, and for the definition of philosophy given in the *De Officiis* (XXXIX 34).

In Cicero's time, in addition to Stoicism and Epicureanism, there was also the *New Academy*, which, in contrast with the Academy of Plato, held that knowledge could only be probable, never certain, and recommended reconciliation of opposing principles and suspension of judgement in doubtful cases (XXIX 16).

Thus the Greeks had already dealt with the three great questions, God, Immortality and Duty, and it had come to be recognised that philosophy was, as Cicero defines it, 'the knowledge of all things human and divine, and their causes'.

III Cicero's Philosophical Works

In spite of opposition from diehards like Cato, the Censor, Greek literature and thought had been familiar at Rome from the beginning of the second century B.C., and Cicero had a wide acquaintance with the chief works of the Epicureans, Stoics, and Academics. The first he rejected entirely, was much attracted to the second, but often followed the third in refusing to dogmatise. He had early become interested in Greek thought through his youthful studies under Greek teachers at Rome and later at Rhodes and Athens, but his career as an orator, begun with his first speech in 81 B.C., and his entry into politics with his first magistracy in 75 B.C., had diverted him from the life of a student. Apart from two early works, his philosophical writings all date from the years 45–44 B.C. The circumstances of his return to philosophy are explained in a passage from the *De Officiis* (XXXIX). Forced to retire from politics by the ascendancy of Caesar, and saddened by the divorce of his wife Terentia, and by the death of his daughter Tullia in 45 B.C., he devoted his enforced leisure to private study, and to the realisation of his ambition of putting Greek speculation into a Roman dress for the benefit of his contemporaries, an ambition narrowly achieved in the last three years of his life. The most important of these works were the following:

(i) *De Re Publica*, in six books, was published about 51 B.C. Only the first two books survive more or less complete. The text even of these depends on a single MS., discovered by Cardinal Mai on a palimpsest in the Vatican Library in 1820. Like Plato's *Republic*, on which it is modelled, the work sets out to outline an ideal state, but from a practical Roman standpoint. The chief speaker is Scipio Aemilianus (185–129 B.C.), famous not only as a soldier and destroyer of Carthage, but as a writer and patron of the arts. For Cicero he is the Roman Socrates and his age the nearest realisation of his political ideal of the *concordia ordinum*. The best known passage in the work is the myth, called *Somnium Scipionis* (XXV).

(ii) *De Legibus*, begun in 52 B.C., in five books, of which three survive.   Based on the *Laws* of Plato, it is in the form of a dialogue between Cicero, his brother Quintus, and his friend Atticus.   The first book deals with the supreme law, on which all particular laws are based, the next two with religious law and the organisation of government, giving much useful information about Roman institutions.

(iii) *Tusculan Disputations* (45 B.C.), in five books, contain discussions supposed to take place at Cicero's villa at Tusculum on the conditions of happiness.   The subjects include the fear of death, physical and mental pain, and how to overcome them, the control of the passions, and virtue as the highest good.

(iv) *De Finibus Bonorum et Malorum* (45 B.C.), on the definitions of Good and Evil, in five books, consists of a series of dialogues on the *summum bonum*.   The first two books are devoted to the statement and refutation of the Epicurean view that pleasure is the highest good.   In Books III and IV, the Stoic view that virtue is the sole good is discussed and, in its strict form, rejected.   Finally, in the last book, the view of Aristotle is preferred that, while virtue is the *summum bonum*, it is to be defined as the harmonious development of all the faculties.

(v) *De Natura Deorum*, in three books, also dates from 45 B.C.   The subject is the existence and nature of the gods, and the discussion is supposed to take place in 76 B.C. at the house of C. Aurelius Cotta, pontifex and orator.   After the Epicurean view of the gods has been set forth in Book I, Book II proceeds to expound divine providence according to the Stoics, and the work concludes with the more critical view of the New Academy.   The long argument for the existence of the gods in Book II contains some of Cicero's most splendid passages.

(vi) *De Divinatione* (44 B.C.) discusses in two books the arguments for and against the possibility of divination. The dialogue is between Cicero and his brother Quintus.

(vii) *De Amicitia* and *De Senectute* (45-44 B.C.) are two short works on friendship and old age. The speaker in the first is Laelius, the friend of Scipio, the Younger, in the second, Cato, the Censor.

(viii) *De Officiis*, Cicero's last philosophical work, dates from 44 B.C. after Caesar's murder. It is addressed to his son, Marcus, then a student at Athens. The subjects are moral duty, the four cardinal virtues, wisdom, justice, courage, and temperance, and how morality is to be reconciled with expediency when the two conflict. The argument is largely illustrated by examples from Roman history.

By the time he had finished the *De Officiis*, Cicero was preparing to make his final stand against Antony in the *Philippic Orations*. These contain some of his finest passages in defence of freedom against tyranny (XVIII).

IV The Thought of Cicero

Works written at such speed and under such conditions were bound to have their defects. It is generally said, and indeed admitted by Cicero himself, that they are not original compositions, but copies of Greek works. It is obvious that they are sometimes superficial and even at times misunderstand the originals, and that Cicero was often eclectic, holding no consistent view, but picking what he pleased out of different systems. Yet it would be as absurd to despise a Roman work for not being Greek, as it would be to refuse to look at the Pantheon because it is not the Parthenon. If Cicero had done no more than give Greek thought a Latin form, supplying it with a vocabulary which secured its transmission through the Middle Ages to become part of the modern heritage, adding at the same time the attraction of a beautiful style, he would still have been worthy of our attention. But he can claim more than this. To Greek abstractions he added something typically Roman, the practical interest in character and conduct. What attracted him about Socrates was that he 'set philosophy in cities and made it enquire about morals and about good and evil' (II 34). When he uses words like *sapientia*, *fides*, *pietas*, he is not just translating Greek, but adding to Greek speculation the great Roman moral conceptions.

In this he is the spokesman of his age. But he also speaks for himself. There is an outlook recognisably Ciceronian. Dreading superstition and sceptical in doubtful matters (*e.g.* his views on divination XXIX), he has a noble interest in the highest questions and a positive opinion on many. He has, for instance, a high regard for truth for its own sake. Man is a rational animal whose function is to know (III). Virtue is for him the highest ideal: he decisively rejects Epicureanism and accepts all that is best in Stoicism (VII and VIII). In politics, he upholds patriotism (XIII), and personal responsibility (XXXIX), opposes tyranny (XVI and XVII) and supports freedom (XVIII). He frankly criticises Roman imperialism, ascribing the ills of the Republic to the brutalities of its generals (XVI 24, '*iure igitur plectimur*'). He believes in the worth and destiny of the individual soul, which he describes with his most splendid eloquence (XXXVI), and he is more than half convinced of its immortality (XXV). Religion purified from superstition is his ideal (XXIX 6), and he considers the existence of God an inevitable conclusion from the beauty and order of the universe (XXX and XXXI). Perhaps his most important legacy to later thought is his formulation of 'Natural Law' (XX and XXI). His language rises to its highest eloquence when he speaks of the supreme law, prior to all human laws, the same everywhere in the world and recognised by all men, whose sanction is divine.

Cicero's influence in transmitting these conceptions to western civilisation has been profound. It is not surprising that Christian thinkers found him at times very close to themselves. Augustine, for example, in his *Confessions* (III 7) attributes to the reading of Cicero's lost dialogue *Hortensius*, on the study of philosophy, a part in his own conversion. But this is counterbalanced by the more penetrating distinction, which the same writer makes (*Serm.* 150), between the pagan philosophies and the religion of Grace:

> '*Quid ergo? Iam constitutis ante oculos nostros tribus, Epicureo, Stoico, Christiano, interrogemus singulos. Dic, Epicuree, quae res facit beatum? Respondet: Voluptas corporis. Dic, Stoice: virtus animi. Dic, Christiane: Donum Dei.*'

> Let us then set before our eyes these three, the Epicurean, the Stoic, and the Christian, and question them in turn. 'Tell us, Epicurean. What makes man happy?' He answers, 'The pleasure of the senses.' 'Tell us, Stoic.' 'Virtue.' 'Tell us, Christian.' 'The Gift of God.'

Above all, it is by his Latin that Cicero triumphs. It was his aim to convince by speaking with eloquence '*velut e superiore loco*'. 'His copious, majestic, musical flow of language', says a great nineteenth century writer (Newman: *Idea of a University*), 'even if sometimes beyond what the subject-matter demands, is never out of keeping with the occasion or with the speaker. It is the expression of lofty sentiments in lofty language, the '*mens magna in corpore magno*'. It is the development of the inner man. . . . As the exploits of Scipio or Pompey are the expression of this greatness in deed, so the language of Cicero is the expression of it in word. And as the acts of the Roman ruler or soldier represent to us, in a manner special to themselves, the characteristic magnanimity of the lords of the earth, so do the speeches or treatises of her accomplished orator bring it home to our imaginations as no other writing can do. Neither Livy, nor Tacitus, nor Terence, nor Seneca, nor Pliny, nor Quintilian, is an adequate spokesman for the Imperial City. They write Latin; Cicero writes Roman.'

COGNITIONEM PRUDENTIAMQUE SEQUETUR CONSIDERATA ACTIC

Cicero: *de Officiis I* 45

PHILOSOPHY OR
THE LOVE OF KNOWLEDGE

☆

I

The Sirens' Song

Every man by nature desires knowledge. This desire may be observed in the child as well as in the student, and Homer recognises it, when he makes the Sirens offer the bait of universal knowledge to the sailors whom they draw on to the rocks. It is found in the highest degree in such thinkers as Archimedes and Plato.

Tantus est igitur innatus in nobis cognitionis amor et scientiae ut nemo dubitare possit quin ad eas res hominum natura nullo emolumento invitata rapiatur. Videmusne ut pueri ne verberibus quidem a contemplandis rebus perquirendisque deterreantur? ut pulsi recurrant? ut   5 aliquid scire se gaudeant? ut id aliis narrare gestiant? ut pompa, ludis atque eiusmodi spectaculis teneantur ob eamque rem vel famem vel sitim perferant? Quid vero? qui ingenuis studiis atque artibus delectantur, nonne videmus eos nec valetudinis nec rei familiaris habere 10 rationem omniaque perpeti ipsa cognitione et scientia captos et cum maximis curis et laboribus compensare eam quam ex discendo capiant voluptatem? Mihi quidem Homerus huiusmodi quiddam vidisse videtur in iis quae de Sirenum cantibus finxit. Neque enim vocum suavitate 15

videntur aut novitate quadam et varietate cantandi
revocare eos solitae qui praetervehebantur, sed quia multa
se scire profitebantur, ut homines ad eorum saxa discendi
cupiditate adhaerescerent. Ita enim invitant Ulixem
20 (nam verti, ut quaedam Homeri, sic istum ipsum locum):
    O decus Argolicum, quin puppim flectis, Ulixes,
    auribus ut nostros possis agnoscere cantus?
    Nam nemo haec unquam est transvectus caerula cursu,
    quin prius astiterit vocum dulcedine captus,
25   post, variis avido satiatus pectore musis,
    doctior ad patrias lapsus pervenerit oras.
    Nos grave certamen belli clademque tenemus,
    Graecia quam Troiae divino numine vexit,
    omniaque e latis rerum vestigia terris.
30 Vidit Homerus probari fabulam non posse, si cantiunculis
tantus irretitus vir teneretur; scientiam pollicentur quam
non erat mirum sapientiae cupido patria esse cariorem.

    Quem ardorem studii censetis fuisse in Archimede, qui
dum in pulvere quaedam describit attentius, ne patriam
35 quidem captam esse senserit! quantum Aristoxeni ingenium
consumptum videmus in musicis! quo studio Aristophanem
putamus aetatem in litteris duxisse! Quid de Pythagora,
quid de Platone aut de Democrito loquar? a quibus propter
discendi cupiditatem videmus ultimas terras esse peragratas.
40 Quae qui non vident, nihil unquam magnum ac cognitione
dignum amaverunt.

De Finibus V 48–50

II

THE THREE LIVES

On the analogy, attributed to Pythagoras, of the visitors to the
Greek Games, mankind is divided into three classes. The ambition of

the first is profit (pecunia), *of the second fame* (gloria), *of the third,*
wisdom (sapientia). *The last is the study of the universe for its*
own sake (contemplatio rerum), *the ideal of the 'philosopher'*
or 'lover of wisdom' (*Greek* φιλόσοφος). *We may be reminded*
here of Bunyan's Christians in Vanity Fair: '*One chanced*
mockingly, beholding the carriage of the men, to say unto them,
"*What will ye buy?*" *But they, looking gravely upon him, answered,*
"*We buy the Truth*".'

Pythagoram autem Phliuntem ferunt venisse eumque
cum Leonte, principe Phliasiorum, docte et copiose disseruisse quaedam; cuius ingenium et eloquentiam cum
admiratus esset Leon, quaesivisse ex eo, qua maxime arte
confideret; at illum artem quidem se scire nullam, sed esse   5
philosophum. Admiratum Leontem novitatem nominis
quaesivisse quinam essent philosophi et quid inter eos et
reliquos interesset; Pythagoram autem respondisse similem
sibi videri vitam hominum et mercatum eum qui haberetur
maximo ludorum apparatu totius Graeciae celebritate;   10
nam ut illic alii corporibus exercitatis gloriam et nobilitatem coronae peterent, alii emendi aut vendendi quaestu
et lucro ducerentur, esset autem quoddam genus eorum,
idque vel maxime ingenuum, qui nec plausum nec lucrum
quaererent, sed visendi causa venirent studioseque per-   15
spicerent quid ageretur et quo modo, item nos quasi in
mercatus quandam celebritatem ex urbe aliqua, sic in hanc
vitam ex alia vita et natura profectos alios gloriae servire,
alios pecuniae; raros esse quosdam, qui ceteris omnibus pro
nihilo habitis rerum naturam studiose intuerentur; hos se   20
appellare sapientiae studiosos (id est enim philosophos); et
ut illic liberalissimum esset spectare nihil sibi acquirentem,
sic in vita longe omnibus studiis contemplationem rerum
cognitionemque praestare.

Nec vero Pythagoras nominis solum inventor, sed rerum   25

etiam ipsarum amplificator fuit. Qui cum post hunc
Phliasium sermonem in Italiam venisset, exornavit eam
Graeciam quae magna dicta est et privatim et publice
praestantissimis et institutis et artibus. Cuius de disciplina
30 aliud tempus fuerit fortasse dicendi. Sed ab antiqua
philosophia usque ad Socratem numeri motusque tracta-
bantur, et unde omnia orerentur quove reciderent, studioseque ab iis siderum magnitudines, intervalla, cursus
anquirebantur et cuncta caelestia. Socrates autem primus
35 philosophiam devocavit a caelo et in urbibus collocavit et
in domus etiam introduxit et coegit de vita et moribus
rebusque bonis et malis quaerere.

Tusculan Disputations V 8-10

III

MAN A RATIONAL AND SOCIAL BEING

*We now come naturally to the question: 'What is Man?'
Cicero's answer is given in the following account of human nature
and its powers. Sharing with other living beings the instincts of
self-preservation and reproduction of his kind, he differs from them
in the possession of reason, which enables him to:—*

1. View the past and future as well as the present.
2. Trace the chain of cause and effect.
3. Communicate by speech.
4. Form associations with his fellows.
5. Desire knowledge for its own sake.

Principio generi animantium omni est a natura tributum,
ut se, vitam corpusque tueatur, declinet ea, quae nocitura
videantur, omniaque quae sint ad vivendum necessaria
anquirat et paret, ut pastum, ut latibula, ut alia generis

eiusdem. Commune item animantium omnium est coni-   5
unctionis appetitus procreandi causa et cura quaedam
eorum, quae procreata sint. Sed inter hominem et
beluam hoc maxime interest, quod haec tantum quantum
sensu movetur, ad id solum quod adest quodque praesens
est se accommodat, paulum admodum sentiens praeteritum   10
aut futurum. Homo autem, quod rationis est particeps,
per quam consequentia cernit, causas rerum videt, similitudines comparat rebusque praesentibus adiungit atque
annectit futuras, facile totius vitae cursum videt ad eamque
degendam praeparat res necessarias.   15

Eademque natura vi rationis hominem conciliat homini
et ad orationis et ad vitae societatem, ingeneratque in
primis praecipuum quemdam amorem in eos qui procreati
sunt, impellitque ut hominum coetus et celebrationes et esse
et a se obiri velit ob easque causas studeat parare ea quae   20
suppeditent ad cultum et ad victum, nec sibi soli sed
coniugi liberis ceterisque quos caros habeat tuerique debeat:
quae cura exsuscitat etiam animos et maiores ad rem
gerendam facit.

In primisque hominis est propria veri inquisitio atque   25
investigatio. Itaque cum sumus necessariis negotiis curis-
que vacui, tum avemus aliquid videre audire addiscere,
cognitionemque rerum aut occultarum aut admirabilium
ad beate vivendum necessariam ducimus. Omnes enim
trahimur et ducimur ad cognitionis et scientiae cupiditatem,   30
in qua excellere pulchrum putamus, labi autem, errare,
nescire, decipi et malum et turpe ducimus. In hoc genere
et naturali et honesto duo vitia vitanda sunt: unum ne
incognita pro cognitis habeamus iisque temere assentiamur,
quod vitium effugere qui volet (omnes autem velle debent)   35
adhibebit ad considerandas res et tempus et diligentiam.
Alterum est vitium, quod quidam nimis magnum studium
multamque operam in res obscuras atque difficiles con-

ferunt easdemque non necessarias.   Quibus vitiis declinatis
quod in rebus honestis et cognitione dignis operae curaeque
40 ponetur, id iure laudabitur.

De Officiis I 11–13; 18

SUMMUM BONUM OR
THE GOOD LIFE

☆

IV

THE CHOICE OF HERCULES, OR THE TWO PATHS

Of special interest to every philosopher is the question, 'What is the Summum Bonum, *the Supreme Good, the highest life for Man?' For the Epicureans the answer was 'Pleasure,'* (nihil bonum nisi voluptatem), *for the Stoics, 'Virtue,' or Moral Uprightness* (honestum). *The Stoic view is here illustrated by an incident from the career of Hercules.*

Haec igitur omnia, cum quaerimus quid deceat, complecti animo et cogitatione debemus; in primis autem constituendum est, quos nos et quales esse velimus et in quo genere vitae; quae deliberatio est omnium difficillima. Ineunte enim adulescentia, cum est maxima imbecillitas 5 consilii, tum id sibi quisque genus aetatis degendae constituit, quod maxime adamavit. Itaque ante implicatur aliquo certo genere cursuque vivendi quam potuit, quod optimum esset, iudicare. Nam quod Herculem Prodicus dicit, ut est apud Xenophontem, cum primum pubesceret, 10 exisse in solitudinem atque ibi sedentem diu secum multumque dubitasse, cum duas cerneret vias, unam Voluptatis, alteram Virtutis, utram ingredi melius esset, hoc Herculi 'Iovis satu edito' potuit fortasse contingere, nobis non item, qui imitamur quos cuique visum est, atque ad eorum studia 15

23

institutaque impellimur. Plerumque autem parentium
praeceptis imbuti ad eorum consuetudinem moremque
deducimur. Alii multitudinis iudicio feruntur, quaeque
maiori parti pulcherrima videntur, ea maxime exoptant:
20 nonnulli tamen sive felicitate quadam sive bonitate naturae
sine parentium disciplina rectam vitae secuti sunt viam.

De Officiis I 117–118

V

TYRANT AND SCHOLAR

*The moral choice is further illustrated by a comparison between
two famous Sicilian Greeks, Dionysius, the tyrant, and Archimedes,
the scientist. The apparent happiness of the former is shown to be
illusory, while the latter finds the search for truth the 'sweetest
nurture of the mind.'*

Duodequadraginta annos tyrannus Syracusanorum fuit
Dionysius, cum quinque et viginti natus annos dominatum
occupavisset. Qua pulchritudine urbem, quibus autem
opibus praeditam servitute oppressam tenuit civitatem!
5 Atqui de hoc homine a bonis auctoribus sic scriptum accepimus, summam fuisse eius in victu temperantiam in rebusque
gerendis virum acrem et industrium, eundem tamen
maleficum natura et iniustum. Ex quo omnibus bene
veritatem intuentibus videri necesse est miserrimum. Ea
10 enim ipsa quae concupiverat, ne tum quidem, cum omnia
se posse censebat, consequebatur. Qui cum esset bonis
parentibus atque honesto loco natus (etsi id quidem alius
alio modo tradidit) abundaretque et aequalium familiari-
tatibus et consuetudine propinquorum, credebat eorum
15 nemini, sed iis quos ex familiis locupletium servos delegerat

et quibusdam convenis et feris barbaris corporis custodiam committebat. Ita propter iniustam dominatus cupiditatem in carcerem quodam modo ipse se incluserat. Quin etiam, ne tonsori collum committeret, tondere filias suas docuit. Ita sordido ancillarique artificio regiae virgines ut tonstri- 20 culae tondebant barbam et capillum patris. Et tamen ab his ipsis, cum iam essent adultae, ferrum removit instituitque ut candentibus iuglandium putaminibus barbam sibi et capillum adurerent. Cumque duas uxores haberet, Aristomachen, civem suam, Doridem autem Locrensem, 25 sic ad eas ventitabat ut omnia specularetur et perscrutaretur ante. Et cum fossam latam cubiculari lecto circumdedisset eiusque fossae transitum ponticulo ligneo coniunxisset, eum ipsum, cum forem cubiculi clauserat, detorquebat. Idemque cum in communibus suggestis consistere non auderet, 30 contionari ex turri alta solebat. Atque is cum pila ludere vellet (studiose enim id factitabat) tunicamque poneret, adulescentulo quem amabat tradidisse gladium dicitur. Hic cum familiaris iocans dixisset: 'Huic quidem certe vitam tuam committis,' adrisissetque adulescens, utrum- 35 que iussit interfici, alterum quia viam demonstravisset interimendi sui, alterum quia dictum id risu approbavisset. Atque eo facto sic doluit nihil ut tulerit gravius in vita; quem enim vehementer amarat, occiderat. Sic distrahuntur in contrarias partes impotentium cupiditates. 40

Quamquam hic quidem tyrannus ipse iudicavit quam esset beatus; nam cum quidam ex eius assentatoribus, Damocles, commemoraret in sermone copias eius, opes, maiestatem dominatus, rerum abundantiam, magnificentiam aedium regiarum negaretque umquam beatiorem 45 quemquam fuisse, 'Visne, igitur,' inquit, 'O Damocle, quoniam te haec vita delectat, ipse eam degustare et fortunam experiri meam?' Cum se ille cupere dixisset, collocari iussit hominem in aureo lecto strato pulcherrimo textili

50 stragulo, magnificis operibus picto, abacosque complures
ornavit argento auroque caelato. Tum ad mensam
eximia forma pueros delectos iussit consistere eosque nutum
illius intuentes diligenter ministrare. Aderant unguenta,
coronae, incendebantur odores, mensae conquisitissimis
55 epulis exstruebantur; fortunatus sibi Damocles videbatur.
In hoc medio apparatu fulgentem gladium e lacunari saeta
equina aptum demitti iussit, ut impenderet illius beati
cervicibus. Itaque nec pulchros illos ministratores aspiciebat nec plenum artis argentum nec manum porrigebat in
60 mensam, iam ipsae defluebant coronae: denique exoravit
tyrannum ut abire liceret quod iam beatus nollet esse.
Satisne videtur declarasse Dionysius nihil esse ei beatum cui
semper aliqui terror impendeat?

Non ego iam cum huius vita, qua taetrius, miserius,
65 detestabilius excogitare nihil possum, Platonis aut Archytae
vitam comparabo, doctorum hominum et plane sapientium; ex eadem urbe humilem homunculum a pulvere et
radio excitabo, qui multis annis post fuit, Archimedem.
Cuius ego quaestor ignoratum ab Syracusanis, cum esse
70 omnino negarent, saeptum undique et vestitum vepribus
et dumetis indagavi sepulchrum. Tenebam enim quosdam
senariolos, quos in eius monumento esse inscriptos accepe-
ram, qui declarabant in summo sepulcro sphaeram esse
positam cum cylindro. Ego autem cum omnia collus-
75 trarem oculis (est enim ad portas Agrigentinas magna
frequentia sepulcrorum), animum adverti columellam non
multum e dumis eminentem in qua inerat sphaerae figura
et cylindri. Atque ego statim Syracusanis (erant autem
principes mecum) dixi me illud ipsum arbitrari esse quod
80 quaererem. Inmissi cum falcibus multi purgarunt et
aperuerunt locum. Quo cum patefactus esset aditus, ad
adversam basim accessimus. Apparebat epigramma exesis
posterioribus partibus versiculorum dimidiatis fere. Ita

nobilissima Graeciae civitas, quondam vero etiam doctis-
sima, sui civis unius acutissimi monumentum ignorasset, 85
nisi ab homine Arpinate didicisset.

Sed redeat, unde aberravit oratio. Quis est omnium,
qui modo cum Musis, id est cum humanitate et cum
doctrina, habeat aliquod commercium, qui se non hunc
mathematicum malit quam illum tyrannum? Si vitae 90
modum actionemque quaerimus, alterius mens rationibus
agitandis exquirendisque alebatur cum oblectatione sollertiae, qui est unus suavissimus pastus animorum, alterius
in caede et iniuriis cum et diurno et nocturno metu.

Tusculan Disputations V 57-62; 64-66

VI

REGULUS, OR HONOUR VERSUS SELF-INTEREST

*The theme of this famous story is the binding power of an oath.
To keep one's word, in spite of the attraction of self-interest*
(utilitas), *requires the highest moral courage* (magnitudo animi).

M. Atilius Regulus, cum consul iterum in Africa ex
insidiis captus esset duce Xanthippo Lacedaemonio,
imperatore autem patre Hannibalis Hamilcare, iuratus
missus est ad senatum, ut, nisi redditi essent Poenis captivi
nobiles quidam, rediret ipse Carthaginem. Is cum Romam 5
venisset, utilitatis speciem videbat, sed eam, ut res declarat,
falsam iudicavit: quae erat talis: manere in patria, esse
domui suae cum uxore, cum liberis, quam calamitatem
accepisset in bello, communem fortunae bellicae iudicantem
tenere consularis dignitatis gradum. Quis haec negat esse 10
utilia? Quem censes? Magnitudo animi et fortitudo
negat; num locupletiores quaeris auctores? Harum enim

est virtutum proprium nihil extimescere, omnia humana despicere, nihil quod homini accidere possit intolerandum
15 putare. Itaque quid fecit? In senatum venit, mandata exposuit, sententiam ne diceret recusavit: quam diu iure iurando hostium teneretur, non esse se senatorem. Atque illud etiam ('o stultum hominem' dixerit quispiam 'et repugnantem utilitati suae') reddi captivos negavit esse
20 utile: illos enim adulescentes esse et bonos duces, se iam confectum senectute. Cuius cum valuisset auctoritas, captivi retenti sunt, ipse Carthaginem rediit neque eum caritas patriae retinuit nec suorum. Neque vero tum ignorabat se ad crudelem hostem et ad exquisita supplicia
25 proficisci, sed ius iurandum conservandum putabat. Itaque tum, cum vigilando necabatur, erat in meliore causa quam si domi senex captivus, periurus consularis remansisset.

Est enim ius iurandum affirmatio religiosa; quod autem
30 affirmate quasi deo teste promiseris, id tenendum est.

De Officiis III 99–100

VII

Servius Sulpicius—A Noble Roman

The character of this distinguished lawyer and patriot exhibits all that is best in the Roman ideal of devotion to duty (pietas).

Vellem di immortales fecissent, patres conscripti, ut vivo potius Ser. Sulpicio gratias ageremus quam honores mortuo quaereremus. Nec vero dubito quin, si ille vir legationem renuntiare potuisset, reditus eius et vobis gratus
5 fuerit et rei publicae salutaris futurus, non quo L. Philippo et L. Pisoni aut studium aut cura defuerit in tanto officio

tantoque munere, sed, cum Ser. Sulpicius aetate illis
anteiret, sapientia omnibus, subito ereptus e causa totam
legationem orbam et debilitatam reliquit. Quod si
cuiquam iustus honos habitus est in morte legato, in nullo 10
iustior quam in Ser. Sulpicio reperietur. Ceteri qui in
legatione mortem obierunt ad incertum vitae periculum
sine ullo mortis metu profecti sunt: Ser. Sulpicius cum
aliqua perveniendi ad M. Antonium spe profectus est, nulla
revertendi. Qui cum ita affectus esset ut, si ad gravem 15
valetudinem labor accessisset, sibi ipse diffideret, non
recusavit quo minus vel extremo spiritu, si quam opem rei
publicae ferre posset, experiretur. Itaque non illum vis
hiemis, non nives, non longitudo itineris, non asperitas
viarum, non morbus ingravescens retardavit, cumque iam 20
ad congressum colloquiumque eius pervenisset ad quem
erat missus, in ipsa cura ac meditatione obeundi sui
muneris excessit e vita.

Reddite igitur, patres conscripti, ei vitam cui ademistis.
Vita enim mortuorum in memoria est posita vivorum. 25
Perficite ut is quem vos inscii ad mortem misistis immortali-
tatem habeat a vobis. Cui si statuam in rostris decreto
vestro statueritis, nulla eius legationem posteritatis obscura-
bit oblivio. Nam reliqua Ser. Sulpicii vita multis erit
praeclarisque monumentis ad omnem memoriam com- 30
mendata. Semper illius gravitatem, constantiam, fidem,
praestantem in re publica tuenda curam atque prudentiam
omnium mortalium fama celebrabit. Nec vero silebitur
admirabilis quaedam et incredibilis ac paene divina eius in
legibus interpretandis, aequitate explicanda scientia. Omnes 35
ex omni aetate qui in hac civitate intelligentiam iuris
habuerunt si unum in locum conferantur, cum Ser.
Sulpicio non sint comparandi. Nec enim ille magis iuris
consultus quam iustitiae fuit. Ita ea quae proficiscebantur a legibus et ab iure civili semper ad facilitatem 40

aequitatemque referebat, neque instituere litium actiones
malebat quam controversias tollere. Ergo hoc statuae
monumento non eget; habet alia maiora. Haec enim
statua mortis honestae testis erit, illa memoria vitae
45 gloriosae, ut hoc magis monumentum grati senatus quam
clari viri futurum sit.

Philippic IX 1-2; 10-11

VIII

Sapiens or the Stoic Ideal

The Third Book of the De Finibus *(Introd. III 4), concludes
with a description of the ideal 'Wise Man,' expressed in terms of
the Stoic Paradoxes (Introd. II 7). Greatly as he admired this
noble conception, Cicero was aware of its absurd side (see IX).*

Quam gravis vero, quam magnifica, quam constans
conficitur persona sapientis! qui, cum ratio docuerit quod
honestum esset, id esse solum bonum, semper sit necesse est
beatus vereque omnia ista nomina possideat quae irrideri
5 ab imperitis solent. Rectius enim appellabitur rex quam
Tarquinius qui nec se nec suos regere potuit, rectius
magister populi (is enim est dictator) quam Sulla qui trium
pestiferorum vitiorum, luxuriae, avaritiae, crudelitatis
magister fuit, rectius dives quam Crassus qui, nisi eguisset,
10 nunquam Euphraten nulla belli causa transire voluisset.
Recte eius omnia dicentur qui scit uti solus omnibus; recte
pulcher appellabitur (animi enim lineamenta sunt pul-
chriora quam corporis), recte solus liber, nec dominationi
cuiusquam parens nec oboediens cupiditati, recte invictus,
15 cuius etiamsi corpus constringatur, animo tamen vincula
inici nulla possint. Nec expectat ullum tempus aetatis, ut

tum denique iudicetur beatusne fuerit cum extremum vitae
diem morte confecerit; quod ille unus e septem sapien-
tibus non sapienter Croesum monuit, nam si beatus unquam
fuisset, beatam vitam usque ad illum a Cyro exstructum 20
rogum pertulisset.   Quod si ita est ut neque quisquam nisi
bonus vir et omnes boni beati sint, quid philosophia magis
colendum aut quid est virtute divinius?

De Finibus III 75–76

IX

Cato or Stoicism Criticised

*Cicero here takes the opportunity of showing up the absurdity of
Cato's rigid insistence on the Stoic Paradoxes (VIII).*

In M. Catone, iudices, haec bona, quae videmus divina
et egregia, ipsius scitote esse propria: quae nonnunquam
requirimus, ea sunt omnia non a natura, verum a magistro.
Fuit enim quidam summo ingenio vir, Zeno, cuius inventorum aemuli Stoici nominantur.   Huius sententiae et 5
praecepta huius modi: sapientem gratia nunquam moveri,
nunquam cuiusquam delicto ignoscere; neminem miseri-
cordem esse nisi stultum et levem; viri non esse neque
exorari neque placari; solos sapientes esse, si distortissimi
sint, formosos, si mendicissimi, divites, si servitutem 10
serviant, reges: nos autem, qui sapientes non sumus,
fugitivos, exules, hostes, insanos denique esse dicunt; omnia
peccata esse paria, omne delictum scelus esse nefarium, nec
minus delinquere eum, qui gallum gallinaceum, cum opus
non fuerit, quam eum, qui patrem suffocaverit: sapientem 15
nihil opinari, nullius rei paenitere, nulla in re falli, sententiam mutare nunquam.

Haec homo ingeniosissimus, M. Cato, auctoribus eruditissimis inductus arripuit, neque disputandi causa, ut
20 magna pars, sed ita vivendi. Petunt aliquid publicani: 'Cave quidquam habeat momenti gratia.' Supplices aliqui veniunt miseri et calamitosi: 'Sceleratus et nefarius fueris, si quidquam misericordia adductus feceris.' Fatetur aliquis se peccasse et eius delicti veniam petit: 'Nefarium
25 est facinus ignoscere.' At leve delictum est: 'Omnia peccata sunt paria.'

Nostri autem illi (fatebor enim, Cato, me quoque in adulescentia diffisum ingenio meo quaesisse adiumenta doctrinae), nostri, inquam, illi a Platone et Aristotele,
30 moderati homines et temperati, aiunt apud sapientem valere aliquando gratiam: viri boni esse misereri, distincta genera esse delictorum et dispares poenas, esse apud hominem constantem ignoscendi locum, ipsum sapientem saepe aliquid opinari, irasci nonnunquam, exorari eundem et
35 placari, quod dixerit interdum, si ita rectius sit, mutare, de sententia cedere aliquando: omnes virtutes mediocritate quadam esse moderatas.

Hos ad magistros si qua te fortuna, Cato, cum ista natura detulisset, non tu quidem vir melior esses nec fortior nec
40 temperatior nec iustior (neque enim esse potes), sed paulo ad lenitatem propensior.

Pro Murena 61–64

X

THE ROMAN GENTLEMAN

Passing to the level of conventional virtue, Cicero accepts as inevitable the strong traditional prejudice against occupations requiring manual labour, as fit only for slaves. Only such careers

as oratory, politics, and estate management, and business, if 'big',
might engage a free man. Of special interest is the condemnation
of retail trade as inseparable from dishonesty, and of luxury trades,
as 'not respectable.'

Iam de artificiis et quaestibus, qui liberales habendi, qui
sordidi sint, haec fere accepimus. Primum improbantur
ii quaestus, qui in odia hominum incurrunt, ut portitorum,
ut faeneratorum. Illiberales autem et sordidi quaestus
mercenariorum omnium, quorum operae, non quorum artes 5
emuntur. Sordidi etiam putandi qui mercantur a merca-
toribus quod statim vendant: nihil enim proficiant, nisi
admodum mentiantur, nec vero est quicquam turpius
vanitate. Opificesque omnes in sordida arte versantur;
nec enim quicquam ingenuum potest habere officina. 10
Minimeque artes eae probandae quae ministrae sunt
voluptatum:
      Cetarii lanii coqui fartores piscatores,
ut ait Terentius. Adde huc, si placet, unguentarios,
saltatores, totumque ludum talarium. In quibus autem 15
artibus aut prudentia maior inest aut non mediocris
utilitas quaeritur, ut medicina, ut architectura, ut doctrina
rerum honestarum, hae sunt iis quorum ordini conveniunt
honestae. Mercatura autem, si tenuis est, sordida putanda
est: sin magna et copiosa, multa undique apportans 20
multisque sine vanitate impertiens, non est admodum
vituperanda. Omnium autem rerum, ex quibus aliquid
acquiritur, nihil est agri cultura melius, nihil dulcius, nihil
uberius, nihil homine libero dignius.

De Officiis I 150–151

ROME AND GREECE

☆

XI

Cicero at Athens, or the Heritage of Greece

The scene of the Fifth Book of the De Finibus *is laid at Athens in 79* B.C. *Cicero and his friends are attending lectures on philosophy, and in this passage discuss the effect on the imagination of visiting historic places with their memories of the great Greeks, and the rival orators Aeschines and Demosthenes.*

Cum audissem Antiochum, Brute, ut solebam, cum M. Pisone in eo gymnasio quod Ptolemaeum vocatur, unaque nobiscum Q. frater et T. Pomponius Luciusque Cicero, constituimus inter nos ut ambulationem postmeridianam
5 conficeremus in Academia, maxime quod is locus ab omni turba id temporis vacuus esset. Itaque ad tempus ad Pisonem omnes. Inde vario sermone sex illa a Dipylo stadia confecimus. Cum autem venissemus in Academiae non sine causa nobilitata spatia, solitudo erat ea quam
10 volueramus. Tum Piso: 'Naturane nobis hoc,' inquit, 'datum dicam an errore quodam, ut, cum ea loca videamus in quibus memoria dignos viros acceperimus multum esse versatos, magis moveamur quam si quando eorum ipsorum aut facta audiamus aut scriptum aliquod legamus? Velut
15 ego nunc moveor. Venit enim mihi Platonis in mentem, quem accepimus primum hic disputare solitum; cuius etiam illi propinqui hortuli non memoriam solum mihi afferunt sed ipsum videntur in conspectu meo ponere.'

34

Tum Quintus: 'Est plane, Piso, ut dicis,' inquit. 'Nam me ipsum huc modo venientem convertebat ad sese 20 Coloneus ille locus, cuius incola Sophocles ob oculos versabatur, quem scis quam admirer quamque eo delecter. Me quidem ad altiorem memoriam Oedipodis huc venientis et illo mollissimo carmine quaenam essent haec ipsa loca requirentis species quaedam commovit, inaniter scilicet, sed 25 commovit tamen.'

Tum Piso: 'Quid Lucius noster?' inquit, 'an eum locum libenter invisit ubi Demosthenes et Aeschines inter se decertare soliti sunt? Suo enim quisque studio maxime ducitur.'   30

Et ille, cum erubuisset, 'Noli,' inquit, 'ex me quaerere, qui in Phalericum etiam descenderim, quo in loco ad fluctum aiunt declamare solitum Demosthenem ut fremitum assuesceret voce vincere. Modo etiam paulum ad dexteram de via declinavi ut ad Pericli sepulchrum acce- 35 derem. Quamquam id quidem infinitum est in hac urbe; quacumque enim ingredimur, in aliqua historia vestigium ponimus.'

De Finibus V 1-3; 5

XII

Greek Witnesses, or Graecia Mendax

Turning from the brilliant genius and subtle wit of the Greeks, Cicero shows us a different side of their character.

De quibus vos aliis testes esse debetis, de eis ipsi alios testes audietis? At quos testes? Primum dicam, id quod est commune, Graecos; non quo nationi huic ego unus maxime fidem derogem. Nam si quis unquam de nostris

5 hominibus a genere isto studio ac voluntate non abhorrens
fuit, me et esse arbitror et magis etiam tum cum plus erat
otii fuisse.   Sed sunt in illo numero multi boni, docti,
prudentes, qui ad hoc iudicium deducti non sunt, multi
impudentes, illiterati, leves, quos variis de causis video
10 concitatos.   Verum tamen hoc dico de toto genere Graecorum: tribuo illis litteras, do multarum artium disciplinam,
non adimo sermonis leporem, ingeniorum acumen, dicendi
copiam, denique etiam, si qua sibi alia sumunt, non
repugno; testimoniorum religionem et fidem nunquam
15 ista natio coluit, totiusque huiusce rei quae sit vis, quae
auctoritas, quod pondus, ignorant.   Videte quo vultu, qua
confidentia dicant: tum intellegetis qua religione dicant.
Nunquam nobis ad rogatum respondent, semper accusatori
plus quam ad rogatum, nunquam laborant quem ad modum
20 probent quod dicunt, sed quem ad modum se explicent
dicendo.   Graecus testis cum ea voluntate processit ut
laedat, non iuris iurandi, sed laedendi verba meditatur;
vinci, refelli, coargui putat esse turpissimum, ad id se parat,
nihil curat aliud.   Itaque non optimus quisque nec gravis-
25 simus, sed impudentissimus loquacissimusque deligitur.
Vos autem in privatis minimarum rerum iudiciis testem
diligenter expenditis; etiam si formam hominis, si nomen, si
tribum nostis, mores tamen exquirendos putatis.   Qui
autem dicit testimonium ex nostris hominibus, ut se ipse
30 sustentat, ut omnia verba moderatur, ut timet ne quid
cupide, ne quid iracunde, ne quid plus minusve quam sit
necesse dicat!

Pro Flacco 9–12

THE STATE AND POLITICS

☆

XIII

Superiority of the Roman Constitution

This passage is from the beginning of Book II of the De Republica (see Introd. III 1). Scipio Aemilianus has just argued that the Roman constitution is the best, because it combines the advantages of monarchy, aristocracy, and democracy. He now proceeds to point out that it has a long political tradition, and does not depend on a single legislator or founder.

Cum omnes igitur flagrarent cupiditate audiendi, ingressus est sic loqui Scipio: Catonis hoc senis est, quem, ut scitis, unice dilexi maximeque sum admiratus, cuique vel patris utriusque iudicio vel etiam meo studio me totum ab adulescentia dedidi; cuius me nunquam satiare potuit 5 oratio; tantus erat in homine usus rei publicae, quam et domi et militiae cum optime, tum etiam diutissime gesserat, et modus in dicendo et gravitate mixtus lepos et summum vel discendi studium vel docendi et orationi vita admodum congruens. Is dicere solebat ob hanc causam praestare 10 nostrae civitatis statum ceteris civitatibus, quod in illis singuli fuissent fere, qui suam quisque rem publicam constituissent legibus atque institutis suis, ut Cretum Minos, Lacedaemoniorum Lycurgus, Atheniensium, quae persaepe commutata esset, tum Theseus, tum Draco, tum Solo, tum 15 Clisthenes, tum multi alii, postremo exsanguem iam et iacentem doctus vir Phalereus sustentasset Demetrius;

37

nostra autem res publica non unius esset ingenio, sed
multorum, nec una hominis vita, sed aliquot constituta
20 saeculis et aetatibus.   Nam neque ullum ingenium tantum
exstitisse dicebat, ut, quem res nulla fugeret, quisquam
aliquando fuisset, neque cuncta ingenia collata in unum
tantum posse uno tempore providere, ut omnia complecter-
entur sine rerum usu ac vetustate.   Quam ob rem, ut
25 ille solebat, ita nunc mea repetet oratio populi Romani
originem; libenter enim etiam verbo utor Catonis.   Facilius
autem, quod est propositum, consequar, si nostram rem
publicam vobis et nascentem et crescentem et adultam et
iam firmam atque robustam ostendero, quam si mihi
30 aliquam, ut apud Platonem Socrates, ipse finxero.

De Re Publica II 1–3

XIV

The Foundation of the City

*Cicero continues with an account of the foundation of Rome by
Romulus in 753 B.C.   Though he accepts the tradition, he emphasises
the importance of geographical and social factors in the choice of the
site.*

Qua gloria parta, urbem auspicato condere, et firmare
dicitur primum cogitavisse rem publicam.   Urbi autem
locum, quod est ei, qui diuturnam rem publicam serere
conatur, diligentissime providendum, incredibili opportuni-
5 tate delegit.   Neque enim ad mare admovit, quod ei fuit
illa manu copiisque facillimum, ut in agrum Rutulorum
procederet, aut in ostio Tiberino, quem in locum multis
post annis rex Ancus coloniam deduxit, urbem ipse con-
deret, sed hoc vir excellenti providentia sensit ac vidit, non

esse opportunissimos situs maritimos urbibus eis, quae ad 10
spem diuturnitatis conderentur atque imperii, primum
quod essent urbes maritimae non solum multis periculis
oppositae, sed etiam caecis.   Nam terra continens adventus
hostium non modo exspectatos, sed etiam repentinos multis
indiciis et quasi fragore quodam et sonitu ipso ante denun- 15
tiat; neque vero quisquam potest hostis advolare terra,
quin eum non modo esse, sed etiam quis et unde sit, scire
possimus.   Maritimus vero ille et navalis hostis ante adesse
potest, quam quisquam venturum esse suspicari queat, nec
vero, cum venit, prae se fert, aut qui sit aut unde veniat 20
aut etiam quid velit, denique ne nota quidem ulla pacatus
an hostis sit, discerni ac iudicari potest.

Est autem maritimis urbibus etiam quaedam corruptela
ac demutatio morum; admiscentur enim novis sermonibus
ac disciplinis et importantur non merces solum adventiciae, 25
sed etiam mores, ut nihil possit in patriis institutis manere
integrum.   Iam qui incolunt eas urbes, non haerent in suis
sedibus, sed volucri semper spe et cogitatione rapiuntur a
domo longius, atque etiam cum manent corpore, animo
tamen exulant et vagantur.   Nec vero ulla res magis 30
labefactatam diu et Carthaginem et Corinthum pervertit
aliquando quam hic error ac dissipatio civium, quod
mercandi cupiditate et navigandi et agrorum et armorum
cultum reliquerant.   Multa etiam ad luxuriam invita-
menta perniciosa civitatibus suppeditantur mari, quae vel 35
capiuntur vel importantur; atque habet etiam amoenitas
ipsa vel sumptuosas vel desidiosas illecebras multas cupiditatum.   Sed tamen in his vitiis inest illa magna commoditas,
et, quod ubique gentium est, ut ad eam urbem, quam
incolas, possit adnare, et rursus ut id, quod agri efferant 40
sui, quascumque velint in terras, portare possint ac mittere.

Qui potuit igitur divinius et utilitates complecti mari-
timas Romulus et vitia vitare, quam quod urbem perennis

amnis et aequabilis et in mare late influentis posuit in ripa?
45 quo posset urbs et accipere a mari, quo egeret, et reddere,
quo redundaret, eodemque ut flumine res ad victum cultumque maxime necessarias non solum a mari absorberet, sed
etiam invectas acciperet ex terra, ut mihi iam tum divinasse
ille videatur hanc urbem sedem aliquando et domum
50 summo esse imperio praebituram; nam hanc rerum
tantam potentiam non ferme facilius alia ulla in parte
Italiae posita urbs tenere potuisset.

Urbis autem ipsius nativa praesidia quis est tam neglegens
qui non habeat animo notata ac plane cognita? cuius is est
55 tractus ductusque muri cum Romuli, tum etiam reliquorum regum sapientia definitus ex omni parte arduis
praeruptisque montibus, ut unus aditus, qui esset inter
Esquilinum Quirinalemque montem, maximo aggere
obiecto fossa cingeretur vastissima, atque ut ita munita arx
60 circumiectu arduo et quasi circumciso saxo niteretur, ut
etiam in illa tempestate horribili Gallici adventus incolumis
atque intacta permanserit. Locumque delegit et fontibus
abundantem et in regione pestilenti salubrem; colles enim
sunt, qui cum perflantur ipsi, tum afferunt umbram
65 vallibus.

De Re Publica II 5–11

XV

WEALTH AND AMBITION—THE RUIN OF ROME

*Cicero attributes the demoralisation of the last century of the
Republic to the growth of wealth and luxury.*

Expetuntur autem divitiae cum ad usus vitae necessarios,
tum ad perfruendas voluptates. In quibus autem maior

est animus, in iis pecuniae cupiditas spectat ad opes et ad
gratificandi facultatem, ut nuper M. Crassus negabat ullam
satis magnam pecuniam esse ei qui in re publica princeps 5
vellet esse, cuius fructibus exercitum alere non posset.
Delectant etiam magnifici apparatus vitaeque cultus cum
elegantia et copia: quibus rebus effectum est ut infinita
pecuniae cupiditas esset. Nec vero rei familiaris amplificatio nemini nocens vituperanda est, sed fugienda semper 10
iniuria est.

Maxime autem adducuntur plerique, ut eos iustitiae
capiat oblivio, cum in imperiorum, honorum, gloriae
cupiditatem inciderunt. Declaravit id modo temeritas C.
Caesaris, qui omnia iura divina et humana pervertit propter 15
eum, quem sibi ipse opinionis errore finxerat, principatum.
Est autem in hoc genere molestum, quod in maximis
animis splendidissimisque ingeniis plerumque existunt
honoris, imperii, potentiae, gloriae cupiditates. Quo magis
cavendum est ne quid in eo genere peccetur. 20

De Officiis I 25–26

XVI

IURE PLECTIMUR: ROME RIGHTLY JUDGED

*This passage is remarkable both for its expression of Cicero's
ideal of the Roman Empire and his criticism of Roman tyranny.
Misgovernment of subject peoples had recoiled upon their rulers.*

Verum tamen, quam diu imperium populi Romani
beneficiis tenebatur, non iniuriis, bella aut pro sociis aut
de imperio gerebantur, exitus erant bellorum aut mites aut
necessarii, regum, populorum, nationum portus erat et
refugium senatus; nostri autem magistratus imperatoresque 5

ex hac una re maximam laudem capere studebant, si
provincias, si socios aequitate et fide defendissent.   Itaque
illud patrocinium orbis terrae verius quam imperium
poterat nominari.   Sensim hanc consuetudinem et disci-
10 plinam iam antea minuebamus, post vero Sullae victoriam
penitus amisimus; desitum est enim videri quicquam in
socios iniquum, cum exstitisset in cives tanta crudelitas.
Ergo in illo secuta est honestam causam non honesta
victoria.   Est enim ausus dicere, hasta posita cum bona in
15 foro venderet et bonorum virorum et locupletium et certe
civium, 'praedam se suam vendere.'   Secutus est qui in
causa impia, victoria etiam foediore non singulorum civium
bona publicaret, sed universas provincias regionesque uno
calamitatis iure comprehenderet.   Itaque vexatis ac per-
20 ditis exteris nationibus ad exemplum amissi imperii portari
in triumpho Massiliam vidimus et ex ea urbe triumphari,
sine qua nunquam nostri imperatores ex transalpinis bellis
triumpharunt.   Multa praeterea commemorarem nefaria
in socios, si hoc uno quicquam sol vidisset indignius.   Iure
25 igitur plectimur.   Nisi enim multorum impunita scelera
tulissemus, nunquam ad unum tanta pervenisset licentia:
a quo quidem rei familiaris ad paucos, cupiditatum ad
multos improbos venit hereditas.   Nec vero unquam
bellorum civilium semen et causa deerit, dum homines
30 perditi hastam illam cruentam et meminerint et sperabunt.
Itaque parietes modo urbis stant et manent, iique ipsi iam
extrema scelera metuentes, rem vero publicam penitus
amisimus.   Atque in has clades incidimus, dum metui
quam cari esse et diligi malumus.   Quae si populo Romano
35 iniuste imperanti accidere potuerunt, quid debent putare
singuli?

De Officiis II 26–29

XVII

CARITAS: LOVE THE BOND OF SOCIETY

From the fate of Julius Caesar, Cicero draws the revolutionary lesson that love (caritas), not hate, rules the world, and that those who, in a democracy (libera civitas), try to govern by terror, are deceived, for freedom will always break out again. It is not only right, but the best policy to be loved instead of feared.

Omnium autem rerum nec aptius est quicquam ad opes tuendas ac tenendas quam diligi nec alienius quam timeri. Praeclare enim Ennius:

Quem metuunt oderunt; quem quisque odit, periisse expetit.

Multorum autem odiis nullas opes posse obsistere, si antea 5 fuit ignotum, nuper est cognitum.   Nec vero huius tyranni solum, quem armis oppressa pertulit civitas ac paret cum maxime mortuo, interitus declarat (quantum odium hominum valeat ad pestem,) sed reliquorum similes exitus tyrannorum, quorum haud fere quisquam talem interitum 10 effugit. Malus enim est custos diuturnitatis metus, contraque benevolentia fidelis vel ad perpetuitatem.   Sed iis, qui vi oppressos imperio coercent, sit sane adhibenda saevitia, ut eris in famulos, si aliter teneri non possunt: qui vero in libera civitate ita se instruunt ut metuantur, iis 15 nihil potest esse dementius.   Quamvis enim sint demersae leges alicuius opibus, quamvis timefacta libertas, emergunt tamen haec aliquando aut iudiciis tacitis aut occultis de honore suffragiis.   Acriores autem morsus sunt intermissae libertatis quam retentae.   Quod igitur latissime patet neque 20 ad incolumitatem solum, sed etiam ad opes et potentiam valet plurimum, id amplectamur, ut metus absit, caritas retineatur.

De Officiis II 23–24

XVIII

LIBERTAS: NIHIL FOEDIUS SERVITUTE

The motto of this last, eloquent appeal for freedom might be, 'Romans never shall be slaves.'

Hanc igitur occasionem oblatam tenete, per deos immortales, patres conscripti, et amplissimi orbis terrae consilii principes vos esse aliquando recordamini. Signum date populo Romano consilium vestrum non deesse rei
5 publicae, quoniam ille virtutem suam non defuturam esse profitetur. Nihil est quod moneam vos. Nemo est tam stultus qui non intellegat, si indormierimus huic tempori, non modo crudelem superbamque dominationem nobis sed ignominiosam etiam et flagitiosam ferendam esse. Nostis
10 insolentiam Antoni, nostis amicos, nostis totam domum. Libidinosis, petulantibus, impuris, impudicis, aleatoribus, ebriis servire, ea summa miseria est summo dedecore coniuncta. Quod si iam (quod di omen avertant!) fatum extremum rei publicae venit, quod gladiatores nobiles
15 faciunt ut honeste decumbant, faciamus nos, principes orbis terrarum gentiumque omnium, ut cum dignitate potius cadamus quam cum ignominia serviamus. Nihil est detestabilius dedecore, nihil foedius servitute. Ad decus et ad libertatem nati sumus: aut haec teneamus aut cum
20 dignitate moriamur. Nimium diu teximus quid sentiremus; nunc iam apertum est; omnes patefaciunt in utramque partem quid sentiant, quid velint. Sunt impii (pro caritate rei publicae nimium multi, sed contra multitudinem bene sentientium admodum pauci) quorum opprimendorum di
25 immortales incredibilem rei publicae potestatem et fortunam dederunt. Ad ea enim praesidia quae habemus iam

accedent consules summa prudentia, virtute, concordia, multos menses de populi Romani libertate commentati atque meditati. His auctoribus et ducibus, dis iuvantibus, nobis vigilantibus et multum in posterum providentibus, 30 populo Romano consentiente, erimus profecto liberi brevi tempore. Iucundiorem autem faciet libertatem servitutis recordatio.

Philippic III 34–36

LAW AND JUSTICE

☆

XIX

THE LAWS OF WAR

The theme is up-to-date. It is significant that, although nations still ignore or break international law, none has ever yet publicly denied its existence.

Atque in republica maxime conservanda sunt iura belli.
Nam cum sint duo genera decertandi, unum per disceptationem, alterum per vim, cumque illud proprium sit hominis,
hoc beluarum, confugiendum est ad posterius, si uti non
5 licet superiore.   Qua re suscipienda quidem bella sunt ob
eam causam, ut sine iniuria in pace vivatur, parta autem
victoria conservandi ii qui non crudeles in bello, non
immanes fuerunt, ut maiores nostri Tusculanos, Aequos,
Volscos in civitatem etiam acceperunt, at Carthaginem et
10 Numantiam funditus sustulerunt: nollem Corinthum, sed
credo aliquid secutos, opportunitatem loci maxime, ne
posset aliquando ad bellum faciendum locus ipse hortari.
Mea quidem sententia paci, quae nihil habitura sit insidiarum, semper est consulendum.   In quo si mihi esset
15 obtemperatum, si non optimam, at aliquam rem publicam,
quae nunc nulla est, haberemus.   Et cum iis quos vi
deviceris consulendum est, tum ii qui armis positis ad
imperatorum fidem confugient, quamvis murum aries
percusserit, recipiendi.   In quo tanto opere apud nostros
20 iustitia culta est, ut ii, qui civitates aut nationes devictas

bello in fidem recepissent, earum patroni essent more
maiorum. Ac belli quidem aequitas sanctissime fetiali
populi Romani iure perscripta est. Ex quo intellegi potest
nullum bellum esse iustum nisi quod aut rebus repetitis
geratur aut denuntiatum ante sit et indictum. Marci 25
quidem Catonis senis est epistola ad Marcum filium, in qua
scribit se audisse eum missum factum esse a consule, cum
in Macedonia bello Persico miles esset. Monet igitur ut
caveat ne proelium ineat: negat enim ius esse qui miles
non sit cum hoste pugnare. 30

De Officiis I 34–37

XX

The Supreme Law

*Why should we obey the law? Is it simply because a particular
government imposes it? If so, what right would we have to
disobey the laws of a tyrant? To Cicero it seems self-evident that
there must be a law above human law, otherwise society and
morality would break up.*

Iam vero illud stultissimum, existimare iusta esse, quae
sita sint in populorum institutis aut legibus. Etiamne, si
quae leges sint tyrannorum? Si triginta illi Athenis leges
imponere voluissent, aut si omnes Athenienses delectarentur
tyrannicis legibus, num idcirco hae leges iustae haberentur? 5
Nihilo, credo, magis illa, quam interrex noster tulit, ut
dictator, quem vellet civium, indicta causa impune posset
occidere. Est enim unum ius, quo devincta est hominum
societas, et quod lex constituit una: quae lex est recta ratio
imperandi atque prohibendi; quam qui ignorat, is est 10
iniustus, sive est illa scripta uspiam, sive nusquam. Quodsi

iustitia est obtemperatio scriptis legibus institutisque
populorum et si, ut iidem dicunt, utilitate omnia metienda
sunt, negleget leges easque perrumpet, si poterit, is, qui
15 sibi eam rem fructuosam putabit fore. Ita fit ut nulla sit
omnino iustitia, si neque natura est, eaque, quae propter
utilitatem constituitur, utilitate illa convellitur. Atque, si
natura confirmatura ius non erit, virtutes omnes tollentur.
Ubi enim liberalitas, ubi patriae caritas, ubi pietas, ubi bene
20 merendi de altero, aut referendae gratiae voluntas poterit
existere? nam haec nascuntur ex eo, quod natura propensi sumus ad diligendos homines; quod fundamentum
iuris est. Neque solum in homines obsequia, sed etiam in
deos caerimoniae religionesque tollentur; quas non metu,
25 sed ea coniunctione, quae est homini cum deo, conservandas
puto.

De Legibus I 42-43

XXI

NATURAL LAW

*This famous fragment completes the argument of the previous
extract, by showing that the Law of Nature is divine.*

Est quidem vera lex recta ratio naturae congruens,
diffusa in omnes, constans, sempiterna, quae vocet ad
officium iubendo, vetando a fraude deterreat; quae tamen
neque probos frustra iubet aut vetat nec improbos iubendo
5 aut vetando movet. Huic legi nec obrogari fas est neque
derogari ex hac aliquid licet neque tota abrogari potest, nec
vero aut per senatum aut per populum solvi hac lege
possumus, neque est quaerendus explanator aut interpres
eius alius, nec erit alia lex Romae, alia Athenis, alia

nunc, alia posthac, sed et omnes gentes et omni tempore 10
una lex et sempiterna et immutabilis continebit, unusque
erit communis quasi magister et imperator omnium deus,
ille legis huius inventor, disceptator, lator; cui qui non
parebit, ipse se fugiet ac naturam hominis aspernatus hoc
ipso luet maximas poenas, etiamsi cetera supplicia, quae 15
putantur, effugerit.

De Re Publica III (fragment)

DEATH AND IMMORTALITY

☆

XXII

Cato on Old Age

*Old Age is according to nature and, therefore, to be accepted with
its limitations like any other period of life.*

Quattuor robustos filios, quinque filias, tantam domum,
tantas clientelas Appius regebat et caecus et senex; intentum enim animum tamquam arcum habebat nec
languescens succumbebat senectuti; tenebat non modo
5 auctoritatem, sed etiam imperium in suos: metuebant servi,
verebantur liberi, carum omnes habebant; vigebat in
illa domo mos patrius et disciplina. Ita enim senectus
honesta est, si se ipsa defendit, si ius suum retinet, si
nemini emancipata est, si usque ad ultimum spiritum
10 dominatur in suos. Ut enim adulescentem, in quo est
senile aliquid, sic senem, in quo est aliquid adulescentis,
probo; quod qui sequitur, corpore senex esse poterit,
animo nunquam erit. Septimus mihi liber Originum est
in manibus; omnia antiquitatis monumenta colligo;
15 causarum illustrium, quascumque defendi, nunc cum
maxime conficio orationes; ius augurium, pontificium,
civile tracto; multum etiam Graecis litteris utor Pythagore-
orumque more, exercendae memoriae gratia, quid quoque
die dixerim, audierim, egerim, commemoro vesperi. Hae
20 sunt exercitationes ingenii, haec curricula mentis, in his

50

desudans atque elaborans corporis vires non magno opere
desidero. Adsum amicis, venio in senatum frequens
ultroque affero res multum et diu cogitatas easque tueor
animi, non corporis viribus. Quas si exsequi nequirem,
tamen me lectulus meus oblectaret ea ipsa cogitantem, 25
quae iam agere non possem; sed ut possim, facit acta vita.
Semper enim in his studiis laboribusque viventi non
intellegitur quando obrepat senectus. Ita sensim sine
sensu aetas senescit nec subito frangitur, sed diuturnitate
exstinguitur. 30

De Senectute 37–38

XXIII

Death Certain

*Death, like the last act of a play, or the end of a long voyage,
since it is* secundum naturam, *is to be reckoned a good thing*
(habenda in bonis).

Quamquam O di boni! quid est in hominis natura diu?
Da enim supremum tempus, exspectemus Tartessiorum
regis aetatem (fuit enim, ut scriptum video, Arganthonius
quidam Gadibus, qui octoginta regnavit annos, centum
viginti vixit), sed mihi ne diuturnum quidem quicquam 5
videtur, in quo est aliquid extremum. Cum enim id
advenit, tum illud, quod praeteriit, effluxit; tantum
remanet, quod virtute et recte factis consecutus sis; horae
quidem cedunt et dies et menses et anni, nec praeteritum
tempus umquam revertitur, nec quid sequatur sciri potest; 10
quod cuique temporis ad vivendum datur, eo debet esse
contentus.

Neque enim histrioni, ut placeat, peragenda fabula est,

modo in quocumque fuerit actu probetur, neque sapienti
15 usque ad 'Plaudite' veniendum est.   Breve enim tempus
aetatis satis longum est ad bene honesteque vivendum; sin
processerit longius, non magis dolendum est, quam agri-
colae dolent praeterita verni temporis suavitate aestatem
autumnumque venisse.   Ver enim tamquam adulescentiam
20 significat ostenditque fructus futuros, reliqua autem
tempora demetendis fructibus et percipiendis accommodata
sunt.   Fructus autem senectutis est, ut saepe dixi, ante
partorum bonorum memoria et copia.   Omnia autem,
quae secundum naturam fiunt, sunt habenda in bonis.
25 Quid est autem tam secundum naturam quam senibus
emori? quod idem contingit adulescentibus adversante
et repugnante natura.   Itaque adulescentes mihi mori sic
videntur, ut cum aquae multitudine flammae vis opprimi-
tur, senes autem sic, ut cum sua sponte, nulla adhibita vi,
30 consumptus ignis exstinguitur, et quasi poma ex arboribus,
cruda si sunt, vix evelluntur, si matura et cocta, decidunt,
sic vitam adulescentibus vis aufert, senibus maturitas;
quae quidem mihi tam iucunda est, ut, quo propius ad
mortem accedam, quasi terram videre videar aliquandoque
35 in portum ex longa navigatione esse venturus.

De Senectute 69–71

XXIV

Facing Death

*The wise man does not fear death, but faces it with Stoic
fortitude.*

Sed quid ego Socratem aut Theramenem, praestantes
viros virtutis et sapientiae gloria, commemoro? cum

Lacedaemonius quidam, cuius ne nomen quidem proditum
est, mortem tanto opere contempserit, ut cum ad eam
duceretur damnatus ab ephoris et esset voltu hilari atque 5
laeto, dixissetque ei quidam inimicus: 'Contemnisne leges
Lycurgi?' responderit: 'Ego vero illi maximam gratiam
habeo, qui me ea poena multaverit, quam sine mutuatione
et sine versura possem dissolvere.' O virum Sparta
dignum! ut mihi quidem, qui tam magno animo fuerit, 10
innocens damnatus esse videatur. Tales innumerabiles
nostra civitas tulit. Sed quid duces et principes nominem,
cum legiones scribat Cato saepe alacres in eum locum
profectas, unde redituras se non arbitrarentur? Pari
animo Lacedaemonii in Thermopylis occiderunt, in quos 15
Simonides:

> Dic, hospes, Spartae nos te hic vidisse iacentes,
> Dum sanctis patriae legibus obsequimur.

E quibus unus, cum Perses hostis in colloquio dixisset
glorians: 'Solem prae iaculorum multitudine et sagittarum 20
non videbitis,' 'In umbra igitur,' inquit, 'pugnabimus.'
Viros commemoro; qualis tandem Lacaena? Quae cum
filium in proelium misisset et interfectum audisset, 'Idcirco,'
inquit, 'genueram, ut esset, qui pro patria mortem non
dubitaret occumbere.' 25

Quae cum ita sint, magna tamen eloquentia est utendum
atque ita velut superiore e loco contionandum, ut homines
mortem vel optare incipiant vel certe timere desistant.
Nam si supremus ille dies non exstinctionem, sed commu-
tationem affert loci, quid optabilius? Sin autem perimit 30
ac delet omnino, quid melius quam in mediis vitae laboribus
obdormiscere et ita coniventem somno consopiri sempiterno?
Quod si fiat, melior Ennii quam Solonis oratio. Hic enim
noster:

> Nemo me lacrimis decoret, nec funera fletu 35
> Faxit!

at vero ille sapiens:

    Mors mea ne careat lacrimis, linquamus amicis
    Maerorem, ut celebrent funera cum gemitu.

             Tusculan Disputations I 100–102; 117

XXV

Somnium Scipionis

The belief in the immortality of the soul, an open question in the preceding passages, is the chief theme of this famous 'myth.'

(1) Cum in Africam venissem M'. Manilio consuli ad quartam legionem tribunus, ut scitis, militum, nihil mihi fuit potius quam ut Masinissam convenirem regem, familiae nostrae iustis de causis amicissimum. Ad quem
5 ut veni, complexus me senex collacrimavit aliquantoque post suspexit in caelum et: Grates, inquit, tibi ago, summe Sol, vobisque, reliqui Caelites, quod ante quam ex hac vita migro conspicio in meo regno et in his tectis P. Cornelium Scipionem, cuius ego nomine ipso recreor; ita numquam
10 ex animo meo discedit illius optimi atque invictissimi viri memoria. Deinde ego illum de suo regno, ille me de nostra re publica percontatus est, multisque verbis ultro citroque habitis ille nobis consumptus est dies.

(2) Post autem apparatu regio accepti sermonem in
15 multam noctem produximus, cum senex nihil nisi de Africano loqueretur omniaque eius non facta solum, sed etiam dicta meminisset. Deinde, ut cubitum discessimus, me et de via fessum et qui ad multam noctem vigilassem, artior quam solebat somnus complexus est. Hic mihi—
20 credo equidem ex hoc, quod eramus locuti: fit enim fere ut cogitationes sermonesque nostri pariant aliquid in somno tale, quale de Homero scribit Ennius, de quo videlicet

saepissime vigilans solebat cogitare et loqui—Africanus
se ostendit ea forma, quae mihi ex imagine eius quam ex
ipso erat notior, quem ubi agnovi, equidem cohorrui, sed 25
ille: Ades, inquit, animo et omitte timorem, Scipio, et
quae dicam trade memoriae.

(3) Videsne illam urbem, quae parere populo Romano
coacta per me renovat pristina bella nec potest quiescere?
—ostendebat autem Carthaginem de excelso et pleno 30
stellarum, illustri et claro quodam loco—ad quam tu
oppugnandam nunc venis paene miles.   Hanc hoc biennio
consul evertes, eritque cognomen id tibi per te partum,
quod habes adhuc a nobis hereditarium.   Cum autem
Carthaginem deleveris, triumphum egeris censorque fueris 35
et obieris legatus Aegyptum, Syriam, Asiam, Graeciam,
deligere iterum absens consul bellumque maximum con-
ficies, Numantiam exscindes.   Sed cum eris curru Capitol-
ium invectus, offendes rem publicam consiliis perturbatam
nepotis mei.   40

(4) Hic tu, Africane, ostendas oportebit patriae lumen
animi, ingenii consiliique tui.   Sed eius temporis ancipitem
video quasi fatorum viam.   Nam cum aetas tua septenos
octiens solis anfractus reditusque converterit, duoque hi
numeri, quorum uterque plenus alter altera de causa 45
habetur, circuitu naturali summam tibi fatalem confecerint,
in te unum atque in tuum nomen se tota convertet civitas,
te senatus, te omnes boni, te socii, te Latini intuebuntur: tu
eris unus, in quo nitatur civitatis salus, ac, ne multa, dictator
rem publicam constituas oportebit, si impias propinquorum 50
manus effugeris.   Hic cum exclamasset Laelius ingemuissent-
que ceteri vehementius, leniter adridens Scipio: Quaeso,
inquit, ne me e somno excitetis, parumper audite cetera.

(5) Sed quo sis, Africane, alacrior ad tutandam rem
publicam, sic habeto: omnibus, qui patriam conserva- 55
verint, adiuverint, auxerint, certum esse in caelo definitum

locum, ubi beati aevo sempiterno fruantur: nihil est enim
illi principi deo, qui omnem mundum regit, quod quidem
in terris fiat, acceptius quam concilia coetusque hominum
60 iure sociati, quae civitates appellantur: harum rectores et
conservatores hinc profecti huc revertuntur.

(6) Hic ego, etsi eram perterritus non tam mortis metu
quam insidiarum a meis, quaesivi tamen viveretne ipse et
Paulus pater et alii, quos nos exstinctos esse arbitraremur.
65 Immo vero, inquit, ei vivunt, qui e corporum vinculis
tamquam e carcere evolaverunt; vestra vero, quae dicitur,
vita mors est. Quin tu aspicis ad te venientem Paulum
patrem? Quem ut vidi, equidem vim lacrimarum profudi,
ille autem me complexus atque osculans flere prohibebat.
70 (7) Atque ego ut primum fletu represso loqui posse coepi:
Quaeso, inquam, pater sanctissime atque optime, quoniam
haec est vita, ut Africanum audio dicere, quid moror in
terris? quin huc ad vos venire propero? Non est ita,
inquit ille. Nisi enim deus is, cuius hoc templum est omne,
75 quod conspicis, istis te corporis custodiis liberaverit, huc tibi
aditus patere non potest. Homines enim sunt hac lege
generati, qui tuerentur illum globum, quem in hoc templo
medium vides, quae terra dicitur, hisque animus datus est
ex illis sempiternis ignibus, quae sidera et stellas vocatis,
80 quae globosae et rotundae, divinis animatae mentibus,
circulos suos orbesque conficiunt celeritate mirabili. Qua
re et tibi, Publi, et piis omnibus retinendus animus est in
custodia corporis nec iniussu eius, a quo ille est vobis datus,
ex hominum vita migrandum est, ne munus humanum
85 adsignatum a deo defugisse videamini. Sed sic, Scipio, ut
avus hic tuus, ut ego, qui te genui, iustitiam cole et pietatem,
quae cum magna in parentibus et propinquis tum in patria
maxima est; ea vita via est in caelum et in hunc coetum
eorum, qui iam vixerunt et corpore relaxati illum incolunt
90 locum, quem vides, (erat autem is splendidissimo candore

inter flammas circulus elucens), quem vos, ut a Graiis
accepistis, orbem lacteum nuncupatis. (8) Ex quo mihi
omnia contemplanti praeclara cetera et mirabilia vide-
bantur. Erant autem eae stellae, quas numquam ex hoc
loco vidimus, et eae magnitudines omnium, quas esse 95
numquam suspicati sumus, ex quibus erat ea minima, quae
ultima a caelo, citima terris, luce lucebat aliena. Stellarum
autem globi terrae magnitudinem facile vincebant. Iam
vero ipsa terra ita mihi parva visa est, ut me imperii nostri,
quo quasi punctum eius attingimus, paeniteret. 100

(9) Quam cum magis intuerer: Quaeso, inquit Africanus,
quousque humi defixa tua mens erit? Nonne aspicis quae
in templa veneris? Novem tibi orbibus vel potius globis
conexa sunt omnia, quorum unus caelestis est, extimus,
qui reliquos omnes complectitur, summus ipse deus arcens 105
et continens ceteros: in quo sunt infixi illi, qui volvuntur,
stellarum cursus sempiterni: cui subiecti septem, qui
versantur retro contrario motu atque caelum, ex quibus
unum globum possidet illa, quam in terris Saturniam
nominant. Deinde est hominum generi prosperus et 110
salutaris ille fulgor, qui dicitur Iovis: tum rutilus horribilisque terris, quem Martium dicitis: deinde subter
mediam fere regionem Sol obtinet, dux et princeps et
moderator luminum reliquorum, mens mundi et temperatio,
tanta magnitudine, ut cuncta sua luce lustret et compleat. 115
Hunc ut comites consequuntur Veneris alter, alter Mercurii
cursus, in infimoque orbe Luna radiis solis accensa convertitur. Infra autem iam nihil est nisi mortale et caducum
praeter animos munere deorum hominum generi datos,
supra Lunam sunt aeterna omnia. Nam ea quae est media 120
et nona, tellus, neque movetur et infima est, et in eam
feruntur omnia nutu suo pondera.

(10) Quae cum intuerer stupens, ut me recepi: Quis hic,
inquam, est, qui complet aures meas, tantus et tam dulcis

125 sonus? Hic est, inquit, ille qui intervallis coniunctus
imparibus, sed tamen pro rata parte ratione distinctis
impulsu et motu ipsorum orbium conficitur et acuta cum
gravibus temperans varios aequabiliter concentus efficit;
nec enim silentio tanti motus incitari possunt et natura fert
130 ut extrema ex altera parte graviter, ex altera autem acute
sonent. Quam ob causam summus ille caeli stellifer
cursus, cuius conversio est concitatior, acuto et excitato
movetur sono, gravissimo autem hic lunaris atque infimus;
nam terra nona immobilis manens una sede semper haeret
135 complexa medium mundi locum.   Illi autem octo cursus,
in quibus eadem vis est duorum, septem efficiunt distinctos
intervallis sonos, qui numerus rerum omnium fere nodus
est;   quod docti homines nervis imitati atque cantibus
aperuerunt sibi reditum in hunc locum, sicut ealii, qui
140 praestantibus ingeniis in vita humana divina studia
coluerunt. (11) Hoc sonitu oppletae aures hominum obsurduerunt: nec est ullus hebetior sensus in vobis, sicut, ubi
Nilus ad illa, quae Catadupa nominantur, praecipitat ex
altissimis montibus, ea gens, quae illum locum accolit,
145 propter magnitudinem sonitus sensu audiendi caret. Hic
vero tantus est totius mundi incitatissima conversione
sonitus, ut eum aures hominum capere non possint, sicut
intueri solem adversum nequitis eiusque radiis acies vestra
sensusque vincitur.
150   Haec ego admirans referebam tamen oculos ad terram
identidem.
      (12) Tum Africanus: Sentio, inquit, te sedem etiam nunc
hominum ac domum contemplari: quae si tibi parva,
ut est, ita videtur, haec caelestia semper spectato, illa
155 humana contemnito. Tu enim quam celebritatem sermonis hominum aut quam expetendam consequi gloriam
potes? Vides habitari in terra raris et angustis in locis et in
ipsis quasi maculis, ubi habitatur, vastas solitudines

interiectas, eosque, qui incolunt terram, interruptos ita esse,
ut nihil inter ipsos ab aliis ad alios manare possit; a quibus 160
expectare gloriam certe nullam poteris.

(13) Cernis autem eandem terram quasi quibusdam
redimitam et circumdatam cingulis, e quibus duo maxime
inter se diversos et caeli verticibus ipsis ex utraque parte
subnixos obriguisse pruina vides, medium autem illum et 165
maximum solis ardore torreri.   Duo sunt habitabiles, quorum australis ille, in quo qui insistunt adversa vobis
urgent vestigia, nihil ad vestrum genus, hic autem alter
subiectus aquiloni, quem incolitis, cerne quam tenui vos
parte contingat.   Omnis enim terra, quae colitur a vobis, 170
angustata verticibus, lateribus latior, parva quaedam
insula est circumfusa illo mari, quod Atlanticum, quod
magnum, quem Oceanum appellatis in terris, qui tamen
tanto nomine quam sit parvus vides.   (14) Ex his ipsis cultis
notisque terris num aut tuum aut cuiusquam nostrum 175
nomen vel Caucasum hunc, quem cernis, transcendere
potuit vel illum Gangem tranatare?   Quis in reliquis
orientis aut obeuntis solis ultimis aut aquilonis austrive
partibus tuum nomen audiet?   Quibus amputatis cernis
profecto quantis in angustiis vestra se gloria dilatari velit. 180
Ipsi autem, qui de vobis loquuntur, quam loquentur diu?

(15) Quin etiam, si cupiat proles illa futurorum hominum
deinceps laudes unius cuiusque nostrum a patribus acceptas
posteris prodere, tamen propter eluviones exustionesque
terrarum, quas accidere tempore certo necesse est, non modo 185
non aeternam, sed ne diuturnam quidem gloriam adsequi
possumus.   Quid autem interest ab iis, qui postea nascentur,
sermonem fore de te, cum ab eis nullus fuerit, qui ante nati
sunt?   qui nec pauciores et certe meliores fuerunt viri,
(16) praesertim cum apud eos ipsos, a quibus audiri nomen 190
nostrum potest, nemo unius anni memoriam consequi possit.
Homines enim populariter annum tantum modo solis, id

est, unius astri reditu metiuntur, cum autem ad idem,
unde semel profecta sunt, cuncta astra redierint eandemque
195 totius caeli descriptionem longis intervallis rettulerint, tum
ille vere vertens annus appellari potest; in quo vix dicere
audeo quam multa hominum saecula teneantur. Namque
ut olim deficere sol omnibus extinguique visus est, cum
Romuli animus haec ipsa in templa penetravit, quando ab
200 eadem parte sol eodemque tempore iterum defecerit, tum
signis omnibus ad principium stellisque revocatis expletum
annum habeto: huius quidem anni nondum vicesimam
partem scito esse conversam.

(17) Quocirca si reditum in hunc locum desperaveris, in
205 quo omnia sunt magnis et praestantibus viris, quanti tandem
est ista hominum gloria, quae pertinere vix ad unius anni
partem exiguam potest? Igitur alte spectare si voles atque
hanc sedem et aeternam domum contueri, neque te sermonibus vulgi dedideris nec in praemiis humanis spem posueris
210 rerum tuarum: suis te oportet illecebris ipsa virtus trahat
ad verum decus, quid de te alii loquantur ipsi videant, sed
loquentur tamen. Sermo autem omnis ille et angustiis
cingitur eis regionum, quas vides, nec umquam de ullo
perennis fuit et obruitur hominum interitu et oblivione
215 posteritatis extinguitur.

(18) Quae cum dixisset: Ego vero, inquam, Africane, si
quidem bene meritis de patria quasi limes ad caeli aditum
patet, quamquam a pueritia vestigiis ingressus patris et tuis
decori vestro non defui, nunc tamen tanto praemio exposito
220 enitar multo vigilantius. Et ille: Tu vero enitere et sic
habeto, non esse te mortalem, sed corpus hoc: nec enim tu
is es, quem forma ista declarat, sed mens cuiusque is est
quisque, non ea figura, quae digito demonstrari potest.
Deum te igitur scito esse, si quidem deus est, qui viget, qui
225 sentit, qui meminit, qui providet, qui tam regit et moderatur
et movet id corpus, cui praepositus est, quam hunc mundum

ille princeps deus, et ut mundum ex quadam parte mortalem
ipse deus aeternus, sic fragile corpus animus sempiternus
movet.

(19) Nam quod semper movetur aeternum est; quod 230
autem motum adfert alicui quodque ipsum agitatur aliunde,
quando finem habet motus, vivendi finem habeat necesse
est. Solum igitur quod se ipsum movet, quia numquam
deseritur a se, numquam ne moveri quidem desinit. Quin
etiam ceteris, quae moventur, hic fons, hoc principium 235
est movendi. Principii autem nulla est origo; nam ex
principio oriuntur omnia, ipsum autem nulla ex re alia
nasci potest; nec enim esset id principium, quod gigneretur
aliunde; quod si numquam oritur, ne occidit quidem
umquam. Nam principium exstinctum nec ipsum ab alio 240
renascetur nec ex se aliud creabit, si quidem necesse est
a principio oriri omnia. Ita fit ut motus principium ex eo
sit, quod ipsum a se movetur: id autem nec nasci potest
nec mori, vel concidat omne caelum omnisque natura
consistat necesse est nec vim ullam nanciscatur, qua a primo 245
impulsa moveatur.

(20) Cum pateat igitur aeternum id esse, quod se ipsum
moveat, quis est qui hanc naturam animis esse tributam
neget? Inanimum est enim omne, quod pulsu agitatur
externo; quod autem est animal, id motu cietur interiore 250
et suo: nam haec est propria natura animi atque vis.
Quae si est una ex omnibus quae sese moveat, neque nata
est certe et aeterna est. (21) Hanc tu exerce optimis in
rebus! sunt autem optimae curae de salute patriae, quibus
agitatus et exercitus animus velocius in hanc sedem et 255
domum suam pervolabit. Idque ocius faciet, si iam tum,
cum erit inclusus in corpore, eminebit foras et ea, quae extra
erunt, contemplans quam maxime se a corpore abstrahet.
Namque eorum animi, qui se corporis voluptatibus
dediderunt earumque se quasi ministros praebuerunt 260

impulsuque libidinum voluptatibus oboedientium deorum
et hominum iura violaverunt, corporibus elapsi circum
terram ipsam volutantur, nec in hunc locum nisi multis
exagitati saeculis revertuntur. Ille discessit: ego somno
265 solutus sum.

De Re Publica VI (fragment)

RELIGION AND NATURE

☆

XXVI

Universal Belief in Divination

The theme of the De Divinatione *is divination, or the art of foretelling the future by various means, such as prophecy, dreams, and astrology. Widespread among the Greeks and Romans, belief in this power was strong at all times, although its practice by private persons came to be disapproved, and* mathematici *(astrologers) were repeatedly banned during the Empire. For the Stoic, it was important to investigate divination, since, if true, it was thought to prove that the soul transcends time, and is, therefore, divine and immortal.*

The following passage is from Cicero's introduction to Book I.

Vetus opinio est iam usque ab heroicis ducta temporibus, eaque et populi Romani et omnium gentium firmata consensu, versari quandam inter homines divinationem, id est praesensionem et scientiam rerum futurarum. Magnifica quaedam res et salutaris, si modo est ulla, 5 quaque proxime ad deorum vim natura mortalis possit accedere. Gentem quidem nullam video neque tam humanam atque doctam neque tam immanem tamque barbaram, quae non significari futura et a quibusdam intellegi praedicique posse censeat. Principio Assyrii, ut 10 ab ultimis auctoritatem repetam, propter planitiam magnitudinemque regionum, quas incolebant, cum caelum ex omni parte patens atque apertum intuerentur, traiectiones motusque stellarum observitaverunt, quibus notatis, 15 quid cuique significaretur, memoriae prodiderunt. Qua in natione Chaldaei diuturna observatione siderum scientiam effecisse putantur, ut praedici posset, quid cuique eventurum et quo quisquam fato natus esset. Eandem artem etiam Aegyptii longinquitate temporum 20 innumerabilibus paene saeculis consecuti putantur. Cilicum autem et Pisidarum gens et his finitima Pamphylia, quibus nationibus praefuimus ipsi, volatibus avium cantibusque ut certissimis signis declarari res futuras putant. Quam vero Graecia coloniam misit in Aeoliam, Ioniam, Asiam, 25 Siciliam, Italiam sine Pythio aut Dodonaeo aut Hammonis oraculo? aut quod bellum susceptum ab ea sine consilio deorum est? Nec unum genus est divinationis publice privatimque celebratum. Nam, ut omittam ceteros populos, noster quam multa genera complexus est! Principio 30 huius urbis parens Romulus non solum auspicato urbem condidisse, sed ipse etiam optimus augur fuisse traditur. Deinde auguribus et reliqui reges usi, et exactis regibus nihil publice sine auspiciis nec domi nec militiae gerebatur. Cumque magna vis videretur esse monstris interpretandis 35 ac procurandis in haruspicum disciplina, omnem hanc ex Etruria scientiam adhibebant, ne genus esset ullum divinationis, quod neglectum ab iis videretur. Et cum duobus modis animi sine ratione et scientia motu ipsi suo soluto et libero incitarentur, uno furente, altero somniante, 40 furoris divinationem Sibyllinis maxime versibus contineri arbitrati eorum decem interpretes delectos e civitate esse voluerunt. Nec vero somnia graviora, si quae ad rem publicam pertinere visa sunt, a summo concilio neglecta sunt.

De Divinatione I 1–4

XXVII

CASES OF DIVINATION

The speaker is Cicero's brother, Quintus, who adduces examples to prove the truth of divination.

Est profecto quiddam etiam in barbaris gentibus prae-
sentiens atque divinans, siquidem ad mortem proficiscens
Callanus Indus, cum ascenderet in rogum ardentem, 'O
praeclarum discessum,' inquit, 'e vita, cum, ut Herculi
contigit, mortali corpore cremato in lucem animus exces- 5
serit!' Cumque Alexander eum rogaret, si quid vellet, ut
diceret, 'Optime,' inquit; 'propediem te videbo.' Quod
ita contigit; nam Babylone paucis post diebus Alexander
est mortuus.

Est apud Platonem Socrates, cum esset in custodia 10
publica, dicens Critoni, suo familiari, sibi post tertium diem
esse moriendum; vidisse se in somniis pulchritudine eximia
feminam, quae se nomine appellans diceret Homericum
quendam eius modi versum:

Tertia te Phthiae tempestas laeta locabit.   15
Quod, ut est dictum, sic scribitur contigisse.

Adiungamus philosophis doctissimum hominem, poetam
quidem divinum, Sophoclem; qui, cum ex sede Herculis
patera aurea gravis subrepta esset, in somnis vidit ipsum
deum dicentem, quis id fecisset. Quod semel iterumque 20
neglexit. Ubi idem saepius, ascendit in Areum Pagum,
detulit rem; Areopagitae comprehendi iubent eum, qui
a Sophocle erat nominatus; is quaestione adhibita confessus
est pateramque rettulit.

Sed quid aut plura aut vetera quaerimus? Saepe tibi 25
narravi me, cum Asiae pro cos. praeessem, vidisse in quiete,
cum tu equo advectus ad quandam magni fluminis ripam
provectus subito delapsus in flumen nusquam apparuisses,

me contremuisse timore perterritum; tum te repente laetum
30 exstitisse eodemque equo adversam ascendisse ripam, nosque
inter nos esse complexos. Facilis coniectura huius somnii,
mihique a peritis in Asia praedictum est fore eos eventus
rerum, qui acciderunt.

Quid? bello Punico secundo nonne C. Flaminius consul
35 iterum neglexit signa rerum futurarum magna cum clade
rei publicae? Qui exercitu lustrato cum Arretium versus
castra movisset et contra Hannibalem legiones duceret, et
ipse et equus eius ante signum Iovis Statoris sine causa
repente concidit nec eam rem habuit religioni, obiecto
40 signo, ut peritis videbatur, ne committeret proelium.
Idem cum tripudio auspicaretur, pullarius diem proelii
committendi differebat. Tum Flaminius ex eo quaesivit,
si ne postea quidem pulli pascerentur, quid faciendum
censeret. Cum ille quiescendum respondisset, Flaminius:
45 'Praeclara vero auspicia, si esurientibus pullis res geri
poterit, saturis nihil geretur!' Itaque signa convelli et se
sequi iussit. Quo tempore cum signifer signum non
posset movere loco nec quicquam proficeretur, plures cum
accederent, Flaminius re nuntiata suo more neglexit.
50 Itaque tribus iis horis concisus exercitus atque ipse inter-
fectus est.

De Divinatione I 52, 54, 58, 77

XXVIII

Is Divination Possible?

Quintus Cicero states the Stoic argument for divination, based upon the immortality of the soul.

Cum ergo est somno sevocatus animus a societate et a
contagione corporis, tum meminit praeteritorum, prae-

sentia cernit, futura providet; iacet enim corpus dormientis
ut mortui, viget autem et vivit animus.   Quod multo magis
faciet post mortem, cum omnino corpore excesserit. Itaque 5
appropinquante morte multo est divinior.   Nam et id
ipsum vident, qui sunt morbo gravi et mortifero affecti,
instare mortem; itaque iis occurrunt plerumque imagines
mortuorum, tumque vel maxime laudi student, eosque, qui
secus quam decuit vixerunt, peccatorum suorum tum 10
maxime paenitet.   Divinare autem morientes illo etiam
exemplo confirmat Posidonius, quod affert, Rhodium
quendam morientem sex aequales nominasse et dixisse, qui
primus eorum, qui secundus, qui deinde deinceps moriturus
esset.   Sed tribus modis censet deorum appulsu homines 15
somniare, uno, quod provideat animus ipse per sese, quippe
qui deorum cognatione teneatur, altero, quod plenus aer
sit immortalium animorum, in quibus tamquam insignitae
notae veritatis appareant, tertio, quod ipsi di cum dormi-
entibus colloquantur.   Idque, ut modo dixi, facilius evenit 20
appropinquante morte, ut animi futura augurentur.   Ex
quo et illud Homerici Hectoris, qui moriens propinquam
Achilli mortem denuntiat.

De Divinatione I 63–64

XXIX

Cicero's own Opinion

*Cicero, in answer to Quintus, adopts the more rational and
sceptical attitude of the New Academy. (see Introd. II.8). 'Religion
without superstition,' is his principle.*

Explodatur haec quoque somniorum divinatio pariter
cum ceteris.   Nam, ut vere loquamur, superstitio fusa per

gentes oppressit omnium fere animos atque hominum
imbecillitatem occupavit.   Quod et in iis libris dictum est,
5 qui sunt de natura deorum, et hac disputatione id maxime
egimus.   Multum enim et nobismet ipsis et nostris pro-
futuri videbamur, si eam funditus sustulissemus.   Nec vero
(id enim diligenter intellegi volo) superstitione tollenda
religio tollitur.   Nam et maiorum instituta tueri sacris
10 caerimoniisque retinendis sapientis est, et esse praestantem
aliquam aeternamque naturam, et eam suspiciendam
admirandamque hominum generi pulchritudo mundi
ordoque rerum caelestium cogit confiteri.   Quam ob rem,
ut religio propaganda etiam est, quae est iuncta cum
15 cognitione naturae, sic superstitionis stirpes omnes eligendae.
Cum autem proprium sit Academiae iudicium suum nullum
interponere, ea probare, quae simillima veri videantur,
conferre causas et, quid in quamque sententiam dici
possit, expromere, nulla adhibita sua auctoritate iudi-
20 cium audientium relinquere integrum ac liberum, tene-
bimus hanc consuetudinem a Socrate traditam eaque
inter nos, si tibi, Quinte frater, placebit, quam saepissime
utemur.

De Divinatione II 148–150

XXX

ARE THERE GODS?

*The discussion on divination leads naturally to the question
whether gods exist, and, if so, what kind of gods.   This is the
subject of the* De Natura Deorum.

Itaque inter omnes omnium gentium summa constat;
omnibus enim innatum est et in animo quasi insculptum

esse deos. Quales sint, varium est, esse nemo negat.
Cleanthes quidem noster quattuor de causis dixit in animis
hominum informatas deorum esse notiones. Primam 5
posuit eam, de qua modo dixi, quae orta esset ex praesen-
sione rerum futurarum; alteram, quam ceperimus ex
magnitudine commodorum, quae percipiuntur caeli tem-
peratione, fecunditate terrarum aliarumque commoditatum
complurium copia; tertiam, quae terreret animos fulmini- 10
bus, tempestatibus, nimbis, nivibus, grandinibus, vastitate,
pestilentia, terrae motibus et saepe fremitibus lapideisque
imbribus et guttis imbrium quasi cruentis, tum labibus aut
repentinis terrarum hiatibus, tum praeter naturam hominum pecudumque portentis, tum facibus visis caelestibus, 15
tum stellis iis, quas Graeci cometas, nostri cincinnatas vocant,
quae nuper bello Octaviano magnarum fuerunt calamitatum
praenuntiae, tum sole geminato, quod, ut e patre audivi,
Tuditano et Aquilio consulibus evenerat, quo quidem anno
P. Africanus sol alter exstinctus est, quibus exterriti 20
homines vim quandam esse caelestem et divinam suspicati
sunt; quartam causam esse, eamque vel maximam,
aequabilitatem motus conversionumque caeli, solis, lunae
siderumque, omnium distinctionem, varietatem, pulchri-
tudinem, ordinem, quarum rerum aspectus ipse satis 25
indicaret non esse ea fortuita. Ut, si quis domum aliquam
aut in gymnasium aut in forum venerit, cum videat
omnium rerum rationem, modum, disciplinam, non possit
ea sine causa fieri iudicare, sed esse aliquem intellegat, qui
praesit et cui pareatur, multo magis in tantis motionibus 30
tantisque vicissitudinibus, tam multarum rerum atque
tantarum ordinibus, in quibus nihil unquam immensa et
infinita vetustas mentita sit, statuat necesse est ab aliqua
mente tantos naturae motus gubernari.

De Natura Deorum II 13–15

XXXI

THE ARGUMENT FROM DESIGN

The proof of the existence of God, based on the design of the universe, is here stated in a simple form; if a house implies a builder, and a picture an artist, then the order of the world points to a designer, and that designer must be a single, intelligent power. 'Deum agnoscis ex operibus eius,' says Cicero elsewhere: 'God is recognised from his works.'

Qui igitur convenit signum aut tabulam pictam cum aspexeris, scire adhibitam esse artem, cumque procul cursum navigii videris, non dubitare, quin id ratione atque arte moveatur, aut, cum solarium vel discriptum vel ex
5 aqua contemplere, intellegere declarari horas arte, non casu, mundum autem, qui et has ipsas artes et earum artifices et cuncta complectatur, consilii et rationis esse expertem putare? Quodsi in Scythiam aut in Britanniam sphaeram aliquis tulerit hanc, quam nuper familiaris
10 noster effecit Posidonius, cuius singulae conversiones idem efficiunt in sole et in luna et in quinque stellis errantibus, quod efficitur in caelo singulis diebus et noctibus, quis in illa barbaria dubitet, quin ea sphaera sit perfecta ratione? Hi autem dubitant de mundo, ex quo et oriuntur
15 et fiunt omnia, casune ipse sit effectus aut necessitate aliqua an ratione ac mente divina, et Archimedem arbitrantur plus valuisse in imitandis sphaerae conversionibus quam naturam in efficiendis, praesertim cum multis partibus sint illa perfecta quam haec simulata sollertius.

De Natura Deorum II 87–88

XXXII

The Beauty of the Universe

The object of this long description is to refute the materialist theory of the Epicureans, that the world originated from the chance movement of atoms.

For the astronomy of the passage, see also notes on XXV.

Ac principio terra universa cernatur, locata in media sede mundi, solida et globosa et undique ipsa in sese nutibus suis conglobata, vestita floribus, herbis, arboribus, frugibus, quorum omnium incredibilis multitudo insatiabili varietate distinguitur. Adde huc fontium gelidas perennitates, 5 liquores perlucidos amnium, riparum vestitus viridissimos, speluncarum concavas amplitudines, saxorum asperitates, impendentium montium altitudines immensitatesque camporum; adde etiam reconditas auri argentique venas infinitamque vim marmoris. Quae vero et quam varia 10 genera bestiarum, vel cicurum vel ferarum! qui volucrum lapsus atque cantus! qui pecudum pastus! quae vita silvestrium! Quid iam de hominum genere dicam? qui quasi cultores terrae constituti non patiuntur eam nec immanitate beluarum efferari nec stirpium asperitate 15 vastari, quorumque operibus agri, insulae litoraque collucent distincta tectis et urbibus. Quae si, ut animis, sic oculis videre possemus, nemo cunctam intuens terram de divina ratione dubitaret. At vero quanta maris est pulchritudo! quae species universi! quae multitudo et 20 varietas insularum! quae amoenitates orarum ac litorum! quot genera quamque disparia partim submersarum, partim fluitantium et innantium beluarum, partim, ad saxa nativis testis inhaerentium! Ipsum autem mare sic

25 terram appetens litoribus alludit, ut una ex duabus naturis
conflata videatur.   Exin mari finitimus aer die et nocte
distinguitur, isque tum fusus et extenuatus sublime fertur,
tum autem concretus in nubes cogitur umoremque colligens terram auget imbribus, tum effluens huc et illuc ventos
30 efficit.   Idem annuas frigorum et calorum facit varietates,
idemque et volatus alitum sustinet et spiritu ductus alit et
sustentat animantes.

Restat ultimus et a domiciliis nostris altissimus omnia
cingens et coercens caeli complexus, qui idem aether vocatur,
35 extrema ora et determinatio mundi, in quo cum admirabili-
tate maxima igneae formae cursus ordinatos definiunt.
E quibus sol, cuius magnitudine multis partibus terra
superatur, circum eam ipsam volvitur, isque oriens et
occidens diem noctemque conficit et modo accedens, tum
40 autem recedens binas in singulis annis reversiones ab
extremo contrarias facit, quarum in intervallo tum quasi
tristitia quadam contrahit terram, tum vicissim laetificat,
ut cum caelo hilarata videatur.   Luna autem, quae est,
ut ostendunt mathematici, maior quam dimidia pars terrae,
45 iisdem spatiis vagatur, quibus sol, sed tum congrediens
cum sole tum digrediens et eam lucem, quam a sole
accepit, mittit in terras et varias ipsa lucis mutationes
habet, atque etiam tum subiecta atque opposita soli radios
eius et lumen obscurat, tum ipsa incidens in umbram
50 terrae, cum est e regione solis, interpositu interiectuque
terrae repente deficit.   Isdemque spatiis eae stellae quas
vagas dicimus, circum terram feruntur eodemque modo
oriuntur et occidunt, quarum motus tum incitantur, tum
retardantur, saepe etiam insistunt.   Quo spectaculo nihil
55 potest admirabilius esse, nihil pulchrius.   Sequitur stellarum inerrantium maxima multitudo, quarum ita discripta
distinctio est, ut ex notarum figurarum similitudine nomina
invenerint.

Haec omnis discriptio siderum atque hic tantus caeli ornatus ex corporibus huc et illuc casu et temere cursantibus 60 potuisse effici, cuiquam sano videri potest? aut vero alia quae natura mentis et rationis expers haec efficere potuit? quae non modo ut fierent ratione eguerunt, sed intellegi qualia sint sine summa ratione non possunt.

De Natura Deorum II 98–104; 115

XXXIII

THE ADAPTATION OF PLANTS AND ANIMALS

The argument from the wonderful order of nature is continued.

Age, ut a caelestibus rebus ad terrestres veniamus, quid est in his, in quo non naturae ratio intellegentis appareat? Principio eorum, quae gignuntur e terra, stirpes et stabilitatem dant et e terra sucum trahunt, obducunturque libro aut cortice trunci, quo sint a frigoribus et caloribus tutiores. 5 Iam vero vites sic claviculis adminicula tamquam manibus apprehendunt atque ita se erigunt, ut animantes. Quin etiam a caulibus, si propter sati sint, ut a pestiferis et nocentibus refugere dicuntur nec eos ulla ex parte contingere. Animantium vero quanta varietas est, quanta ad 10 eam rem vis, ut in suo quaeque genere permaneat! Pastum autem animantibus large et copiose natura eum, qui cuique aptus erat, comparavit. Dedit autem eadem natura beluis et sensum et appetitum, ut altero conatum haberent ad naturales pastus capessendos, altero secernerent pestifera 15 a salutaribus. Iam vero alia animalia gradiendo, alia serpendo ad pastum accedunt, alia volando, alia nando, cibumque partim oris hiatu et dentibus ipsis capessunt, partim unguium tenacitate arripiunt, partim aduncitate

20 rostrorum, alia sugunt, alia carpunt, alia vorant, alia
mandunt; atque etiam aliorum ea est humilitas, ut cibum
terrestrem rostris facile contingant; quae autem altiora sunt,
ut anseres, ut cygni, ut grues, ut cameli, adiuvantur
proceritate collorum; manus etiam data elephanto est, quia
25 propter magnitudinem corporis difficiles aditus habebat
ad pastum. At quibus bestiis erat is cibus, ut alterius
generis bestiis vescerentur, aut vires natura dedit aut
celeritatem. Data est quibusdam etiam machinatio quaedam atque sollertia, ut in araneolis aliae quasi rete texunt,
30 ut, si quid inhaeserit, conficiant, aliae autem observant et
ex inopinato, si quid incidit, arripiunt idque consumunt.

De Natura Deorum II 120–123

XXXIV

The Human Body and the Senses

*The construction of the human body with its senses and powers
makes man supreme over the natural world.*

Ad hanc providentiam naturae tam diligentem tamque
sollertem adiungi multa possunt, e quibus intellegatur,
quantae res hominibus quamque eximiae tributae sint.
Quae primum eos humo excitatos celsos et erectos consti-
5 tuit, ut deorum cognitionem caelum intuentes capere
possent. Sunt enim in terra homines, non ut incolae atque
habitatores, sed quasi spectatores superarum rerum atque
caelestium, quarum spectaculum ad nullum aliud genus
animantium pertinet. Sensus autem interpretes ac nuntii
10 rerum in capite tamquam in arce mirifice ad usus necessarios et facti et collocati sunt. Nam oculi tamquam
speculatores altissimum locum obtinent, ex quo plurima

conspicientes fungantur suo munere; et aures, cum sonum
percipere debeant, qui natura in sublime fertur, recte in
altis corporum partibus collocatae sunt. Quis vero opifex 15
praeter naturam, qua nihil potest esse callidius, tantam
sollertiam persequi potuisset in sensibus? quae primum
oculos membranis tenuissimis vestivit et saepsit; quas
primum perlucidas fecit, ut per eas cerni posset, firmas autem,
ut continerentur; sed lubricos oculos fecit et mobiles, ut et 20
declinarent, si quid noceret, et aspectum, quo vellent, facile
converterent; aciesque ipsa, qua cernimus, quae pupula
vocatur, ita parva est, ut ea, quae nocere possint, facile
vitet, palpebraeque, quae sunt tegmenta oculorum, mollis-
simae tactu, ne laederent aciem, aptissimae factae et ad 25
claudendas pupulas, ne quid incideret, et ad aperiendas,
idque providit ut identidem fieri posset cum maxima
celeritate.

Iam vero domina rerum, ut vos soletis dicere, eloquendi
vis, quam est praeclara quamque divina! quae primum 30
effecit, ut et ea, quae ignoramus, discere et ea, quae scimus,
alios docere possimus ; deinde hac cohortamur, hac
persuademus, hac consolamur afflictos, hac deducimus
perterritos a timore, hac gestientes comprimimus, hac
cupiditates iracundiasque restinguimus, haec nos iuris, 35
legum, urbium societate devinxit, haec a vita immani et
fera segregavit.   Ad usum autem orationis incredibile est,
si diligenter attenderis, quanta opera machinata sit.
Primum enim a pulmonibus arteria usque ad os intimum
pertinet, per quam vox principium a mente ducens per- 40
cipitur et funditur; deinde in ore sita lingua est finita dentibus; ea vocem immoderate profusam fingit et terminat
atque sonos vocis distinctos et pressos efficit, cum et dentes
et alias partes pellit oris.

Quam vero aptas quamque multarum artium ministras 45
manus natura homini dedit! Digitorum enim contractio

facilis facilisque porrectio propter molles commissuras et
artus nullo in modo laborat. Itaque ad pingendum, ad
fingendum, ad scalpendum, ad nervorum eliciendos sonos
50 ac tibiarum apta manus est admotione digitorum. Atque
haec oblectationis; illa necessitatis, cultus dico agrorum
exstructionesque tectorum, tegumenta corporum texta vel
suta omnemque fabricam aeris et ferri; ex quo intellegitur
ad inventa animo, percepta sensibus adhibitis opificum
55 manibus omnia nos consecutos, ut tecti, ut vestiti, ut salvi
esse possemus, urbes, muros, domicilia, delubra haberemus.
Iam vero operibus hominum, id est manibus, cibi etiam
varietas invenitur et copia. Nam et agri multa efferunt
manu quaesita, quae vel statim consumantur vel man-
60 dentur condita vetustati, et praeterea vescimur bestiis et
terrenis et aquatilibus et volantibus partim capiendo,
partim alendo. Efficimus etiam domitu nostro quadri-
pedum vectiones, quorum celeritas atque vis nobis ipsis
affert vim et celeritatem. Nos onera quibusdam bestiis,
65 nos iuga imponimus, nos elephantorum acutissimis sensibus,
nos sagacitate canum ad utilitatem nostram abutimur, nos e
terrae cavernis ferrum elicimus, rem ad colendos agros
necessariam, nos aeris, argenti, auri venas penitus abditas
invenimus et ad usum aptas et ad ornatum decoras,
70 arborum autem consectione omnique materia et culta et
silvestri partim ad calficiendum corpus igni adhibito et ad
mitigandum cibum utimur, partim ad aedificandum, ut
tectis saepti frigora caloresque pellamus. Magnos vero
usus affert ad navigia facienda, quorum cursibus suppedi-
75 tantur omnes undique ad vitam copiae; quasque res violentissimas natura genuit, earum moderationem nos soli
habemus, maris atque ventorum, propter nauticarum
rerum scientiam, plurimisque maritimis rebus fruimur
atque utimur. Terrenorum item commodorum omnis est
80 in homine dominatus. Nos campis, nos montibus fruimur,

nostri sunt amnes, nostri lacus, nos fruges serimus, nos arbores, nos aquarum inductionibus terris fecunditatem damus, nos flumina arcemus, derigimus, avertimus, nostris denique manibus in rerum natura quasi alteram naturam efficere conamur.   85

De Natura Deorum II 140–142; 148–149; 150–152

MAN AND HIS DESTINY

☆

XXXV

Cosmopolis—Man and the Gods

Man, as a divine being, has community with the gods.

Quid vero? hominum ratio non in caelum usque penetravit? Soli enim ex animantibus nos astrorum ortus, obitus cursusque cognovimus; ab hominum genere finitus est dies, mensis, annus, defectiones solis et lunae cognitae
5 praedictaeque in omne posterum tempus, quae, quantae, quando futurae sint. Quae contuens animus accedit ad cognitionem deorum, e qua oritur pietas, cui coniuncta iustitia est reliquaeque virtutes, e quibus vita beata existit par et similis deorum, nulla alia re nisi immortalitate, quae
10 nihil ad bene vivendum pertinet, cedens caelestibus. Quibus rebus expositis satis docuisse videor, hominis natura quanto omnes anteiret animantes. Ex quo debet intellegi nec figuram situmque membrorum nec ingenii mentisque vim talem effici potuisse fortuna. Restat ut
15 doceam atque aliquando perorem omnia, quae sint in hoc mundo, quibus utantur homines, hominum causa facta esse et parata.

Principio ipse mundus deorum hominumque causa factus est, quaeque in eo sunt, ea parata ad fructum hominum et
20 inventa sunt. Est enim mundus quasi communis deorum atque hominum domus aut urbs utrorumque. Soli enim ratione utentes iure ac lege vivunt. Ut igitur Athenas et

Lacedaemonem Atheniensium Lacedaemoniorumque causa
putandum est conditas esse, omniaque, quae sint in
his urbibus, eorum populorum recte esse dicuntur, sic, 25
quaecumque sunt in omni mundo, deorum atque hominum
putanda sunt.

De Natura Deorum II 153-154

XXXVI

THE PROGRESS OF THE SOUL

The education of the personality through philosophy raises it
above low ambitions to its highest attainment in the individual and
in society.

Nam cum animus, cognitis perceptisque virtutibus, a
corporis obsequio indulgentiaque discesserit, voluptatemque,
sicut labem aliquam dedecoris, oppresserit, omnemque
mortis dolorisque timorem effugerit, societatemque caritatis
coierit cum suis, omnesque natura coniunctos suos duxerit, 5
cultumque deorum et puram religionem susceperit, et
exacuerit illam, ut oculorum, sic ingenii aciem, ad bona
seligenda et reicienda contraria—quae virtus ex providendo
est appellata prudentia—quid eo dici aut cogitari poterit
beatius? Idemque cum caelum, terras, maria, rerumque 10
omnium naturam perspexerit, eaque unde generata, quo
recursura, quando, quo modo obitura, quid in iis mortale et
caducum, quid divinum aeternumque sit, viderit, ipsumque
ea moderantem et regentem paene prehenderit, seque non
unis circumdatum moenibus, popularem alicuius definiti 15
loci, sed civem totius mundi, quasi unius urbis agnoverit, in
hac ille magnificentia rerum atque in hoc conspectu et
cognitione naturae, dii immortales! quam se ipse noscet

(quod Apollo praecepit Pythius), quam contemnet, quam
20 despiciet, quam pro nihilo putabit ea, quae vulgo dicuntur
amplissima! Atque haec omnia, quasi saepimento aliquo,
vallabit disserendi ratione, veri et falsi iudicandi scientia,
et arte quadam intelligendi, quid quamque rem sequatur,
et quid sit cuique contrarium. Cumque se ad civilem
25 societatem natum senserit, non solum illa subtili disputatione
sibi utendum putabit, sed etiam fusa latius perpetua
oratione, qua regat populos, qua stabiliat leges, qua castiget
improbos, qua tueatur bonos, qua laudet claros viros; qua
praecepta salutis et laudis apte ad persuadendum edat suis
30 civibus; qua hortari ad decus, revocare a flagitio, consolari
possit afflictos factaque et consulta fortium et sapientium,
cum improborum ignominia, sempiternis monumentis
prodere.

De Legibus I 60-62

XXXVII

The Medicine of the Soul

An almost modern interest in psychology prompts the question:
Why cannot the mind be healed like the body? After a discussion
on the causes of moral depravity, it is discovered that the answer is
philosophy, used as a self-applied 'mind-cure' and moral discipline.
'The concept of philosophy as an ars vivendi *is Greek. Nothing*
can be further from the truth than to call the Greeks "intellectualists."
The object of philosophy was to teach a man to live well, and with
that object to think rightly about God, the world and himself.'
(Legacy of Greece, p. 45) *Cp., however, II Introductory Note.*

Sunt ingeniis nostris semina innata virtutum, quae si
adolescere liceret, ipsa nos ad beatam vitam natura

perduceret. Nunc autem, simul atque editi in lucem et
suscepti sumus, in omni continuo pravitate et in summa
opinionum perversitate versamur, ut paene cum lacte 5
nutricis errorem suxisse videamur. Cum vero parentibus
redditi, dein magistris traditi sumus, tum ita variis imbuimur
erroribus, ut vanitati veritas et opinioni confirmatae natura
ipsa cedat. Accedunt etiam poetae, qui cum magnam
speciem doctrinae sapientiaeque prae se tulerunt, audiuntur, 10
leguntur, ediscuntur et inhaerescunt penitus in mentibus;
cum vero eodem quasi maximus quidam magister populus
accessit atque omnis undique ad vitia consentiens multitudo,
tum plane inficimur opinionum pravitate a naturaque
desciscimus, ut nobis optime naturae vim vidisse videantur, 15
qui nihil melius homini, nihil magis expetendum, nihil
praestantius honoribus, imperiis, populari gloria iudi-
caverunt. Ad quam fertur optimus quisque veramque
illam honestatem expetens, quam unam natura maxime
anquirit, in summa inanitate versatur consectaturque 20
nullam eminentem effigiem virtutis, sed adumbratam
imaginem gloriae. Est enim gloria solida quaedam res et
expressa, non adumbrata; ea est consentiens laus bonorum,
incorrupta vox bene iudicantium de excellenti virtute, ea
virtuti resonat tamquam imago. Quae quia recte factorum 25
plerumque comes est, non est bonis viris repudianda. Illa
autem, quae se eius imitatricem esse vult, temeraria atque
inconsiderata et plerumque peccatorum vitiorumque
laudatrix, fama popularis, simulatione honestatis formam
eius pulchritudinemque corrumpit. Qua caecitate ho- 30
mines, cum quaedam etiam praeclara cuperent eaque
nescirent nec ubi nec qualia essent, funditus alii everterunt
suas civitates, alii ipsi occiderunt. Atque hi quidem
optima petentes non tam voluntate quam cursus errore
falluntur. Quid? qui pecuniae cupiditate, qui voluptatum 35
bilidine feruntur, quorumque ita perturbantur animi, ut

non multum absint ab insania, his nullane adhibenda
curatio?   Utrum quod minus noceant animi aegrotationes
quam corporis, an quod corpora curari possint, animorum
40 medicina nulla sit?

     Est profecto animi medicina, philosophia, cuius auxilium
non ut in corporis morbis petendum est foris, omnibusque
opibus atque viribus ut nosmet ipsi nobis mederi possimus
elaborandum est.

Tusculan Disputations III 2, 3, 4, 6

XXXVIII

The Guide of Life

*In this eloquent passage, philosophy is personified and almost
identified with Nature: she is not only the guide of life, but the
originator of civilisation.*

     O vitae philosophia dux, o virtutis indagatrix expultrixque
vitiorum! Quid non modo nos, sed omnino vita hominum
sine te esse potuisset?   Tu urbes peperisti, tu dissipatos
in societatem vitae convocasti, tu eos inter se primo
5 domiciliis, deinde coniugiis, tum litterarum et vocum communione iunxisti, tu inventrix legum, tu magistra morum
et disciplinae fuisti; ad te confugimus, a te opem petimus,
tibi nos, ut antea magna ex parte, sic nunc penitus totosque
tradimus.   Est autem unus dies bene et ex praeceptis tuis
10 actus peccanti immortalitati anteponendus.   Cuius igitur
potius opibus utamur quam tuis, quae et vitae tranquilli-
tatem largita nobis es et terrorem mortis sustulisti?

Tusculan Disputations V 5

CICERO SUMS UP

☆

XXXIX

STATESMAN OR PHILOSOPHER?

Cicero here explains why he has returned to the study of philosophy late in life. It was not that he had ever lost interest in the world of thought, which had been his first love, but his devotion to politics, which he had always felt to be his prime duty, had left him little leisure. That leisure he now had, through Caesar's tyranny and the collapse of the Republic.

Quamquam libri nostri complures non modo ad legendi, sed etiam ad scribendi studium excitaverunt, tamen interdum vereor ne quibusdam bonis viris philosophiae nomen sit invisum mirenturque in ea tantum me operae et temporis ponere. Ego autem, quam diu res publica per eos gere- 5 batur, quibus se ipsa commiserat, omnes meas curas cogitationesque in eam conferebam. Cum autem dominatu unius omnia tenerentur neque esset usquam consilio aut auctoritati locus, socios denique tuendae rei publicae, summos viros, amisissem, nec me angoribus dedidi, quibus 10 essem confectus nisi iis restitissem, nec rursum indignis homine docto voluptatibus. Atque utinam res publica stetisset quo coeperat statu nec in homines non tam commutandarum quam evertendarum rerum cupidos incidisset! Primum enim, ut stante re publica facere sole- 15 bamus, in agendo, plus quam in scribendo operae poneremus, deinde ipsis scriptis non ea, quae nunc, sed actiones

83

nostras mandaremus, ut saepe fecimus. Cum autem res
publica, in qua omnis mea cura, cogitatio, opera poni
20 solebat, nulla esset omnino, illae scilicet litterae conticu-
erunt forenses et senatoriae. Nihil agere autem cum
animus non posset, in his studiis ab initio versatus aetatis
existimavi honestissime molestias posse deponi, si me ad
philosophiam rettulissem. Cui cum multum adulescens
25 discendi causa temporis tribuissem, postea quam honoribus
inservire coepi meque totum rei publicae tradidi, tantum
erat philosophiae loci quantum superfuerat amicorum et
rei publicae temporibus. Id autem omne consumebatur in
legendo, scribendi otium non erat. Maximis igitur in
30 malis hoc tamen boni assecuti videmur, ut ea litteris
mandaremus, quae nec erant satis nota nostris et erant
cognitione dignissima. Quid enim est, per deos, optabilius sapientia, quid praestantius, quid homini melius, quid
homine dignius? Hanc igitur qui expetunt philosophi
35 nominantur, nec quicquam aliud est philosophia, si
interpretari velis, praeter studium sapientiae. Sapientia
autem est, ut a veteribus philosophis definitum est, rerum
divinarum et humanarum causarumque, quibus eae res
continentur, scientia, cuius studium qui vituperat haud
40 sane intellego quidnam sit quod laudandum putet.

De Officiis II 2–5

XL

Farewell to the Reader

This epilogue to the De Officiis *is addressed to Cicero's son,*
Marcus, to whom the whole work is dedicated. Marcus was study-
ing at Athens at the time, and Cicero was, with some reason, anxious
about his progress.

Habes a patre munus, Marce fili, mea quidem sententia
magnum, sed perinde erit, ut acceperis. Quamquam hi
tibi tres libri inter Cratippi commentarios tamquam
hospites erunt recipiendi: sed ut, si ipse venissem Athenas,
quod quidem esset factum, nisi me e medio cursu clara 5
voce patria revocasset, aliquando me quoque audires, sic,
quoniam his voluminibus ad te profecta vox est mea,
tribues iis temporis quantum poteris, poteris autem
quantum voles. Cum vero intellexero te hoc scientiae
genere gaudere, tum et praesens tecum propediem, ut 10
spero, et dum aberis, absens loquar. Vale igitur, mi
Cicero, tibique persuade esse te quidem mihi carissimum,
sed multo fore cariorem, si talibus monitis praeceptisque
laetabere.

De Officiis III 121

XLI

FAREWELL TO THE AUTHOR

*This account of Cicero's death we owe to the accidental preserva-
tion of a fragment from one of the lost books of Livy.*

M. Cicero pro certo habens, id quod erat, non Antonio
eripi se posse, primum in Tusculanum fugit, inde in
Formianum, ut ab Caieta navem conscensurus, proficiscitur.
Unde aliquoties in altum provectum cum modo venti
adversi rettulissent, modo ipse iactationem navis pati non 5
posset, taedium tandem eum et fugae et vitae cepit,
regressusque ad superiorem villam, 'Moriar,' inquit, 'in
patria saepe servata.' Satis constat servos fortiter fide-
literque paratos fuisse ad dimicandum; ipsum deponi
lecticam, et quietos pati, quod sors iniqua cogeret, 10
iussisse. Prominenti ex lectica praebentique immotam

cervicem caput praecisum est. Nec satis stolidae crudelitati militum fuit; manus quoque, scripsisse aliquid in Antonium exprobrantes, praeciderunt. Ita relatum caput 15 ad Antonium, iussuque eius inter duas manus in rostris positum, ubi ille consul, ubi saepe consularis, ubi eo ipso anno adversus Antonium, quanta nulla umquam humana vox, cum admiratione eloquentiae auditus fuerat.

Livy (fragment)

EPILOGUE

Rapuisti tum Ciceroni lucem sollicitam et aetatem senilem et vitam miseriorem te principe quam sub te triumviro mortem; famam vero gloriamque factorum atque dictorum adeo non abstulisti, ut auxeris. Vivit 5 vivetque per omnem saeculorum memoriam, dumque hoc, vel forte vel providentia vel utcumque constitutum, rerum naturae corpus—quod ille paene solus Romanorum animo vidit, ingenio complexus est, eloquentia illuminavit— manebit incolume, comitem aevi sui laudem Ciceronis 10 trahet, omnisque posteritas illius in te scripta mirabitur, tuum in eum factum exsecrabitur; citiusque e mundo genus hominum quam Ciceronis memoria cedet.

Velleius Paterculus II, 66, 4–5

NOTES

The references, *e.g.* 'see Note 8 (*e*)', are to the
'Notes on Some Points of Ciceronian Style'.

I

2 **quin . . . rapiatur** : 'that human nature is drawn to these
things without the attraction of profit'.

3 **videmusne** : 'do we not see?' –*ne* has almost the force of
nonne.

4 **ut** : 'how', followed by subj. in ind. question.

6 **gestiant** : 'long to'.

8 **Quid vero?** 'Again'. Introduces a new example.

9 **qui** : antecedent is *eos* below. See Note 4(*b*).

ingenuis studiis atque artibus : 'by the higher branches of
study and learning'. *Ingenuus*, 'freeborn', is applied, like *liberalis*,
to what is worthy of a free citizen, as distinct from a slave. *Ars*,
properly 'the skill of a craftsman', was extended to all branches of
mental activity, such as grammar, literature, and art proper, and
since these studies (*artes* or *studia*) were regarded as necessary to
the education of all Roman freemen or gentlemen, they were
regularly called by Cicero *artes optimae, ingenuae,* or *liberales*. The
Romans took over this idea from Greek education, which, from the
time of Alexander, had come to be based on a regular curriculum
of studies (ἐγκύκλιος παιδεία), comprising grammar, music,
geometry, rhetoric, and dialectic (philosophy). Quintilian,
writing at the end of the first century A.D., calls it *orbis ille doctrinae*.

From Graeco-Roman education are derived the Seven
Liberal Arts of medieval education, consisting of two parts, a
Trivium (Grammar or Literature, Rhetoric, and Dialectic), and
a Quadrivium (Geometry, Arithmetic, Astronomy, and Music).
These formed the traditional curriculum of the 'Arts' faculties of
the universities.

The ancients thought of all knowledge as one, and would
scarcely have approved the specialisation which now separates
mathematics and science from 'Arts' subjects. They would
equally have disapproved a narrowly vocational education : the
essence of the liberal arts was that they conferred knowledge for its
own sake, and corrected and trained the mind in the use of it.

12 **compensare** : 'pay for, make up for'. **eam . . . voluptatem** : see Note 4(*c*).

15 **Sirenum** : The song of the Sirens, fabulous creatures who tried to draw Odysseus on to the rocks with the charm of their voices, comes from Homer, *Od.* XII 184 ff. The attraction, according to Cicero, lay not merely in the beauty of the music (*vocum suavitate*), but in its appeal to human curiosity about the unknown.

20 **verti** : 'translated'. Cicero from time to time inserts in his works his own translations of passages from Homer and the Greek tragedians. The following translation of the Sirens' Song is a good specimen of his competence in versification.

21 **Argolicum** : from *Argolicus*, 'Argive, Greek'. **quin . . . flectis** : 'why do you not turn?' **Ulixes** : Ulysses or Odysseus.

23 **caerula** : 'blue waters'.

24 **quin . . . astiterit** : 'without staying'.

25 **variis . . . musis** : 'all the Muses' charms'.

26 **lapsus** : 'sailing on'.

27 **tenemus** : 'we know'.

28 **Troiae** : dat. 'against Troy'.

29 **rerum vestigia** : 'all that comes to pass'. The Greek is: ὅσσα γένηται ἐπὶ χθονὶ πουλυβοτείρῃ.

30 **probari** : 'win approval'. **cantiunculis** : diminutive of *cantus*, 'mere songs', opposed to *scientiam*.

31 **scientiam** : emphatic: 'it is knowledge which they offer'. For asyndeton, see Note 1(*b*).

quam . . . esse cariorem : acc. and inf. dependent on *non erat mirum*; *cupĭdo*: adj. (note quantity); *patria*: abl. of comparison after *cariorem*. Trans. 'and it was not to be wondered at that to a man desirous of wisdom, this (*i.e.* knowledge) should be dearer than his native land'.

33 **Archimedes** of **Syracuse** (287–212 B.C.), mathematician and astronomer, was killed by a soldier during the Roman sack of the city while engaged upon a geometrical problem (see Note on V 68).

34 **in pulvere**: Ancient mathematicians used a board or abacus covered with fine sand for their calculations.

35 **Aristoxenus** of **Tarentum**, a pupil of Aristotle, wrote works on musical theory.

36 **consumptum . . . in musicis** : 'devoted to music'.

Aristophanem : Not the comic poet. Aristophanes of Byzantium (circ. 195 B.C.), head of the library of Alexandria, was famous for his literary and grammatical studies. He probably invented Greek accents.

37 **in litteris** : 'in literary studies'.

39 **ultimas terras** : Pythagoras, Plato and Democritus (see Introduction II 2, 4) are said to have travelled in Egypt and Asia.

40 **qui** : see Note 4(*e*) for omission of antecedent.

II

1 **Pythagoram** : See Introduction II 2.
Phliuntem : 'to Phlius', a town of the Peloponnese.

2 **copiose** : 'eloquently'. **disseruisse** : 'held some discourse'.

4 **qua . . . confideret** : 'what profession he chiefly followed'.

5 **artem quidem** : See Note 8(*e*).

6 **novitatem nominis** : See Note 3. The 'novel name', which Pythagoras was said to have invented, was φιλόσοφος (lover of wisdom).

8 **similem . . . et** : instead of the more usual *similem atque*, 'the same as'.

9 **mercatum** : properly a 'market', here the assembly at the Greek Games, to which in fact a market was usually attached. The Olympic Games are probably meant. Trans: 'He replied that human life seemed to him to resemble the fair which was held when the Games were celebrated with great splendour amid a great concourse of spectators from all Greece.'

10 **apparatu, celebritate** : abls. of occasion or accompanying circumstances.

11 **ut** : 'just as', is taken up by *item=sic*, line 16 below. The subjs, *peterent* etc. are due to the indirect speech.
illic : 'there', *i.e.* at the games.
nobilitatem coronae : 'the glorious crown of victory', *i.e.* the laurel wreath given as the prize to athletes. See Note 3.

13 **autem** : adversative, 'while'. See Note 8(*d*).

14 **idque** : 'and that too'. See Note 4(*f*).

16 **quasi** : answered by *sic* below. Trans. 'so (*item*) we, like (*quasi*) visitors from some city to a crowded national assembly, had

come into this world from some other sphere of life'. (For the hendiadys in *vita et natura*, see Note 2.) There is a reference here to Pythagoras' belief in metempsychosis or transmigration of souls. (See Introduction II 2.)

18 **alios . . . alios** : in apposition to *nos*, 'some of us . . . others of us'. **servire:** 'devote oneself to'.

20 **rerum naturam** : 'the universe'.

22 **illic** : *i.e.* at the games. **liberalissimum** : 'most worthy of a free man'. See Note on I 9. **acquirentem** agrees with *hominem* understood.

25 **inventor . . . amplificator** : Cicero is fond of nouns ending in *–tor*, denoting the doer of an action. They may often be rendered by verbs in English. Trans. 'Pythagoras not only originated the name "philosophy", but developed the study itself'.

28 **Graeciam quae Magna dicta est** : 'what is called Magna Graecia', *i.e.* the southern part of Italy, fringed with Greek colonies, such as Tarentum.

29 **disciplina** : 'system of thought'.

30 **fuerit** : fut. pf. 'there will be an opportunity later'.

31 **numeri motusque** : 'mathematics and theories of motion'. Pythagoras thought that the universe obeyed the laws of number and harmony, while the earliest Greek philosophers, like Thales of Miletus (see Introduction II 1), sought for a physical substance, such as air or water, out of which all things arose (*orerentur*) and to which they returned (*reciderent*).

34 **Socrates** (Introduction II 3) tells us in the *Phaedo* how, in his youth, he read a book by Anaxagoras (Introduction II 1), but found that the author, while claiming that Mind governed all things, seemed more interested in physical speculation about air and water. Disappointed, he turned from science to human conduct, and, as Cicero says, 'brought philosophy down from the heavens', and made it concern itself with questions of 'life and character, good and evil' (*de vita et moribus rebusque bonis et malis*).

III

1 **principio** : 'in the first place'. **natura** : 'Nature', the power behind the world personified.

2 **vitam corpusque tueatur** : contrasts with *declinet ea quae . . .*

videantur. Note the absence of conjunction after *tueatur*, and the word order. See Notes 1(*b*) and (*c*).

5 **commune** : noun, 'common property'.

8 **hoc . . . quod** : 'there is this great difference that'. See Note 5.

tantum : The full construction is: *tantum (movetur) quantum sensu movetur*, 'is influenced (only) so far as (it is influenced) by the senses', 'by nothing more than the senses'.

9 **quod adest quodque praesens est** : 'what is immediately present'.

11 **autem** : See Note 8(*d*). **rationis** : 'reason'.

12 **consequentia cernit** : 'traces effects'.

13 **similitudines comparat** : 'observes likenesses or analogies', *i.e.* detects the common elements in things, or, in philosophical language, forms universals.

16 **eadem** : lit. 'the same', adds another attribute to 'nature'. *Cp.* Note 4(*f*). Trans: 'nature, too; nature likewise'.

17 **orationis** : 'speech'.

19 **impellit ut . . . velit** : 'prompts men to desire associations and festivals and join in them themselves'.

20 **ea quae suppeditent** : see Note 6 (*a*); *suppeditare* is here intr. = 'be sufficient'.

21 **ad cultum et ad victum** : 'for civilised life'. See Note 2.

23 **maiores ad rem gerendam** : 'more active in the affairs of life'.

26 **cum . . . tum** : 'it is when we are free', or 'when (at last) we are free'. See Note 8(*a*).

27 **avemus** : 'we long'. **videre, audire, addiscere** : see Note 1(*a*)

31 **pulchrum** : sc. *esse*. **autem** : see Note 8(*d*).

labi . . . errare, nescire, decipi : The four verbs are arranged in pairs. See Note 1(*a*).

32 **in hoc genere** : 'in this pursuit', lit. 'in this (class of things), sphere'.

33 **naturali** : 'natural', *i.e.* in accordance with the nature of man. **honesto** : 'praiseworthy'.

duo vitia : In his regard for truth, Cicero warns against two opposite faults: 1. The hasty acceptance of the unproved, and 2. Waste of effort in investigating the unknowable or trivial.

35 **qui** : see Note 4(*e*).

39 **easdemque** : see Note 4(*f*).

40 **quod . . . id** : see Note 4(*b*). **rebus honestis** : 'profitable subjects', *i.e.* those concerned with virtuous conduct (*honestum*). **operae curaeque** : partitive genit. after *quod*.

IV

1 **haec omnia** : 'all these considerations'.   **cum quaerimus** : 'in our search'.

quid deceat : *i.e. decorum*, what befits a human being, what is best in behaviour, or (as here) in the choice of a career.

4 **deliberatio** : 'subject for discussion, question'.

5 **cum est . . . tum . . . constituit** : see Note 8(*a*).
imbecillitas consilii : 'weakness of judgement'.

6 **id** : anticipates *quod*. See Note 4(*a*).

7 **ante** : with *quam*, 'before'.

8 **quod (genus) optimum esset** : 'what career was best'.

9 **nam quod** : introduces a long dependent clause, resumed by *hoc* below (see Note 5). Trans. 'what Prodicus relates about Hercules, that he went into a desert place . . . this (*hoc*) might perhaps have happened to Hercules . . . (but) not to us . . .'
Hercules : the most popular of Greek heroes, was adopted by the Stoics as the type of the Wise Man, and his labours were interpreted as allegories of the victory of virtue over the passions.

Prodicus *of* **Cos** : a sophist, or professional teacher of popular knowledge, and contemporary of Socrates, was the author of a famous myth, 'The Choice of Hercules', a version of which is given by Xenophon (*Mem.* II 1 21). According to this, the young Hercules is confronted by two women, Pleasure and Virtue, who try to win his favour by opposing arguments.

13 **hoc** : resumes *quod* above.

14 **Iovis satu edito** : quoted from some poet. Trans. 'Sprung of the seed of Jupiter'.
nobis : contrasts with *Herculi*. See Note 1(*b*).

15 **visum est** : impers., 'has seemed good'. Supply *imitari*.

18 **quaeque . . . ea** : see Note 4(*b*).

20 **bonitate naturae** : 'goodness of natural disposition'.

V

2 **Dionysius** : tyrant of Syracuse (405–367 B.C.), established a regime notorious for its combination of oppression and great external splendour.

4 **praeditam** : emphatic. Trans : 'How fair and splendid was that city which he held in the subjection of slavery'.

5 **atqui** : 'and yet'.

6 **victu** : 'way of life.'.

7 **eundem tamen** : 'but at the same time'. See Note 4(*f*).

8 **maleficum** : 'wicked'. **ex quo** : 'judging from this'.

9 **miserrimum** : agrees with *eum* understood.

10 **cum . . . censebat** : for indic. see Note 8(*a*).

12 **etsi id quidem . . .** : 'although it is true that authorities differ from one another about this'. For *quidem* see Note 8(*e*).

16 **convenis** : 'foreigners'.

19 **quin etiam** : 'moreover'.

20 **sordido . . . artificio** : 'fulfilling the degraded duties of female slaves'. **tonstriculae** : 'female barbers'.

23 **candentibus** : 'glowing (with heat)'. **iuglandium putaminibus** : 'walnut shells'.

25 **Aristomachen** : Greek Acc. of *Aristomache*.
Doridem : nom. *Doris*. **Locrensem** : 'of Locri', a S. Italian town.

26 **sic . . . ut** : restrictive, 'only in such a way that', 'never without'.

27 **lecto cubiculari** : 'the couch in his bedchamber'.

28 **eum ipsum** : 'even that', *i.e.* the bridge.

29 **cum . . . clauserat** : *cum* with pluperf. ind. ='whenever'.
detorquebat : 'he would swing to one side'.
idemque : 'moreover'. See Note 4(*f*).

30 **communibus suggestis** : 'public platforms'.

31 **pila ludere** : 'play ball'. Ball games were combined with physical training among the Greeks.

32 **factitabat** : frequentative, 'was accustomed to do'.

34 **quidem** : modifies preceding word. See Note 8(*e*). 'You trust your life to *him* at any rate (*certe*)'.

36 **demonstravisset ... approbavisset** : subjs. of alleged reason:
'for having shown ... approved'.

38 **nihil** : obj. of *tulerit*.

39 **quem enim** : see Note 4(*e*). **amarat** : *amaverat*.

40 **impotentium** : 'powerless to control themselves, despotic'.

41 **quamquam** : here co-ordinating conj. = *tamen* (and yet).

43 **Damocles** : The moral of the famous story of the sword of
Damocles is summed up in the line:
   Uneasy lies the head that wears a crown.
copias eius etc. : see Note 1 (*a*).

49 **hominem** : *i.e.* Damocles. **strato** : participle with *lecto*.
textili stragulo : 'woven couch-cover'. Abl. with *strato*.

50 **picto** : 'embroidered'. **abacos** : 'side-boards'.

51 **caelato** : 'embossed', of gold and silver plate.

52 **nutum ... ministrare** : 'wait at his beck and call'.

54 **odores** : 'perfumes', here 'incense'. **conquisitissimis** : 'choice,
expensive'.

56 **lacunari** : 'panelled ceiling'. **saeta equina aptum** : 'sus-
pended on a horse-hair'.

58 **nec ... aspiciebat** : 'he had no eye for'.

60 **defluebant** : 'threatened to fall off'.

63 **aliqui** : adj. form of *aliquis*.

65 **Archytas** of **Tarentum** : circ. 400 B.C., mathematician, and
contemporary of Plato.

67 **ex eadem urbe** : Syracuse. **pulvere** : 'counting-board'. See
Note on I 35.

68 **radio** : 'pointer'. **excitabo** : 'summon'.
Archimedes of **Syracuse**, mathematician and engineer. His
saying, 'Eureka' (I have found it), on discovering the law of
specific gravity, is well-known. Less known, but more striking,
is: δός μοι πᾶ στῶ, καὶ κινήσω τὸν κόσμον (Give me a place to
stand, and I will move the world). He wrote a treatise on the
relationship between the volumes of a cylinder and a sphere
inscribed in it, and ordered this discovery to be commemorated on
his tomb. He perished in the Roman sack of Syracuse in 212 B.C.
(See Note on I 33.)

69 **quaestor** : Cicero was quaestor in Sicily in 75 B.C.
cum ... negarent : 'for they absolutely denied its existence'.

70 **vestitum . . . dumetis** : 'overgrown with bushes and brambles'.

71 **tenebam** : 'I remembered'.

72 **senariolos** : 'iambic lines', consisting of six iambic feet.

75 **portas Agrigentinas** : gate of Syracuse leading to Agrigentum, an important town on the S. coast of Sicily.

80 **inmissi** : 'set to work'.

82 **ad adversam basim** : 'direct to the pedestal'.

exesis . . . fere : 'almost the whole of the second halves of the lines being eaten away'.

86 **homine Arpinate** : Cicero himself, born at Arpinum.

88 **qui modo . . . habeat . . . qui . . . malit** : note the double *qui* with subj. *Qui modo* has a restrictive sense, 'provided that he, if only he'. *qui . . . malit* is consecutive after *quis est omnium* (see Note 6(*a*)). The meaning is: 'Who is there that has any acquaintance (*commercium*) whatever with the Muses—that is, with culture and learning, who would not prefer . . .' **musis** : The nine Muses presided over different branches of literature and the arts.

humanitate : *Humanitas* means basically 'human nature', the qualities and feelings of mankind; then 'humane conduct, kindness, politeness', and finally 'mental cultivation befitting a man, liberal education, culture'. In the last sense, it is used by Cicero to express his educational ideal, which combined an aversion from war and civil strife with intellectual culture and an admiration for Greek literature and science, and which valued character as well as learning. From this sense of the word is derived the modern term 'Humanities', applied to the Greek and Latin Classics.

91 **actionem** : 'way of life'. **rationibus** : 'the principles of things'.

92 **oblectatione sollertiae** : 'satisfaction of intellectual exercise'.

93 **qui** : drawn into agreement with the predicate '*pastus*'. Trans. 'which (exercise) is by far the most delightful nurture of the mind'. **unus** : strictly redundant, has the effect of strengthening the superlative.

VI

1 **M. Atilius Regulus** was sent during the First Punic War to attack Carthage (255 B.C.). Defeated and taken prisoner, he was sent back to Rome on parole to urge the Romans to ransom their

prisoners and make peace. He advised the Senate to refuse, and returned, faithful to his word, to be cruelly put to death. *Cp.* Horace's version of the story (*Odes* III 5).

consul iterum : 'consul for the second time'.

2 ex insidiis : 'as the result of an ambush'.

Xanthippus was a Spartan general called in by the Carthaginians.

3 iuratus : active meaning, 'on oath'.

4 ut : '(on condition) that', with *iuratus*.

6 utilitatis : 'expediency, self-interest'.

speciem : 'attractiveness'. ut res declarat : 'as the sequel shows'.

7 falsam : 'delusive'.

quae : antecedent is '*utilitatis*'. talis : 'as follows'.

8 domui : =*domi* (locative).

quam calamitatem = *eam calamitatem, quam* . . . see Note 4(*b*).

9 communem fortunae bellicae : 'as part of the fortunes of war'. iudicantem : agrees with *se* understood.

10 consularis dignitatis gradum : 'the honour of consular rank'.

11 utilia : 'advantageous'.

magnitudo animi (greatness of soul) is an active type of courage, shown in undertaking great and dangerous tasks, especially in facing death and tyranny. (*De Off.* I 66).

fortitudo (courage) consists primarily in despising outward fortune, and enduring hardship. Regulus exhibited both types of courage.

12 num locupletiores quaeris auctores : 'do you ask for more trustworthy authorities (than these virtues)?' *Locuples* usually means 'rich'.

harum . . . proprium : 'it is the essence of these virtues'.

16 ne diceret : after *recusavit*, 'he refused to give his vote'.

quam diu . . . senatorem : ind. speech. Supply *dixit*.

18 atque illud etiam : 'and what is more'. *illud* anticipates the whole sentence, '*reddi . . . negavit . . . utile*'. See Note 5.

dixerit quispiam : 'someone may say'. Perf. subj. in polite assertion.

19 repugnantem . . . suae : 'enemy of his own interests'.

20 illos . . . se : see Note 1(*b*).

21 valuisset : 'had prevailed'. auctoritas : 'influence', power to command based on reputation, position, or personality.

22 **captivi** . . . **ipse** : see Note 1(*b*).

24 **exquisita** : 'carefully devised, refined'.

26 **tum cum necabatur** : see Note 8(*a*). **vigilando** : 'by lack of sleep'. **in meliore causa** : 'in a more honourable position'.

27 **senex** . . . **consularis** : for chiasmus, see Note 1(*c*).

29 **religiosa** : 'morally binding'. **quod** . . . **id** : see Note 4(*b*). **affirmate** : 'expressly'.

30 **promiseris** : ideal second per. sing., 'one'. For subj. see Note 6(*a*).

VII

Six months after Caesar's murder, Cicero, casting off all compromise, came out as the declared opponent of the consul M. Antonius. In the period Sept. 44 to April 43 B.C., he delivered the fourteen *Philippic Orations*, urging the Senate to take action against Antony as an enemy of the Republic. The famous *Second Philippic* (Nov. 44 B.C.), published at the time of Antony's departure for Cisalpine Gaul, was a slashing attack on his personality and policy. On 1st Jan. 43 B.C., the Senate appointed Octavian, together with the consuls Hirtius and Pansa, to undertake the campaign against Antony, at the same time sending an embassy in a last minute effort to make terms. One of the ambassadors was the famous lawyer, Servius Sulpicius Rufus, who though he knew himself to be in bad health, insisted on fulfilling his duty, but died during the course of the embassy. The *Ninth Philippic* (Feb. 43 B.C.), is a brilliant and moving panegyric (*laudatio*), in which the orator asks for a public funeral and a statue on the Rostra in his honour. Sulpicius was a personal friend of Cicero, and the author of a famous letter of consolation to him on the death of his daughter, Tullia.

1 **vellem** : potential subj. followed by a jussive subj. (*fecissent*). 'I could wish that heaven had granted that (*ut*). . . .'

4 **legationem renuntiare** : 'report the result of his mission'.

5 **fuerit** . . . **futurus** : 'would have been', represents *fuisset* of the direct speech in a past impossible condition.

non quo : with subj., 'not because', gives the reason rejected by the writer, in contrast with *sed* (*quod*) . . . *reliquit*, the accepted reason. Philippus and Piso were fellow ambassadors with Sulpicius.

7 **aetate . . . sapientia** : for asyndeton, see Note 1(*b*).

8 **causa** =*negotium* : 'business', here, 'his commission as ambassador'.

10 **legato** : goes with *cuiquam*. **in nullo** : 'in the case of no one'.

14 **aliqua . . . revertendi** : see Note 1(*b*). *Aliqua* contrasts with *nulla*, *perveniendi* with *revertendi*.

15 **affectus** : sc. *morbo*. **si . . . accessisset** : depends on *sibi ipse diffideret*. *Accessisset* represents the fut. perf. of the direct speech. Trans: 'that he had no confidence in himself (*i.e.* in his ability to endure), should any additional burden be put upon his weakened health'.

18 **experiretur** : probably governs *rem* understood.

21 **eius** : *i.e.* Antony.

22 **meditatione . . . muneris** : 'preparation for performing his task'.

25 **posita est** : 'depends upon'.

29 **reliqua vita** : 'his future life', *i.e.* his immortality of fame.

30 **omnem** =*omnium*.

31 **semper illius gravitatem . . .** : The virtues ascribed to Sulpicius make up that strength of character which was the Roman ideal. *Gravitas*, literally 'weight', comes to mean 'dignity, seriousness', the quality that makes a man morally impressive. It is akin to *auctoritas*, influence based on character or position, but contains an element of severity. *Constantia* is 'firmness, steadfastness, consistency of character'. Cato, the Younger, in addition to extraordinary *gravitas*, showed *constantia* in a high degree by his fidelity to principle and his preference of death to tyranny (*De Off.* I 112) (see IX introductory Note). *Fides*, the quality that inspires confidence, faithfulness to the pledged word, is said by Cicero (*De Off.* I 23) to be the foundation of justice. A notable example of *fides* is Regulus (see VI). *Prudentia* is practical wisdom, the power of deciding between right and wrong, especially, as here, in the conduct of public affairs.

33 **silebitur** : 'cease to be heard of, fall into oblivion'.

35 **in legibus interpretandis, aequitate explicanda** : For the asyndeton, see Note 1(*b*). Trans: 'not only in interpreting laws, but in expounding the principles of justice'. *Aequitas* means 'fairness', the application to individual cases of the principles of justice rather than the mere letter of the law. Sometimes, as below, it implies beneficence or generosity as opposed to strictness.

38 **iuris consultus** : a jurist, or legal expert, whose duty it was to interpret the law in disputed cases. Sulpicius, however, was not merely skilled in the statute law (*ius*), but was equally concerned to observe its spirit (*iustitia*). *Iustitia*, according to Cicero (*De Off.* I 20), means to give each man his due, to injure none unless injured oneself, and to respect the rights and property of individuals.

39 **ea quae proficiscebantur** : 'matters arising from'.

40 **iure civili** : the Civil Law or body of Roman Law concerned with the rights of private citizens, their status, property, etc.

ad facilitatem aequitatemque referebat : 'judged on the side of leniency and fairness'.

41 **litium actiones** : 'law-suits'.

43 **alia maiora** : sc. *monumenta*.

44 **illa memoria** : 'his other memorial will be the record of a distinguished life'.

VIII

1 **gravis . . . constans** : see Note on VII 31.

2 **conficitur** : 'is represented', *i.e.* by the Stoics.

persona : 'character'. Originally applied to the mask worn by actors in the Greek drama, the word came to mean the character represented by the mask, and, by a later weakening, no more than 'individual, person'. The classical use always keeps the idea of 'character'. **ratio** : 'reason'.

3 **quod honestum esset, id esse solum bonum** : Cicero's translation of the first Stoic Paradox ὅτι μόνον τὸ καλὸν ἀγαθόν, 'that virtue is the sole good'. *Honestus* is regularly used to translate καλός in the moral sense of 'virtuous'. *quod . . . id*: see Note 4(*b*).

4 **nomina** : The Stoics claimed for the virtuous man the titles of all possible perfections. Thus he was said to be king, dictator, rich, handsome, free, etc.

6 **Tarquinius** : last king of Rome, expelled as a tyrant in 509 B.C.

7 **magister populi** : 'Master of the People', an old title of the dictator. There is an ironical contrast between Tarquin, master of the people, and Sulla, 'master of three deadly vices'. There is perhaps also a play on a second meaning of *magister*, 'teacher'.

Lucius Cornelius Sulla : the dictator (138–78 B.C.). Cicero's unfavourable judgement of him is expressed more fully in XVI 10 where he ascribes the ruin of the old Roman ideal of government to Sulla's cruelty in the provinces and the proscriptions at Rome.

9 **M. Licinius Crassus**, famous for his wealth and avarice, was a member of the First Triumvirate in 60 B.C. along with Caesar and Pompey. In 53 B.C., as commander of the eastern armies, he rashly crossed the Euphrates, to be killed by the Parthians in the disaster at Carrhae.

nisi eguisset : 'had he not wanted (something)'.

10 **Euphraten** : Greek accusative.

11 **eius** : possessive genit. after *dicentur*. 'All things will rightly be called his, who alone knows how to use (*uti*) them'. See Note 4(*a*).

16 **ullum tempus aetatis** : 'any particular moment of life'.

17 **tum denique . . . cum** : see Note 8(*a*).

18 **quod** : antecedent is the whole preceding sentence. Translate: 'I mean the warning so unwisely given to Croesus by one of the Seven Wise Men'.

ille unus : Solon, the Athenian lawgiver, reckoned among the seven traditional wise men. His famous saying, 'Call no man happy until he is dead', was said to have been uttered on a visit to Croesus, the wealthy king of Lydia. Croesus remembered it on his funeral pyre, when about to be burnt alive by Cyrus, and called three times on the name of Solon. Hearing him, and himself taking Solon's saying to heart, Cyrus spared him.

19 **non sapienter** : In the Stoic view, Solon's warning was absurd, since the wise man's happiness is a quality independent of time or fortune. He does not need to wait for the end of his life to know whether he is happy or not.

21 **quod si ita est . . .** : The point of the paradox is to show that human personality, guided by goodness, can be superior to all outward circumstances. **neque . . . et** : see Note 8(*c*).

IX

The speech *Pro Murena* was delivered in Nov. 63 B.C., immediately before the Catilinarian orations. The defendant, L. Licinius Murena, was accused of corruption at the consular elections of

63 B.C. The prosecutors were Servius Sulpicius Rufus (see VII) and M. Porcius Cato, great-grandson of Cato, the Censor. Cato was a die-hard supporter of the Republic and ended his own life after Caesar's victory at Thapsus in 46 B.C. A convinced Stoic, he exhibited the supremacy of virtue by extraordinary personal integrity and often with a rigid adherence to theory. He is said to have spent his last night alive in studying the arguments for the immortality of the soul in Plato's *Phaedo*.

1 **bona** : 'qualities'.

2 **ipsius . . . esse propria** : 'are personal to himself'. **scitote** : 2nd pers. pl. imperat. of *scio*. **quae** : see Note 1(*b*). Contrasts with *quae videmus* above.

3 **requirimus** : 'we miss', i.e. *desideramus*. The expression is peculiar, but the meaning is: What we miss in Cato is generosity: we find hardness instead. This hardness is due not to himself, but to his teachers. The whole sentence may be translated: 'What we would wish to see otherwise in him is due, not to his natural inclination, but to his teacher', *i.e.* Zeno, who founded the Stoic school at Athens in the fourth century B.C. The name 'Stoic' is derived from the Stoa (colonnade) where he taught. (See Introduction II 7.)

ea : antecedent *quae*. See Note 4(*b*).

4 **inventorum** : 'tenets'.

5 **aemuli** : 'students'.

5 **sententiae** : 'dogmas'. **praecepta** : 'teachings'. **huiusmodi** (**sunt**) : 'are as follows'. Cicero proceeds to enumerate some of the Stoic Paradoxes.

6 **gratia** : 'personal favour, influence'.

8 **viri non esse** : 'that it is unmanly'.

9 **exorari** : 'to give way to appeals'. **si distortissimi sint** : 'even if they should be deformed'.

10 **servitutem serviant** : cognate acc.: 'are in slavery'.

13 **paria** : neut. plur. of *par* = equal.

14 **gallum gallinaceum** : 'poultry-cock'.

15 **suffocaverit** : 'strangled'.

16 **nihil opinari** : 'never merely supposes anything'.

19 **arripuit** : 'eagerly adopted', *i.e.* from his Stoic teachers (*auctoribus*). In what follows Cicero confronts Cato with a number of situations, to which Cato is supposed to give the Stoic response.

The purpose is to show that Cato's principles do not apply to real situations.

20 **petunt aliquid publicani**: '(Suppose) the tax-gatherers ask for a concession'. Cato replies: 'Beware of letting personal influence have the slightest weight (*momenti*)'.

21 **supplices** : predicative. Trans: 'some wretched and unfortunate men come begging for aid'.

23 **fueris** : The fut. perf. in the apodosis emphasises the completion of the future action. 'You will show yourself, prove yourself to be'.

25 **at** : introduces an objection, 'But surely'.

27 **nostri . . . illi** : 'those teachers of mine', *i.e.* the philosophers of the New Academy, whose lectures Cicero attended in his youth (see Introduction II 8).

28 **adiumenta doctrinae** : 'the support of philosophy'.

29 **a Platone et Aristotele** : 'of the Platonic and Aristotelian school'.

30 **moderati et temperati** : 'balanced and judicious thinkers'.

31 **aliquando** : emphatic—'from time to time'. **distincta genera:** in answer to the Stoic assertions that there were no degrees in sin and that all sins were equally punishable.

32 **esse apud . . . locum** : 'that even a man of strict principle admits room (*locum*) for pardon'.

35 **(id) quod dixerit . . .** : governed by *mutare*. See Note 4(*e*).

36 **mediocritate** : Virtue, according to Aristotle, lay in the 'mean' between two extremes. Thus, for example, courage is half-way between rashness and cowardice.

37 **moderatas** : passive sense, 'governed'.

38 **hos ad magistros** : *i.e.* Platonic and Aristotelian teachers, instead of the Stoics.
        cum ista natura : 'with those natural endowments of yours'.

X

1 **artificiis** : 'trades'. **quaestibus** : 'occupations'. **liberales** : 'gentlemanly'; opp. *sordidi*, 'base'. See Note on I 9. **qui . . . qui . . . sint** : indirect question, dependent on *accepimus*.

2 **haec** : 'the following (account)'. **accepimus** : 'we have heard'.

3 **improbantur** : 'are disapproved'. **portitorum** : 'collectors of customs duties'.

4 **faeneratorum** : 'money-lenders'. **mercenariorum** : 'hired workmen'. **quorum . . . emuntur** : 'who are paid for their labour (*operae*), not for their skill (*artes*)'.

7 **vendant** : see Note 6(*a*). **nihil proficiant** : 'they would make no profit'.

9 **vanitate** : 'falsehood'. **opifices** : 'craftsmen'.

10 **ingenuum** : i.e. *liberalem*, 'honourable'. **officina** : 'workshop'.

11 **voluptatum ministrae** : 'handmaidens of pleasure'.

12 **cetarii** : 'dealers in salt fish'. **lanii** : 'butchers'. **coqui** : 'cooks'. **fartores** : 'sausage-makers'. **piscatores** : 'fish-mongers'.

14 **P. Terentius Afer** : second century B.C. Roman dramatist, who wrote Latin adaptations of Greek comedy, some of which have survived. **unguentarios** : 'perfumers'.

15 **saltatores** : 'dancers'. **ludum talarium** : 'dicing'. **in quibus artibus . . . hae**—*hae artes in quibus . . .* : *cp*. Note 4(*b*).

16 **prudentia . . . quaeritur** : 'which exhibit greater skill or aim at some more than ordinary benefit'.

17 **doctrina rerum honestarum** : 'instruction in useful subjects'. *i.e.* education of youth.

18 **iis . . . honestae** : 'respectable for those whose rank they suit'.

19 **tenuis** : 'on a small scale'.

20 **copiosa** : 'extensive'.

21 **sine vanitate** : 'without false pretences'. **impertiens** : 'conferring'.

XI

1 **Antiochus of Ascalon** was a representative of the Academic school and one of Cicero's first teachers. He was actually head of the Academy in 79 B.C.
    M. Junius Brutus : the murderer of Caesar. The *De Finibus* is dedicated to him.

2 **gymnasio . . . vocatur :** 'which is called the School of Ptolemy'.

3 **Q. frater :** Cicero's brother Quintus. **T. Pomponius Atticus:** Cicero's close friend and correspondent. **Lucius Cicero :** a cousin of Cicero.

5 **Academia :** the famous grove near Athens where Plato taught.

6 **id temporis :** i.e. *eo tempore* (*diei*). **ad tempus :** 'in good time'.

7 **omnes :** supply '*venimus*'. **Dipylo :** the Dipylon Gate of Athens, leading to Eleusis. **sex stadia :** 'three-quarters of a mile'. A stadion was about a furlong.

9 **spatia :** 'open spaces, walks'. **ea :** see Note 4(*a*).

10 **naturane . . . dicam :** 'Shall I say that it is a gift we owe to nature or to some accident, that (*ut*). . . .' For *hoc*, anticipating *ut*, see Note 5.

14 **velut :** 'as, for instance'.

18 **ipsum :** 'Plato himself'.

20 **modo :** 'just'. **convertebat ad sese :** 'attracted my attention'.

21 **Coloneus ille locus :** Colonus is a hill, a mile north of Athens, birth-place of Sophocles, the tragic poet. **ob oculos :** 'before my eyes'.

22 **quam . . . quamque :** used without an adj. or adv. in the sense of 'how much'.

23 **altiorem :** 'earlier'. **Oedipodis :** genit. of *Oedipous*. In the *Oedipus Coloneus* of Sophocles, the aged and blind Oedipus arrives at Colonus and asks for Athenian protection. To his question where he is, the chorus reply in a famous ode in praise of Colonus, apparently referred to in '*illo mollissimo carmine*'.

25 **species :** 'a vision', goes with *Oedipodis* above. **inaniter :** 'idly'. **scilicet :** concessive, 'I admit'.

26 **tamen** : 'all the same'.

28 **invisit** : perf. from *inviso* = 'visit'. **Aeschines** : fourth century B.C. Attic orator and opponent of the more famous Demosthenes in his policy of resistance to Philip of Macedon.

32 **in Phalericum (Portum)** : the harbour of Phalerum, adjoining the Piraeus, the main port of Athens. **descenderim** : causal subj. See Note 6(*b*).

34 **modo** : 'just now'.

35 **Pericles** (500–429 B.C.) : the great Athenian statesman and founder of the fifth century Athenian Empire.

36 **quamquam . . . urbe** : 'Yet (*quamquam* = *tamen*) it (*id*) is an endless pursuit (*i.e.* visiting historic spots) in this city'.

XII

The speech in defence of L. Valerius Flaccus dates from 59 B.C. Flaccus was accused of extortion when governor of Asia. Having a weak case, Cicero tried to discredit the prosecution by questioning the reliability of its witnesses, who were all Greeks. He gives the Greeks full credit for genius and learning, but accuses them, as a people, of dishonesty. That this was a generally accepted view in his time appears from other passages in Cicero. Thus, in *Verr.* II 7, speaking of the Sicilians, he attributes to them almost Roman qualities, and continues: '*nihil ceterorum simile Graecorum, nulla desidia, nulla luxuries*'. ('There is nothing in them like the rest of the Greeks, no laziness, no luxury'.)

This contemptuous attitude may perhaps be partly explained by the fact that the Roman conquest had completed the ruin of the Greeks politically and financially, and many were forced to earn their living as tutors and philosopher companions to wealthy Romans or in lower employments. It is hardly surprising that they should have become demoralised, and that the Romans came to feel for them all the scorn of the honourable citizen for the immoral foreigner. A century and a half later, the satirist Juvenal writes contemptuously of a Greek Rome which he cannot endure. (See Mahaffey: *Silver Age of the Greek World*, p. 162 ff.)

1 **de quibus . . . de eis** : see Note 4(*b*). The meaning is: 'Will you (Roman jurymen) listen to the evidence of others (Greeks) about those matters (the character of Flaccus) about which you yourselves should be giving evidence to others?' Cicero expresses

surprise that a Roman jury should be ready to listen to Greek provincial witnesses as to the character of a Roman governor.

2 **at quos testes?** : *at* introduces an objection: 'But, you say, what witnesses?'

id quod commune : 'a thing which they all have in common', *i.e.* they are all Greeks.

3 **non . . . derogem** : 'not that I in particular wish to deprive the whole Greek nation of their reputation for honour'. *quo* with subj. often expresses a rejected reason or, as here, purpose; lit. 'not in order that'.

5 **genere** : 'nation'. **studio . . . non abhorrens** : 'not without sympathy and good-will'.

6 **me . . fuisse** : 'I reckon that I myself am such, and was still more when'. **tum cum** : see Note 8(*a*).

7 **in illo numero** : 'among them'. **multi** : the second *multi* (line 8) contrasts with the first. See Note 1(*b*).

11 **litteras** : 'literature'. **multarum artium disciplinam** : 'distinction in many branches of learning'.

12 **leporem** : 'charm'. **dicendi copiam** : 'eloquence'.

13 **qua** : neut. plur. of indefinite *qui*. Trans. 'if they claim for themselves any other qualities'.

14 With **testimoniorum** begins a contrasting clause. See Note 1(*b*) **religionem et fidem** : 'sacred and binding obligation'. See Note 2.

15 **vis** : 'meaning'.

16 **pondus** : 'importance'.

17 **religione** : 'scrupulousness'.

18 **ad rogatum** : neut., 'to the question put'.

19 **laborant** : 'worry, concern themselves'.

20 **probent** : here 'are to prove'. Deliberative subj. **explicent** : 'extricate themselves (from a difficulty)'.

21 **ea voluntate . . . ut** : 'with the intention of'. See Note 4(*d*).
processit : perf. indic. after *cum* frequentative: 'whenever a Greek witness comes forward . . . he thinks (*meditatur*)'.

23 **coargui** : 'to be refuted'. **ad id** : 'for that purpose', *i.e.* of deception.

26 **vos autem** : 'you, on the other hand'. **in privatis minimarum rerum iudiciis** : '(even) in private cases concerning the most trivial matters'.

27 **expenditis** : 'weigh up'.

28 **tribum** : The urban population of Rome was divided into local 'tribes' or parishes for the purpose of taxation, voting, etc.
nostis = *novistis*: 'You are acquainted with'.
qui : antecedent *is* (understood) is subject of *sustentat*. See Note 4(*e*). Trans. 'whenever any of our own people (*i.e.* Romans) gives evidence, how (*ut*) he restrains himself!' (a rare meaning of *sustentat*).

XIII

2 **ingressus est** : 'began', governs *loqui*.
Catonis hoc senis est : 'What I am going to say (*hoc*) is the opinion held by Cato in his old age'.
M. Porcius Cato (234–149 B.C.), the Censor, was born at Tusculum. During his censorship, he upheld the old Roman morality with the utmost rigour, opposing luxury and Greek culture, though he himself learned Greek in his old age. His ideal of life was that of the old-fashioned farmer ruling his slaves with a rod of iron. It was described in his work *De Re Rustica* on agriculture. His work *Origines*, now lost, on the early history of Rome and Italy, was important as one of the first histories written in Latin. He was also distinguished as an orator. His implacable enmity against Carthage is expressed in the famous saying, in which he repeatedly urged its destruction, '*Delenda est Carthago*'. He sometimes shocked even ancient sentiment by his severity, as, for instance when, on leaving Spain, he sold his war-horse which had worn itself out in his service. To posterity he became a proverbial example of *gravitas Romana*. His descendant, Cato of Utica (see IX introductory Note), was a worthy representative of the family tradition.
quem . . . unice dilexi : 'for whom I had an extraordinary affection'.

4 **patris utriusque** : 'of both my fathers'. Scipio was the son of Aemilius Paulus, conqueror of Macedonia, but had been adopted as the son of P. Scipio, son of the elder Africanus. (See XXV introductory Note.) **totum** : predicative, 'entirely'.

6 **usus rei publicae** : 'experience of public affairs'.

7 **cum . . . tum etiam** : see Note 8(*b*).

8 **modus** : 'moderation'. **lepos** : 'humour'.

9 **orationi . . . congruens** : 'a manner of life consistent with his speech'.

10 **is dicere solebat . . . :** a complicated sentence. *Ob hanc causam* introduces a long *quod* clause. This consists of two contrasting parts, of which the second begins with *nostra autem res publica*. With *ut Cretum* begins a long subordinate clause extending as far as *Demetrius*, after which the *quod* construction is resumed. Trans. 'He used to say that the superiority of our own constitution to that of other states consisted in this, that in the latter it had generally been individual lawgivers who had devised for each its own particular laws and institutions, as, for example, Minos in Crete and Lycurgus at Sparta, while Athens, which had gone through many phases, had had a succession of lawgivers, Theseus, Draco, Solon, Cleisthenes and many others, and, finally, when prostrate and bleeding to death, had been revived by the skill of Demetrius of Phalerum: our own state, on the other hand . . . (*nostra autem res publica*)'.

13 **Cretum :** genit. pl. of *Cres, Cretis*, 'a Cretan'. **Minos :** legendary king of pre-historic Crete.

14 **Lycurgus :** early Spartan legislator.

15 **Theseus :** early king of Athens, united the Attic communities into one state. **Draco :** seventh century Athenian legislator. The severity of his code is the origin of the expression 'Draconian Laws'. **Solon :** famous Athenian statesman and poet of the sixth century (see Note on VIII 18).

16 **Cleisthenes :** founder of Athenian democracy (sixth century).

17 **Demetrius** of **Phalerum :** Macedonian viceroy at Athens after the death of Alexander, in 323 B.C. The list of Athenian lawgivers appears hardly consistent with the inclusion of Athens among the states which owed their constitutions to one man. The meaning, however, is that, although both Athens and Rome experienced constitutional changes, these changes at Rome were not associated with individual names so much as at Athens. The distinction is rather superficial.

18 **esset . . . constituta :** dependent on *quod* (l. 11). Subj. is due to ind. speech.

19 **nec una . . . aetatibus :** 'dependent, not on the life of one man, but on many generations and ages'.

20 **nam neque ullum . . . :** Shorten the rather redundant expression. 'Never, he used to say, had there existed in the world asingle man of such genius that . . .'. **ingenium :** 'man of genius'.

21 **quem :** antecedent *quisquam*. **fugeret :** 'would escape the notice of'. For the subj., see Note 6(*a*).

22 **cuncta ingenia collecta in unum** : 'all the men of genius in the world concentrated into one'.

23 **tantum providere** : 'exercise such foresight'.

24 **sine . . . usu ac vetustate** : for hendiadys see Note 2. 'without the help of a long tradition of experience'. Cicero means the *mos maiorum*, as opposed to the legislation of particular lawgivers.

26 **libenter . . . Catonis** : 'it is a pleasure to use Cato's word', *i.e.* 'origin'. The reference is to Cato's *Origines*: see Note on line 2 above.

27 **quod est propositum** : 'my object'.

28 **nascentem . . . robustam** : The metaphor is drawn from the growth of a human being from birth (*nascentem*), through childhood (*crescentem*) to maturity (*adultam*) and manhood (*firmam, robustam*). Trans. 'in its origin, development, full growth and assured strength of maturity'.

29 **quam . . . si finxero** : 'than if I invent some imaginary state, as Socrates does in Plato's dialogue', *i.e.* in the *Republic*, in which Socrates, being asked to define justice, answers by outlining an imaginary state, where it is fully realised, and where every man is educated according to his ability and function, from the rulers or Guardians down to the ruled.

XIV

1 **qua gloria parta** : 'after this glorious exploit'. The reference is to Romulus' conquest of Alba Longa.

auspicato : 'after taking the auspices', *i.e.* with religious sanction. Impers. abl. abs.

firmare . . . rem publicam : 'establish a permanent state'. Both *condere* and *firmare* depend on *cogitavisse*.

2 **dicitur** : subject. 'Romulus'.

3 **quod** : i.e. *id quod*. **serere** : i.e. *condere*.

4 **incredibili opportunitate** : abl. of quality. Lit: 'as for the site . . . he chose (one) of extraordinary fitness'. Trans. 'he made an extraordinarily appropriate choice'.

5 **quod** : i.e. *id quod*.

6 **illa** : i.e. *tali*: 'which he could have done very easily with such numbers and resources as he had'.

ut . . . procederet : explanatory of the preceding clause: 'by advancing into Rutulian territory'. The Rutuli were a Latin people living near the mouth of the Tiber.

8 **Ancus** : fourth king of Rome.

9 **hoc** : anticipates the acc. and inf. *non esse.* . . . See Note 5. **sensit ac vidit** : 'had the insight to realise'. See Note 2.

10 **quae ad spem diuturnitatis** . . . **atque imperii** : 'cities destined to be centres of lasting empires'. For the hendiadys see Note 2.

13 **caecis** : passive sense, 'unknown'. **terra continens** : 'inland site'.

15 **quasi** . . . **denuntiat** : 'gives warning by some audible disturbance'. See Note 2.

16 **advolare** : 'swoop down upon'.

17 **quin** : 'without'.

18 **ille** : contrasts with the land enemy mentioned in the previous sentence. Trans. 'on the other hand, the enemy who comes by sea with a fleet'. **ante** : belongs to following *quam*.

19 **queat** : for *possit*, as often in negative expressions.

20 **venit** : perf. ind. after *cum*, 'whenever'. **nec** . . . **prae se fert** : 'nor does he declare'.
qui sit : *qui* (adj.) is not uncommon for *quis* (pron.) in indirect questions. It may have the sense of *qualis* here, 'what he is'.

21 **nŏtā** : abl. 'by any sign'. **pacatus** : supply *utrum* before this word: 'whether he is a friend or foe'.

22 **discerni ac iudicari** : see Note 2.

24 **demutatio** : 'degradation'. A rare word. **admiscentur** : subject *urbes maritimae* (understood). **sermonibus** : abl. Trans. 'they (the coastal cities) suffer an admixture (lit. are intermingled with) of foreign tongues and ways'.

25 **adventiciae** : 'foreign'.

27 **qui** : antecedent *ii* (understood). See Note 4(*e*).

28 **volucri** . . . **rapiuntur** : 'they are borne away on the swift wings of hope and imagination'.

29 **manent** : for *cum* with ind. see Note 8(*a*). Here there is a slightly concessive sense marked by *tamen*. Trans. 'even when they do remain in the body, their minds are far away'.

31 **labefactatam** : 'undermined'. **pervertit** : 'overthrew'. Carthage and Corinth both fell to Roman arms in the same year, 146 B.C.

32 **aliquando** : 'finally'. **error** : 'wandering'. Not common in this sense. **dissipatio** : 'dispersal'.

35 **quae . . . importantur** : 'in the form of spoil of war or ordinary imports'.

36 **amoenitas** : 'beauty of nature'.

37 **sumptuosas . . . illecebras** : 'brings with it a variety of pleasures to ensnare into luxury or idleness'.

38 **commoditas** : followed by a double explanatory clause, *et ut . . . possit* and *et rursus ut . . . possint*.

39 **quod ubique gentium est** : 'all the nations of the earth'. The whole clause, though placed before *ut*, is subject of *possit*. *Cp.* Note 7.

ad eam urbem, quam incolas : 'to the particular (coastal) city in which one (ideal 2nd pers. sing.) is dwelling'.

40 **incolas, efferant,** and **velint** : attracted into the mood of the *ut* clause. **quod . . . sui** : 'the produce of their own lands'. Obj. of *portare*.

42 **qui** : 'how'. Archaic abl. of *qui*. **divinius** : 'more admirably'. **complecti** : 'seize'.

43 **perennis amnis et aequabilis** : genit. after *ripa*, 'a river with unfailing and steady current'.

44 **in mare late influentis** : 'with wide estuary'.

45 **quo** : antecedent *amnis*. **posset** : final subj. Trans. 'so that by this route (*i.e.* the river) the city might be able to receive'.

quo egeret . . . quo redundaret : Supply *id* as antecedent for both clauses. See Note 4(*e*). Both verbs are attracted into the mood of *posset*.

46 **eodem** : goes with *flumine*. The *ut* clause continues the final construction begun by *quo posset* above.

47 **a mari absorberet** : this is the MSS. reading. Though doubtful, it may be translated: 'draw in from the sea'.

48 **ut . . . videatur** : consecutive.

50 **hanc rerum tantam potentiam** : 'so great an empire as this'.

51 **non ferme** : almost the same as *vix*, 'scarcely'.

53 **nativa** : 'natural', *i.e.* not artificial.

54 **habeat** : see Note 6(*a*).
is : = *talis*, and introduces the long consecutive clauses, *ut . . . cingeretur* and *ut . . . niteretur*. See Note 4(*d*).

55 **tractus ductusque** : 'extent and course'.

muri : The original fortified settlement at Rome was built on the Palatine by Romulus. Later, the seven hills were included, and surrounded by the Servian Wall, attributed to the sixth king, Servius Tullius. This remained the city boundary until the late Republic. **cum . . . tum etiam :** see Note 8 (*b*).

56 **definitus :** 'marked out'. Agrees with *ductus*, the second of the two subjects.

ex omni parte . . . montibus : 'along a line of hills, at every point, high and steep'. The hills with their steep cliffs, now levelled by time and erosion, in ancient times formed a natural defence, except where the low-lying ground between the Esquiline and the Quirinal left a gap which had to be filled with an earthwork (*agger*).

59 **ita :** introduces a fresh consecutive clause, *ut . . . permanserit*. **arx :** the Capitoline hill.

60 **circumiectu . . . niteretur :** 'resting upon a circuit of rocks, steep and cut almost sheer away (*circumciso*)'.

61 **Gallici adventus :** the Gallic invasion of 390 B.C., in which most of Rome was taken except the Capitol.

64 **cum . . . tum :** with slightly adversative force. See Note 8(*a*).

XV

Cicero here gives four reasons why men desire wealth: 1. As a necessity of life. 2. For the enjoyment of pleasure. 3. As a means of prestige and power. 4 For luxurious and cultured living.

1 **cum . . . tum :** see Note 8 (*b*).

2 **in quibus . . . animus :** 'in men of aspiring minds'.

3 **in iis :** see Note 4(*b*). **spectat . . . facultatem :** 'aims at the accumulation of wealth and the power to confer favours'.

4 **M. Crassus :** see Note on VIII 9. Crassus was an extreme example of the wealthy upper class, which owed its riches to the plunder of provinces and financial speculation, and which used its power for personal ambition and political ascendancy (*principatus*). Crassus was said to own most of the house property of Rome, which he had bought cheap from owners eager to sell through fear of fire.

nuper : Crassus had been dead ten years at the time the *De Officiis* was written (44 B.C.).

5 **pecuniam** : 'property'. **princeps** : The *principes civitatis* were prominent members of the senatorial or pro-consular class, who attained an unofficial position of power through personal achievement or *auctoritas*, *e.g.* Pompey, Crassus and Caesar. The Republic perished through the attempts of one individual or another to make himself sole *princeps*. Thus *principatus*, as below, often meant *dominatus* (tyranny).

6 **cuius . . . posset** : see Note 6(*a*). Trans. 'unless he could maintain an army on its income (*fructibus*)'.

7 **magnifici apparatus** : 'luxurious establishments'.

vitaeque . . . copia : 'refined and affluent style of living.' One of the great defects of Roman republican society was the wide gap between the wealthy aristocracy, enjoying a pretentious luxury and the vast mass of the impoverished or unemployed proletariat.

10 **nemini nocens** : conditional meaning, 'provided it injures no one'.

13 **imperiorum** : 'military commands'. **honorum** : 'civil offices' For asyndeton of nouns see Note 1(*a*).

14 **inciderunt** : indic. after *cum* meaning 'whenever'. **modo** : 'recently'.

temeritas C. Caesaris : This was written in 44 B.C. just after Caesar's murder. *Cp.* what Cicero says elsewhere of Caesar's tyranny in XVI 16 f., XVII 6 f.

16 **eum** : with *principatum*, 'supreme power'. See Note 4(*c*).

17 **in hoc genere** : 'in this regard'. **quod** : '(the fact) that'.

18 **ingeniis** : 'men of genius'.

19 **honoris . . . gloriae** : note asyndeton and arrangement of four nouns in pairs. See Note 1(*a*).

XVI

1 **quam diu** : 'as long as'. The dependent clause extends as far as *necessarii*. Asyndeton of both kinds is noticeable in this sentence. See Notes 1(*a*) and (*b*).

2 **tenebatur** : 'was maintained'.

aut pro sociis aut de imperio : Examples of wars in defence of allies would be the Samnite and Second Punic Wars, the first of which originated in the defence of Capua, the second in that of

Saguntum. Of wars fought for the preservation of the empire
(*de imperio*), the Mithridatic Wars may, perhaps, be cited. The
distinction is a fine one.

3 **Mites** : Examples would be the Second Macedonian War,
which ended with the proclamation of the freedom of Greece by
Flamininus (196 B.C.), or the earlier wars against the Latins which
resulted in their enfranchisement.

4 **necessarii** : Roman severity was especially shown in the
treatment of Carthage and Corinth, whose destruction in 146 B.C.
is elsewhere defended by Cicero as inevitable. (See XIX 9 f.)
    portus et refugium : 'harbour of refuge'. See Note 2.

6 **ex hac una re** : anticipates *si defendissent*, *si* being almost
equivalent to *quod*. This use of *si* is found after verbs of expecting
or trying. Trans. 'were anxious to claim credit for this alone, that
they had defended provinces and allies with justice and honour'.

8 **patrocinium** : the protection afforded to a client by a patron
or by a victorious *imperator* as a favour to a whole community.
Thus the family of the Metelli were patrons of the province of
Sicily.
    imperium : the absolute right of the victor to rule. Cicero's
ideal of the empire views Rome rather as the protector than the
ruler of the world. Compare the modern distinction between
empire and commonwealth. Trans. 'a protectorate of the world
rather than an empire'. See Note on XIX 21.

9 **sensim hanc consuetudinem** : The decline of Roman morals
is a constant theme of writers of this age: *e.g.* Sallust, like Cicero,
makes Sulla's eastern victories a landmark in degeneracy. He
says: '*Ibi primum insuevit exercitus populi Romani amare potare, signa
tabulas pictas vasa caelata mirari, ea privatim et publice rapere. . . .*' The
theme of moral deterioration becomes a commonplace in the
Augustan writers, Livy, Vergil and Horace.

10 **Sulla** (138–78 B.C.) distinguished himself first as a soldier
by his victories over Rome's foreign enemies, Jugurtha in Africa
and Mithridates in Asia. On his return to Italy in 83 B.C., he
fought a civil war against the popular party, and after his victory
employed against them ruthless measures of extermination and
confiscation (proscriptions). During his dictatorship, he introduced a number of conservative measures intended to restore the
weakened authority of the Senate.

11 **desitum est** : The passive form of *desino* is often used when the
dependent infinitive is itself passive.

13 **in illo** : 'in his (Sulla's) case'. **honestam causam** : Sullas'

cause against the tyranny of the popular party was good, but not his adoption of cruel methods.

14 **hasta posita** : 'by auction', *i.e.* of the property of the proscribed. An auction sale was held near a spear set upright in the ground.

16 **secutus est qui** : Julius Caesar. This wholesale denunciation of Caesar's policy can hardly be justified. Rhetorical exaggeration must be allowed for. As Cicero himself had pointed out in the *Pro Marcello* (46 B.C.), there had been many notable examples of Caesar's *clementia* towards opponents. It is true, however, that the disastrous civil war against the Pompeians (49–45 B.C.) extended from Spain and Africa to Asia Minor and Egypt. For subjs. after *qui*, see Note 6(*a*).

18 **uno calamitatis iure** : 'in a common rule of destruction'.

20 **ad exemplum . . . imperii** : 'in token of an empire forfeited'.

21 **Massiliam** : Marseilles joined the Pompeians in the Civil War and was taken by siege in 49 B.C. A model of the town was carried in Caesar's Gallic triumph of 45 B.C. This humiliating treatment of an ancient Greek colony and one of Rome's earliest allies, was felt to be particularly outrageous on Caesar's part.

ex ea urbe triumphari : 'a triumph celebrated over that city'.

22 **sine qua** : 'without whose help'. **ex transalpinis bellis** : 'after wars beyond the Alps'.

24 **si . . . indignius** : 'if the sun had witnessed an outrage more shameful than this', *i.e.* if this had not surpassed all the others.

iure . . . plectimur : 'we are justly punished'. The argument is that respect for human rights is indivisible: if the Romans had not permitted tyranny to be exercised against their subjects, they would not have had to suffer it themselves.

26 **unum** : Julius Caesar.

27 **paucos** : In his will, Caesar named as his heir M. Octavius, his grand-nephew, the future Augustus.

28 **multos** : Antony and his supporters, who, Cicero suggests, were the heirs of Caesar's ambitions (*cupiditatum*). See Note 1(*b*).

29 **bellorum civilium** : The horror of the Civil Wars was even more deeply felt by the Augustan writers. To Vergil it appeared that the world had gone mad: see the concluding passage of *Georgic* I 510–514, where he compares it to a chariot out of control.

semen et causa : 'root cause'. See Note 2.

30 **hastam illam** : *i.e.* the Sullan proscriptions. Ironically, Cicero himself was to be a victim of the proscriptions introduced by Antony, Octavian and Lepidus in 43 B.C.

31 **iique ipsi** : 'and even they'. See Note 4(*f*).

32 **extrema . . . metuentes** : *i.e.* the very walls dread the fire-brands of revolutionaries.

33 **dum . . . malumus** : 'through preferring'.

XVII

2 **alienius** : 'more unfavourable'.

3 **Quintus Ennius** : (239–169 B.C.), the father of Roman poetry. Among his works, which survive only in fragments, were the *Annales*, a history of Rome in hexameter verse and a number of tragedies, to one of which belongs the line quoted. He was much admired by Cicero.

4 **(eum) periisse expetit** : 'aims at the ruin', *i.e.* of the man he hates.

6 **opes** : 'power'.

7 **nuper** : a reference to Caesar's assassination, which was 'recent' at the time Cicero was writing. **huius tyranni** : *i.e.* Caesar.

8 **cum maxime** : usually 'at the very time when', sometimes, as here, 'at this very time'. Trans. 'to whom, though dead, the state is even now subservient'. In Cicero's view, the dead Caesar lived on in Antony. *Cp.* Shakespeare:

> O Julius Caesar, thou art mighty yet!
> Thy spirit walks abroad . . .
>
> *Julius Caesar* V, 3

10 **valeat ad pestem** : 'how powerful it is as a destructive force'.

11 **haud fere** : i.e. *vix*.

12 **diuturnitatis** : 'duration', *i.e.* of power.

13 **benevolentia** : 'good will'.

fidelis (custos) vel ad perpetuitatem : 'a sure guarantor even of its permanence'.

14 **iis** : 'by those'. Dat. of agent. **sit adhibenda** : concessive, 'granted that it must be employed'.

15 **eris** : 'masters'. Dat. of agent. Trans. 'as by masters'. **in famulos** : 'towards their servants'. **si possunt** : 'if they cannot otherwise be controlled'. **qui** : antecedent *iis* in next line. See Note 4(*b*).

16 **libera civitate** : To the end Cicero remained faithful to the idea of republican freedom.

ita se instruunt ut metuantur : 'set out to make themselves feared'. **iis** : abl. of comparison after *dementius*.

17 **demersae** : 'overwhelmed'.

18 **alicuius opibus** : 'by the ascendancy of some individual'. **emergunt** : 'come to the surface'.

19 **haec** : *i.e. leges et libertas.* **aliquando** : 'some day'. **aut iudiciis . . . suffragiis** : 'as a result of the silent verdict (of the people), or the secret choice of the ballot'.

20 **acriores . . . retentae** : 'freedom for a while suppressed has sharper fangs than freedom preserved'.

21 **quod** : antecedent *id* below. See Note 4(*b*).

23 **ut . . . retineatur** : explanatory of *id*. **metus . . . caritas** : see Note 1(*b*).

caritas : esteem or affection shown towards gods, parents, or country. It is distinct from *amor*, which is personal love for wife, family or children. Used in the Vulgate version of the New Testament to translate ἀγάπη, it came to denote specifically Christian love: hence English 'charity'. Trans. 'Let us adhere to the principle which is of the widest application and is the strongest guarantee not only of security, but also of power and position, I mean, the renunciation of fear (as a motive) and its replacement by love'.

XVIII

The *Third Philippic* was delivered before the Senate on December 20th, 44 B.C. In November, Antony had already marched north into Cisalpine Gaul against Decimus Brutus. At Rome, the Senate, supported by Octavian and the consuls for 43 B.C., Hirtius and Pansa, was preparing to resist him. Cicero warns that the cause of constitutional freedom calls for immediate action. Note that in the popular view, *libertas* stood for 'the spirit and practice of republican government', also for 'freedom from a tyrant or a faction'. But it could also be twisted to suit a party: thus Caesar claimed to assert the freedom of the Republic. Here it stands for the Republican ideal, which all Cicero's eloquence could not save. (See R. Syme: *The Roman Revolution* p. 155).

1 **tenete** : 'seize'. **occasionem oblatam** : 'the opportunity offered you'.

2 **amplissimi . . . consilii** : 'the noblest assembly in the world'.

3 **aliquando** : 'at last'.

6 **moneam** : see Note 6(a).

7 **intellegat** : see Note 6(a). **indormierimus** : lit. 'fall asleep over this crisis (*huic tempori*)'. Trans. 'slumber through this hour of destiny'.

8 **dominationem** : 'tyranny'.

9 **nostis** :=*novistis*, 'you are acquainted with'.

11 **libidinosus**: 'lustful'. **petulans**: 'impudent'. **impurus**: 'foul'. **impudicus**: 'lewd, sensual'. **aleator**: 'gambler'. **ebrius**: 'drunkard'.

12 **servire** : 'to be in slavery to' (dat.). Note the rhetorical vocabulary of abuse!

ea : =*id*, resuming *servire*, but drawn into agreement with the predicate *miseria*.

13 **quod si** : 'but if'. **fatum extremum** : 'the day of ruin'.

14 **venit** : perf., 'has already come'. **quod** : antecedent *id* understood as obj. of *faciamus*. See Note 4(e). Trans. 'Let us, the leaders (*principes*) of the world, do what noble gladiators do, who wish to (*lit.* in order to) die (*decumbant*) with honour, and let us rather fall with dignity than submit to the disgrace of slavery'.

21 **in utramque partem** : 'on one side or the other'.

22 **impii** : 'disloyal'. **pro caritate rei publicae** : lit. 'more, than in one's love for one's country one would desire'. Trans. 'gauged by patriotism too many, but few indeed compared with the host of the loyal'.

28 **commentati atque meditati** : 'who have been thinking and planning'.

XIX

Cicero here deals with war and the rules which govern it. The *Ius Gentium*, the usage which regulated actual relations between Rome and foreign states, was recognised from early times. Thus Livy (V 27) in telling the story of the treacherous schoolmaster, who offered to betray the sons of the chief men of Falerii to the Romans, makes Camillus reject the offer with the words: '*Sunt et belli, sicut pacis, iura*', 'War has its laws as well as peace'. The *Ius Gentium* readily developed into the *Ius Humanum*, 'Common Justice', what all men would recognise as just and right.

1 **in re publica** : 'in affairs of state'.

2 **decertandi** : 'of settling a dispute'. **disceptationem** : 'arbitration'.

3 **illud** : 'the former'. **proprium** : 'the mark of'.

4 **hoc** : 'the latter'. **confugiendum est** : 'recourse must be had'. **si** : '(only) if'.

5 **quidem** : concessive, 'indeed', balanced by *autem* below. See Note 8(*e*). **ob eam causam ut** : 'to the end that'.

6 **ut . . . vivatur** : impersonal passive; final subj. Trans. 'that one may live'.

7 **conservandi** : 'ought to be spared'. In the examples from history which follow, Cicero tries to show that Roman conquests are not inconsistent with the principle of the 'just war'. But he is clearly uneasy about Corinth.

8 **Tusculanos . . .** : Tusculum was the oldest *municipium* or provincial township in Italy, having received Roman citizenship in 381 B.C. The Aequi and the Volsci were central Italian peoples admitted to full or partial citizenship by the beginning of the third century B.C. Roman policy was to 'spare the vanquished' (Vergil's *parcere subiectis*) and eventually admit them to political privilege. The grant of citizenship originally confined to Italians, had, by the third century A.D., been extended to the whole empire.

9 **in civitatem accipere** : 'grant citizenship to'. **Carthage** : destroyed by Scipio Africanus Minor in 146 B.C., and **Numantia,** a Spanish town, also by Scipio in 134 B.C.

10 **nollem** : potential subj. After *Corinthum* supply *sustulissent*, 'I would they had not (destroyed) Corinth'. Corinth was plundered and destroyed by the consul Mummius in 146 B.C., and robbed of its art treasures, which were carried off to Italy. It was a particularly bad example of Roman ruthlessness, although the Greeks had given provocation and the city was in fact afterwards rebuilt. The treatment of Carthage, Corinth and Numantia is a good commentary on the second half of Vergil's famous line, '*debellare superbos*' (to subdue the proud).

11 **aliquid secutos** : lit. 'followed something', *i.e.* 'had some good in view'. Subj. is *maiores nostros*. **opportunitatem loci** : 'favourable site'. See Note 3.

13 **quae . . . sit** : 'such a peace as'. See Note 6(*a*).

14 **consulendum est** : with *paci*, lit. 'regard must be had to'. Trans. 'One must always work for a peace which is likely to leave no opening for double-dealing'. **in quo** : 'in this matter'.

 si . . . obtemperatum : 'if I had been listened to'. Cicero is no doubt thinking of his efforts to prevent the Civil War between Caesar and Pompey, which had led to the breakdown of the Republic.

 15 **si non optimam . . . est** : 'we should have had, if not the ideal government, at least some kind of constitution (*at aliquam*), which we at present altogether lack'. Observe the emphatic predicative use of *nulla*, 'non-existent'. For *res publica* see Note on **XXXIX** 18.

 16 **cum . . . tum** : 'both . . . and'. See Note 8(*b*).

 17 **deviceris** : fut. perf., 'one conquers'. Note ideal 2nd pers. sing. = 'one'.

 ad fidem . . . confugient : in this phrase, *fides* = *tutela* (protection). To put oneself under the protection of a Roman general was equivalent to unconditional surrender. At the same time, the Roman assumed a certain obligation (*fides*) to afford protection to the defeated.

 19 **murum aries percusserit** : It was the practice of the Romans to grant terms to an enemy who surrendered before the battering-ram touched the walls. In *B. G.* II 32, Caesar accepts the surrender of the Aduatuci on this condition. Cicero takes a more liberal view and proposes to relax it. **in quo** : 'in this regard'.

 21 **patroni** : Besides the private relationship by which a wealthy or powerful citizen could become the patron, or legal adviser, guardian and protector of a client or dependent, there was also a traditional *patrocinium* (see Note on **XVI** 8), by which a victorious general might become the public patron of towns or whole provinces. This obligation descended from father to son in the same family: thus the Marcelli were patrons of Sicily, Aemilius Paulus of Spain and Macedonia. By granting this patronage, the Romans, according to Cicero, more than fulfilled the claims of *iustitia*.

 22 **belli aequitas** : 'the law of war'. **sanctissime** : 'most strictly'.

 fetiali populi Romani iure : 'in the diplomatic law of the Roman people'. The fetials were priestly officials, dating from regal times, who performed the sacred rites connected with declarations of war and treaties of peace or alliance.

 24 **rebus repetitis** : 'after satisfaction has been demanded'. When a war was waged for the recovery of violated rights, a formal demand for restitution had first to be made by the fetials, who called down the wrath of the gods on themselves, if their demands were unjust. Ten to thirty days after their return to

Rome, war was formally notified (*denuntiatum*) and declared (*indictum*). Without this, no legal state of war existed.

nullum bellum esse iustum : The conditions laid down for a just war are:—1, that it must have a just cause; 2, that it must be formally declared; 3, that it must have as its object the establishment of a just peace; and 4, that it must be waged without unnecessary cruelty. All of these appear in the medieval definition of the just war, and are still recognised, though not always observed, to-day. The modern undeclared war of aggression, for example, is contrary to ancient standards.

25 **M. Porcius Cato** : see Note on XIII 2.

27 **missum factum** : 'released (from the ranks)'.

28 **bello Persico** : 'the war against Perseus', king of Macedonia, defeated 168 B.C.

29 **qui** : antecedent *eum* understood. See Note 4(*e*).

30 **(eum) pugnare** : acc. and inf. after *ius*.

    hoste : Note that *hostis* means an officially declared enemy: a personal enemy is *inimicus*. Cato's insistence on a legal point is characteristically Roman.

XX

For the *De Legibus*, see Introduction III (ii). At the beginning of Book I, Cicero sets out to explain to his friend Atticus and his brother Quintus what it is that makes laws morally binding. The argument is briefly as follows. Behind the *leges scriptae et instituta populorum* (the enactments of particular states) there lies *ius universum* (universally recognised justice). Justice is recognised by all men, because it is inherent in human nature (*insita in natura*). Now the highest quality of man is reason (*ratio, mens*), by which he distinguishes right from wrong. What reason decrees is *Ius* or *Lex*, law in the sense of supreme and binding obligation, than which there is no higher sanction. In the present extract, Cicero calls this *ius unum* (line 8) and *una lex*, defined as *recta ratio imperandi atque prohibendi*, 'the right rule of commanding and forbidding', the law of right and wrong. This is the bond of society, and a guarantee against the decrees of tyrants. It is to this unwritten law that Antigone, in the play of Sophocles, appeals against the arbitrary command of King Creon not to bury her brother Polyneices: the tyrant forbids her to do what *pietas*, enjoined by the law of nature, commands. She expresses this in the famous lines:

οὐ γάρ τι νῦν γε κἀχθές, ἀλλ' ἀεί ποτε
ζῇ ταῦτα, κοὐδείς οἶδεν ἐξ ὅτου 'φάνη.

Ant. 456.

for these (the unwritten laws) are not of to-day or yesterday, but live for all time, and no one knows when they were first put forth.

This whole conception of 'natural law' is further developed in the next extract.

1 **iam vero** : 'moreover'. **illud** : supply *est*. See Note 5.

2 **sita sint** : 'are founded on'.

populorum . . . **legibus** : 'usages or laws of particular peoples'.

etiamne : expresses incredulity. 'What, if they should be laws imposed by tyrants?'

3 **triginta illi** : the 'Thirty' tyrants, an oligarchy imposed on defeated Athens by the Spartan Lysander in 404 B.C.

5 **idcirco** : '(merely) on this account', picks up the preceding *si*– clauses.

6 **illa** : nom., sc. *lex*. Supply *iusta haberetur*.

interrex : In 82 B.C., L. Valerius Flaccus, acting as *interrex* or regent in default of consuls, proposed a bill (*Lex Valeria*), making Sulla dictator for the purpose of reforming the constitution without any time limit on his tenure of the office. (Six months had been the limit in early times). He was thus practically a dictator in the modern sense. *Cp.* what Cicero says of Sulla in XVI.

ut . . . **occidere** : after *tulit*: 'conferring on the dictator the power of executing without penalty and without a trial any citizen he wished'.

8 **unum ius** . . . **una lex** . . . **recta ratio** : see introductory Note.

10 **qui** . . . **is** : see Note 4(*b*).

11 **scripta** : Natural law (*illa*) is equally valid, whether written or not. Compare St. Paul's *Epistle to the Romans*, II 14, where he speaks of the Gentiles obeying a law written on their hearts (γραπτὸν ἐν ταῖς καρδίαις αὐτῶν), *i.e.* the law of nature. This, however, he regards as incomplete without the written Jewish Law, which is revealed by God.

13 **iidem** : the Epicureans, who regarded the law as merely the interest (*utilitas*) of society, based on a kind of social contract.

metienda sunt : 'are to be measured, reckoned'.

14 **negleget** : subject is *is qui . . . fore.*

16 **neque . . . eaque** : see Notes 8(*c*) and 4(*a*).

natura : abl. '(based) on nature', *i.e.* of things, including man. Greek thinkers were much concerned with the question whether law exists only by the convention of society (νόμῳ), and therefore differs from place to place, as the Epicureans supposed, or by nature (φύσει), according to Plato and the Stoics.

17 **illa** : The reading is doubtful: some texts have *alia*. Trans. 'This means (*ita fit ut*) that there is no such thing (*nulla*) as justice if it is not based on nature, and that kind of (*ea*) 'justice' which is set up (*constituitur*) by expediency (*utilitate*), is liable to be overthrown (lit. 'uprooted') by that same (*illa*) expediency'.

18 **virtutes** : see Note on XXXV 8.

19 **liberalitas** : the quality one expects in a free man: then nobility of spirit, kindness, generosity.

caritas : see Note on XVII 23.

pietas : 'duty to parents, country, or gods'. Cicero here specially mentions the virtues which are the bond of social life.

bene merendi . . . voluntas : 'the will to do good to one's neighbour and to return thanks for good received'.

21 **ex eo quod** : 'from the fact that'. **propensi** : 'inclined to'.

23 **in homines obsequia** : 'allegiance to men'.

24 **caerimoniae religionesque** : 'religion and its rites'.

25 **coniunctione** : The kinship of man with God was one of the main beliefs of Stoicism.

XXI

The Third Book of the *De Re Publica*, of which only fragments survive (Introduction III i), deals, like *De Legibus* I, with the nature of justice. In opposition to the view that justice is only a human convention, Scipio Aemilianus holds that it is something absolute, and ends his argument with this famous exposition of natural law (*recta ratio*) (see XX introductory Note). It is said to be in accordance with the nature of things (*naturae congruens*), universal (*diffusa in omnes*), and divine, since its creator is God (*deus, ille legis inventor*): it is unchangeable and invariable by time or place, and its penalties are inescapable. Thus, since man shares in God's reason, the Supreme Law is also the law of all mankind, at once human and divine. The classical conception, transmitted by Cicero, greatly influenced the medieval thinkers, *e.g.* Aquinas, who says of natural law '*nihil aliud est quam impressio divini luminis in nobis*'. The Greek Stoics were naturally led from this point to the idea of a world-state (*Cosmopolis* XXXV). Under their influence the Roman lawyers like Sulpicius (VII introductory Note), and his successors down to the time of Justinian (sixth century A.D.) extended the Roman *ius gentium* (XIX introductory Note), into a true international law.

The content of Natural Law is implied in several passages in this book. It sanctions everything to which man is naturally inclined, *e.g.* 1, the preservation of life; 2, the procuring of the necessities of life and the means to them; 3, marriage and the care of children; 4, the desire for social life; 5, the duties, commanded by *pietas* towards relatives, country and gods; 6, the precepts of *iustitia*, such as giving every man his due, and respecting the lives and rights of others; 7, the regulations of the *ius gentium e.g.* especially in regard to war. (See XIX.) 'Thou shalt not steal', 'Thou shalt not kill', are precepts of the Natural Law, as well as of the Mosaic Law.

Natural Law has ever since been an accepted part of western thought. Think, for instance, of Roosevelt's 'Four Freedoms', and consider the question: by what right were the Nazi war criminals condemned at Nuremberg?

Observe, however, that not all such notions, *e.g.* 'the inalienable rights of man', would have been recognised without qualification by Cicero: his emphasis is not on rights, but on duties and divine sanction.

3 **fraude** : here 'offence, wrong'.

5 Note the force of the prefixes: **obrogare**, 'propose a new law in place of an old one, invalidate, replace': **derogare**, 'restrict, modify, diminish': **abrogare**, 'annul (wholly)'. **Huic legi**: dat. after *obrogari*. Trans. 'this law may not be invalidated by an opposing one, nor can it be modified by restrictions nor wholly repealed'.

8 **explanator** : 'interpreter'.

9 **erit** : This and the following future tenses seem to imply that Cicero foresees a time, when divine law will be universally recognised.

12 **magister** : Originally a military term, like *imperator*, 'general, and supreme commander'. The remarkable language used of the Supreme Being recalls Hebrew monotheism and seems almost to anticipate Christianity, but it must be remembered that the Stoic God is identical with the universe, not, like the Christian

God, its Creator. The Hymn of Cleanthes speaks of the 'Lord of nature, ruling all things in accordance with law'. (See Note on XXX 4.) Cicero was also inspired by Plato, whose *Laws* he had certainly read. In *Laws* (713 E), it is said that 'in states which are ruled by a mortal and not by God, there is never any escape from evils'. A little later (716 A), the Athenian legislator thus addresses the citizens of his future state: 'God, who holds the beginning and end and middle of all things that are, goes straight onward pursuing his course according to nature, while upon him ever attends Justice, who punishes those who depart from the divine law'.

13 **inventor** : Cicero is fond of nouns in –*tor*, denoting the doer of an action. They may be translated by verbs: 'and the God who shall prescribe, administer, and promulgate this law, shall be the one common Lord and Supreme Ruler of all'.

14 **ipse se fugiet** : 'will be trying to escape from himself'.
hoc ipso : 'by this very fact'.

15 **quae putantur** : 'which are (popularly) supposed', *i.e.* the punishments of criminals in Hades. The offender against the Supreme Law, even if he escapes external penalties, will be punished by the very fact of his defiance of human nature (*naturam hominis*).

XXII

For the *De Senectute*, see Introduction III vii. The speaker is Cato, the Censor (234–149 B.C.) (see Note on XIII 2), who, after a preliminary dialogue with Scipio Aemilianus and his friend Laelius, argues at length that old age is no disadvantage. The date of the dialogue is supposed to be about 150 B.C., when Cato was eighty-four years old.

2 **clientelas** : plur. in a concrete sense, 'such a vast number of dependants'.
Appius Claudius Caecus : Censor in 312 B.C. and constructor of the *Via Appia*.
intentum : 'stretched, alert'.

3 **arcum** : 'bow'.

4 **tenebat** : Note asyndeton from here down to *disciplina*. See Note 1 (*a*).

5 **auctoritatem** : 'moral, personal authority'.

imperium : 'military discipline'. *Imperium* is the power to command an army.

7 **mos patrius :** i.e. *mos maiorum,* 'ancestral tradition'.
ita with **si :** 'on condition that, if only'.

8 **honesta :** 'respected'.

9 **nemini . . . emancipata :** 'enslaved to no one, subject to no one's authority'. *Emancipo* means 'to free from the *patria potestas*', i.e. the absolute right of the *pater familias* or head of the household to dispose of sons, slaves, or property. He could voluntarily renounce his right over a slave by emancipating him or declaring him free outright. But the same verb could also mean to emancipate with the object of transferring into the *potestas* of another master, and so could acquire, as here, the opposite sense of 'enslave'.

usque . . . spiritum : 'to his last breath', i.e. as long as he lived.

11 **senile aliquid :** 'something of the old man'.

12 **probo :** 'approve', the usual meaning of this verb.
quod : obj. of *sequitur* ('aims at'); antecedent is the whole preceding sentence.
qui : antecedent *is* omitted. See Note 4(e).
corpore . . . animo : asyndeton. See Note 1(b).

13 **Originum :** for the *Origines,* see Note on XIII 2.
mihi . . . est in manibus : 'I am working on the seventh book'. Note asyndeton from *colligo* onwards. See Note 1(a).

15 **causarum . . . orationes :** 'speeches delivered in the famous cases'. **cum maxime :** 'at this very moment'.

16 **conficio :** 'I am putting the finishing touches to my speeches', i.e. for publication.
ius augurium, pontificium, civile : The augural law laid down regulations for the observation and expiation of omens, the flight of birds, lightning, etc. The pontifical law was concerned with sacrifice, the calendar, and the organisation of the state religion. The civil law dealt with the rights, duties, and relations of citizens.

17 **tracto :** 'I am engaged upon'. **Graecis litteris :** It was only late in life that Cato gave up his original prejudice against the study of Greek literature.
Pythagoreorum more : For the Pythagoreans see Introduction II 2. Daily self-examination was part of the discipline practised in their communities. Cicero no doubt had in mind the following lines, traditionally ascribed to Pythagoras:

μηδ'ὕπνον μαλακοῖσιν ἐπ'ὄμμασι προσδέξασθαι·
πρὶν τῶν ἡμερινῶν ἔργων τρὶς ἕκαστον ἐπελθεῖν·
πῇ παρέβην; τί δ'ἔρεξα; τί μοι δέον οὐκ ἐτελέσθη;

Let not your soft eyes close in sleep, before thrice reviewing
each of the day's deeds: Where did I transgress? What have
I done? What duty have I left undone?

18 **gratia** : like *causa*, 'for the purpose of'.

20 **curricula** : 'training-ground'.

21 **desudans atque elaborans** : 'with much sweat and toil'.

22 **desidero** : 'to desire something one has not, to miss'.
adsum amicis : 'I support my friends'. *i.e.* in the courts.
frequens : here with adverbial sense, 'frequently'.

23 **ultro** : 'on my own initiative'. An example would be the
famous *Delenda est Carthago*.
affero : 'propose motions long and carefully prepared', *i.e.*
in the Senate.

25 **lectulus** : 'couch', *i.e.* for reading.

26 **ut possim . . . vita** : *facit* governs *ut possim*: 'that I can live an
active life, is the result of my previous career'.

27 **viventi** : dat. of person interested after *obrepat*.

28 **non intellegitur** : impers. pass. Trans. 'living amid these
studies and occupations, one does not notice when old age creeps
on'. **sensim sine sensu** : 'gradually and unobserved'.

29 **frangitur** : 'snuffed out'. **diuturnitate** : 'finally', lit. 'with
the lapse of time'.

30 **exstinguitur** : 'flickers out'.

XXIII

1 **quamquam** : here for *tamen*, 'and yet'. **hominis natura** :
'human affairs'. **est . . . diu** : 'is (lasts) for long'.

2 **da . . . tempus** : 'Grant life its longest possible span'.
Tartessiorum : Tartessus was near Gades in S.W. Spain,
the most westerly of Mediterranean colonies, settled in turn by
Greeks and Phoenicians.

3 **ut scriptum video** : Cicero's authority for Arganthonius and
his age is the Greek historian, Herodotus (I 163).

5 **diuturnum** : 'lasting'.

6 **aliquid** : 'any end'. **id** : *i.e.* the end. **cum . . . tum** : for ind. with *cum*, see Note 8(*a*).

7 **effluxit** : 'has passed (for ever)'.

8 **recte factis** : 'by good deeds'. **consecutus sis** : The subj. is used in indefinite sentences with the ideal 2nd pers. sing. or imaginary 'you'.
 e.g. *Ubi consulueris, mature facto opus est.*
  Whenever you have deliberated, you need speedy action.
               Sall. Cat. I 6.

11 **quod . . . eo** : see Note 4(*b*). **temporis** : partitive genit. with *quod*.

13 **histrioni . . .** : 'The actor need not wait until the play's end for his applause, provided (*modo* with subj.) he wins favour in whatever act he has appeared'.

14 **sapienti** : 'the wise men need not stay (on the stage) until the fall of the curtain'.

15 **plaudite** : '(now) applaud', quoted from the request for applause usually made by one of the actors, known as the Cantor, who came forward to utter a few lines addressed to the audience as a sign that the play was over.

16 **honeste** : 'virtuously'. **sin** : 'but if'.

19 **ver . . . significat** : Difficult. Reading *adulescentiam*, the meaning appears to be: ' "Spring" signifies a time of growth, so to speak'. There may be a reference to the derivation of *adulescentia* from *adolesco* (to grow up), and to some doubtful etymology of *ver*, such as Varro's, who derives it from *vireo* (to flourish).

20 **ostendit** : 'promises'.

21 **demetendis fructibus** : 'for reaping the harvest'.

23 **partorum** : from *pario*, 'win, gain'. **memoria et copia** : 'richly stored memory'. Hendiadys, see Note 2.

24 **secundum naturam** : 'according to the nature of things'. **sunt habenda in bonis** : 'are to be reckoned as good'.

26 **quod idem** : i.e. *mori*.

28 **ut cum** : 'as when', with indic. in similes. **aquae multitudine** : 'a flood of water'. **flammae vis** : 'a blazing fire'. See Note 3.

30 **consumptus** : 'burned out'.
 et quasi . . . : for asyndeton in this sentence, see Note 1(*b*). *quasi*: unusual for *ut* or *quemadmodum*, 'just as': resumed by *sic.*

31 **cruda** : 'unripe'. **evelluntur** : 'are plucked'. **cocta** : from *coquo*, 'ripened'.

33 **quae quidem** : see Note 8(*e*).
For the comparison of life with a voyage, *cp*. M. Aurelius, (*Med*. III 3 1):—Ἐνέβης, ἔπλευσας, κατήχθης· ἐκβῆθι. ('Thou hast embarked and hast voyaged, and now art come to land: disembark'.) ; and Spenser, *Faerie Queen* (I IX 40):—

Is not short paine well borne, that brings long ease,
And layes the soule to sleepe in quiet grave?
Sleepe after toyle, port after stormie seas,
Ease after warre, death after life does greatly please.

XXIV

The philosophic attitude to death is the theme of *Tusculan Disputations I*. Examples of courage in the face of death are given as part of the proof that it is not to be feared. One of the main arguments is that with which Socrates ends his *Apology*, that, whether death means extinction or not, it is in either case good. This subject had a personal interest for Cicero, since his daughter Tullia's death in 45 B.C., the same year in which the book was written, had plunged him into grief, which cried out for philosophic consolation. His own death, faced with something of the fortitude he here recommends, was to take place at the hands of Antony's assassins only two years later in the proscriptions of 43 B.C.

1 **Socrates** : see Introduction II 3.
Theramenes : Athenian statesman during the last stages of the Peloponnesian War. A moderate oligarch, he was a member of the 'Thirty', but quarrelled with their leader, Critias, and was condemned to death by drinking hemlock in 404 B.C. The dramatic story is told by the Greek historian Xenophon in his *Hellenica* (II iii). As he raised the cup, he poured out some of the poison on the ground, as though at a banquet, with the words: Κριτίᾳ τοῦτ' ἔστω τῷ καλῷ, 'a libation to the fair Critias'.

2 **cum** : with the subj. sometimes has an adversative force, 'when at the same time', 'whereas'. Here the sense is: 'why do I mention Socrates and Theramenes, when (I can mention such examples as) a certain unknown Spartan. . . .'

5 **ephoris** : The Ephors were a body of five supreme magistrates at Sparta, who exercised control even over the kings. **voltu** : abl. of quality with *esset*. **hilaris**, 'joyful'.

7 **Lycurgus** : early Spartan lawgiver.

8 **ea poena quam** : 'such a penalty as', *i.e.* death. See Note 4(*d*).

multaverit : causal subj. See Note 6(*b*). *multare*: 'punish'.

sine mutuatione et sine versura : 'without begging or borrowing further'. *Versura* means 'raising a fresh loan to pay a debt'.

9 **possem** : Secondary sequence after a perf. subj. is quite frequent in Cicero.

dissolvere : 'discharge', *i.e.* without further complications.

Sparta dignum : *i.e.* worthy of his native Sparta's reputation for valour, a true Spartan reply. Sparta was a military state, run under the strictest discipline, the object of which was to maintain the distinction between the privileged Spartiates, the warrior caste, the middle class or Perioeci, and the serfs or Helots. 'Spartan endurance' has become proverbial.

10 **mihi quidem** : 'for my part'. Dat. of *equidem*. **qui** : antecedent *is* omitted. See Note 4(*e*). **fuerit** : causal subj. See Note 6(*b*).

12 **tulit** : 'has produced'.

13 **eum locum . . . unde** : 'into such a position that they could not expect to return'. See Note 4(*d*).

15 **Thermopylis** : The pass of Thermopylae controlled the route from northern to southern Greece. Here in 480 B.C., 300 Spartan warriors under Leonidas made a last stand in defence of Greece against the Persian invaders under Xerxes. Their position was betrayed from the rear, and all were wiped out fighting to the last.

occiderunt : Note quantity of stem vowel, derived from *ob-cădo*, i.e. *occĭdo*: 'to fall in battle'. **in quos** : 'upon whom'. Supply *scripsit*.

16 **Simōnides** : (circa 500 B.C.), Greek lyric poet, wrote a famous epigram on the Spartan dead at Thermopylae, here translated by Cicero:—

ὦ ξεῖν', ἀγγέλλειν Λακεδαιμονίοις ὅτι τῇδε
κείμεθα, τοῖς κείνων ῥήμασι πειθόμενοι.

19 **e quibus** : 'one of whom', *i.e.* the Spartans. **Perses** : nom. sing. 'a Persian'.

20 **prae** : 'because of' in negative sentences.

22 **qualis** : 'of what spirit?' Trans. 'What do you think of the spirit of the Spartan mother . . .?' **tandem** : in emphatic questions, 'I ask you'. **Lacaena** : 'Spartan woman'. Supply *erat*.

23 **idcirco** : with *ut*, 'to the end that'.

24 **genueram** : 'I gave you birth'. From *gignĕre*, *gĕnui*, *gĕnitum*.

25 **dubitaret** : see Note 6(*a*). With inf., 'hesitate'.
mortem occumbere : like *mortem obire*, 'meet death (in battle)'.

26 **cum . . . sint** : 'though this be so', *i.e.* though these examples prove that death is not to be feared. An unusual sense for *cum* in this phrase, where it almost always means 'since'.

27 **velut e superiore loco** : 'as from a position of authority', a phrase used of a judge giving an authoritative judgement from the bench. **contionari**: 'speak (to a public audience)'.

28 **certe** : 'at any rate'.

29 **supremus ille dies** : 'the last day (of life)'.

32 **obdormiscere** : 'fall asleep'. **coniventem** : 'closing his (one's) eyes', agrees with an indefinite pronoun such as *aliquem* understood. **consopiri** : 'to be lulled into an endless sleep'.

33 **quod si fiat** : 'should this be so', *i.e.* should death turn out to be a sleep.
Ennii : see Note on XVII 3 **Solonis** : for Solon see Note on VIII 18.
oratio : here, 'saying', referring to the epigram quoted below.

34 **hic noster** : (sc. *poeta*) *i.e.* 'our own (native) Ennius'.

36 **faxit** : archaic pres. subj. of *facio*, formed from *fac-sim*.
The lines from Ennius, in elegiac metre, are from his epitaph on himself. Trans. 'Let no one honour me with tears nor conduct my funeral with mourning'. The full version of the last line is: *Faxit. Cur? Volito vivu' per ora virum.* 'Why? I float still living on the lips of men', *i.e.* enjoy the immortality of fame.

37 **at vero ille sapiens** : 'But the famous Wise Man (wrote) . . .' Solon was one of the seven traditional Wise Men of Greece. Cicero implies that he wanted his death mourned as an evil in itself. The original of the epigram is:

μήδ' ἐμοὶ ἄκλαυστος θάνατος μόλοι, ἀλλὰ φίλοισι
καλλείποιμι θανὼν ἄλγεα καὶ στοναχάς.

XXV

The piece known as '*Somnium Scipionis*' is the only considerable surviving fragment of Book VI of the *De Re Publica*. It owes its preservation to the interest shown in it by the grammarian

Macrobius (fifth century A.D.) and by Christian writers, who valued its doctrine of the immortality of the soul. The *Somnium* formed the conclusion of the whole work, and was clearly meant to correspond to the 'myth', an imaginary narrative illustrating

GENEALOGY OF THE SCIPIONES

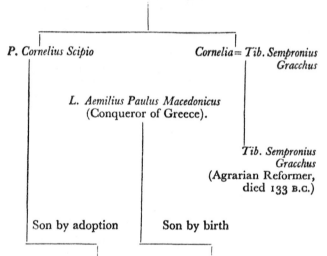

1. *P. Cornelius Scipio Africanus Maior*
(236–183 B.C.). Victor of Zama 202 B.C.

P. Cornelius Scipio

Cornelia = *Tib. Sempronius Gracchus*

L. Aemilius Paulus Macedonicus
(Conqueror of Greece).

Tib. Sempronius Gracchus
(Agrarian Reformer,
died 133 B.C.)

Son by adoption   Son by birth

2. P. Cornelius Scipio Aemilianus Africanus Minor
(185 B.C.–129 B.C.). Destroyer of Carthage, 146 B.C.
Victor of Numantia, 133 B.C.

1. Referred to as 'Africanus'.   2. Called 'Aemilianus'.

a philosophical truth, with which Plato ends his *Republic*. Here Socrates describes the experience of a certain Er, son of Armenius, who is taken for dead, but revives when placed upon the funeral pyre. His soul having been in Hades in the interval, he is able to assure his hearers of the immortality of the soul and to describe the destiny of the departed. In Cicero's version, the speaker is the 'Younger' Scipio Aemilianus, (185–129 B.C.), Greek scholar and gentleman as well as soldier, who in a conversation with his friends, supposed to take place in 129 B.C., the year of his death, recounts a vision he had had in 149 B.C., when on campaign against Carthage. He tells how his adoptive grandfather, the famous Scipio Africanus the 'Elder', (236–183 B.C.), the conqueror of Hannibal at Zama in 202 B.C., and his father Aemilius Paulus had both appeared to him, assured him of their continued existence, and revealed to him the glorious destiny which awaited just and pious Romans after death. The philosophy of the *Somnium* is a mixture of Platonism and Stoicism and resembles in many respects Vergil's famous *Aeneid VI.*, in which Aeneas descends into Hades and hears from his father Anchises a similar account of the soul's destiny.

1 *Scipio relates his visit to Masinissa*

1 **Africam** : the land round Carthage, later the province of Africa, modern Tunisia.

M'. Manilio : Manius Manilius, consul 149 B.C., was unsuccessful in his assault on Carthage in the Third Punic War, and was superseded in 148 B.C. by Scipio.

consuli : '(as tribune) to the consul'.

2 **tribunus** : Though only a junior officer, Scipio showed superior ability in command, was elected consul in 147 B.C., and took and destroyed Carthage in the next year.

nihil . . . potius : 'my first desire was to . . .'

3 **Masinissa** : a Numidian king, who had aided Scipio the Elder in the campaign of Zama (204–202 B.C.), became his personal friend, and was rewarded with extra territory. His later aggression against Carthage, encouraged by Rome, led to the Third Punic War.

6 **grates ago** : 'I thank'.

7 **Sol** : Sun-worship was natural to Masinissa, as a half-Oriental, half-Hellenised monarch. **Caelites** : moon and stars, thought of as gods.

8 **migro** : pres. ind. is usual with *antequam*, when the main clause is affirmative. Trans. 'Before I leave this life'. Masinissa died in 148 B.C.

9 **ita nunquam . . .** : 'so little does the memory of that noble man and unconquered soldier fade from my mind'.

10 **illius . . . viri** : the Elder Scipio.

12 **percontatus est** : 'he questioned, enquired'. **ultro citroque** : 'on both sides'.

2 *Scipio's Dream*

14 **apparatu** : 'splendour, magnificence'.

15 **in multam noctem** : 'until late in the night'.

17 **cubitum** : supine, 'to sleep'.

18 **et de via fessum et qui** : both *de via* and *qui* with subj. are causal (see Note 6(*b*), 'as I was weary after my journey and had stayed up besides until late in the night (*ad multam noctem*)'.

19 **artior** : 'deeper' (sleep), lit. 'tighter'.

20 **ex hoc quod** : 'as a result of what'.

22 **de Homero** : Ennius (239–169 B.C.) took Homer as his model for his *Annales* (see XVII 3), and is said to have had supernatural communication with him not only in dreams but when awake, and even to have held a Pythagorean belief that he himself was a re-incarnation of the Greek poet. He mentions this in a fragmentary line quoted from the *Annales*: '*Visus Homerus adesse poeta*'.

24 **imagine** : The *imagines*, or death-masks, of famous ancestors decorated the atrium of the Roman house. Scipio could hardly have known his adoptive grandfather personally, since the latter died about the year of his birth in 185 B.C.

26 **ades . . . animo** : (abl.) 'be of good courage'.

27 **trade memoriae** : 'see that you remember'.

3–5 *Scipio's future is foretold by Africanus*

28 **illam urbem** : Carthage.

29 **per me** : with *coacta*. He refers to his victory at Zama in 202 B.C.

renovat : Carthaginian aggression, here blamed for the Third Punic War, was largely provoked by Roman encouragement of her local enemies.

32 **nunc** : 149 B.C. **paene miles** : '(as yet) hardly more than a private'. **hoc biennio** : 'within the next two years'.

33 **cognomen** : *i.e.* Africanus. **per te** : 'by your own efforts'.

34 **a nobis hereditarium** : 'as an inheritance from me'.

35 **censor** : 142 B.C.

36 **obieris** : 'have gone on missions to'. **legatus** : about 140 B.C., or later, Scipio was appointed ambassador to settle the affairs of Greece and the Middle East.

37 **deligĕre** : *i.e.* *deligĕris* 2nd sing. fut. pass. **iterum absens consul** : he held his second consulship in 134 B.C. by special dispensation from the law requiring personal canvassing.

bellumque maximum : The war of conquest in Spain, which Rome had waged with varied success since 190 B.C., was brought to a decisive point by Scipio's capture of Numantia in 133 B.C.

39 **offendes** : 'meet with, find'.

40 **nepotis mei** : Tiberius Gracchus, son of Cornelia, daughter of Scipio, the Elder. His land reforms were opposed by the Senate, and he was forced into revolutionary courses which led to his death in a riot in 133 B.C.

42 **ancipitem . . . viam** : 'I see two paths of destiny, as it were, before you'.

43 **aetas . . . converterit** : 'when your life has completed 8 times 7 (*i.e.* 56) circuits of the sun', lit. 'windings and returns'. See Note 2.

44 **duoque hi numeri** : 7 and 8. Mystic ideas about numbers were derived from Pythagoras (Introduction II 2). There seems to be a special reference here to the music of the planets, described in Sect. 10. This is produced by the movement of the eight spheres, with their seven distinct notes, and these numbers are, therefore, perfect (*pleni*), each of their own kind (lit. 'for different reasons'). Consequently, their multiple, fifty-six, is of special significance.

46 **circuitu naturali** : 'in due course of their revolutions'.

46 **summam . . . confecerint** : 'have completed the sum which is destined for you'.

47 **in te unum** : Scipio is to be the man of the hour in his country's crisis, like his grandfather in the Second Punic War, and Cicero himself in 63 B.C. against Catiline.

48 **omnes boni** : 'all good citizens'. By *boni* Cicero means good sound conservatives, as opposed to *seditiosi* or *perditi cives*, revolutionaries or irresponsibles.

intuebuntur : 'will look to you (for help)'.

49 **unus, in quo nitatur**; 'the one man, upon whom the national welfare depends'. See Note 6(*a*).

ne multa: sc. *dicam*, 'in short'.

dictator: The dictatorship had originally been a constitutional office, held for six months to deal with a particular crisis (*rei gerundae causa*), but gradually fell into disuse after 216 B.C. In 81 B.C., Sulla was appointed to an extraordinary dictatorship to reconstruct the constitution (*rei publicae constituendae*), and Caesar was destined to go still further by assuming the office in perpetuity in 44 B.C. Although *constituas* suggests the Sullan title, Cicero, writing of an earlier time, appears to mean the original office, which Scipio is to hold as an elder statesman, to restore settled government after the Gracchan crisis, and deal with the revolt of Rome's Latin allies (*Latini*), who objected to losing their lands under the proposed reforms.

50 **constituas** : dep. on *oportebit*, 'it will be your duty to restore'.

impias . . . effugeris : This anticipates Scipio's actual death, which took place late in the year 129 B.C. It was supposed that he had been murdered by his opponents, possibly by members of the family of the Gracchi, his own relatives (*propinquorum*).

51 **Caius Laelius Sapiens** was a close friend and associate of Scipio, whose political and cultural interests he shared.

55 **sic habeto** : 2nd sing. imperat., 'be assured of this'.

58 **illi principi deo** : the transcendent God, who moves and rules the universe (*cp.* Sect. 18).

59 **fiat** : limiting subj. after *quod*: 'at any rate which happens on earth'. *Cp. quod sciam*, 'so far as I know'.

60 **civitates** : The ancient *civitas* was a community of citizens, either of a single city or of several united in one state, in accordance with a social contract (*iure sociati*). For both Greeks and Romans, man was a 'social animal' (πολιτικὸν ξῷον), as Aristotle called him.

rectores : Whether Cicero meant by '*rector*', which he uses elsewhere in the *De Re Publica*, a single office above the Senate and ordinary magistrates, thus foreshadowing the Augustan system, or analogous, in modern times, to that of the American President, is doubtful. It is more likely that he is thinking of statesmen of the type of Scipio, who by their abilities exercise the *auctoritas* of personal prestige. They are, in his view, the true Romans, and no doubt he at one time hoped that Pompey would prove to be such. (See G. H. Poyser: *Selections from De Re Publica*, Introduction pp. 23 ff.)

61 **hinc . . . huc** : 'go hence and return hither', *i.e.* from our world to yours and back again.

6–8 *Scipio meets his father Paulus, who warns him against suicide and bids him observe* pietas. *He looks down upon the earth.*

62 **tam . . . quam** : 'so much . . . as'.

63 **a meis** : with *insidiarum*.

64 **Paulus** : Aemilius Paulus, conqueror of Greece, and **actual** father of Aemilianus, who was later adopted into the family of the Scipiones.

65 **immo vero** : 'on the contrary'.   **vinculis** : 'from the bonds'.

66 **quae dicitur** : 'so called'.

67 **quin** : with pres. ind., lit. 'why not?'; almost *nonne?* 'Do you not see?'

68 **equidem** . . . **profudi** : 'for my part, I shed a flood of tears'.

74 **templum** : *i.e.* the heavens, a region of the sky marked out by the augurs.

75 **istis** . . . **custodiis** : 'the prison-house of your body', or, perhaps, 'your (*istis*) post as sentinel (*custodiae* pl.) of your body'.

76 **hac lege** . . . **qui** : 'on this condition that.' *qui*: for *ut.*

77 **tuerentur** : 'guard', here almost, 'dwell'.   **globum** : 'globe, sphere', *i.e.* the earth.

78 **medium** : 'at the centre'. The earth is stationary at the centre of the universe. **animus** : 'soul'.

79 **quae** : neut. plur., drawn into agreement with the predicate '*sidera*'.

80 **divinis** . . . **mentibus** : The god of Stoicism, the divine reason, has not only framed the body of the universe, but endowed it with a rational soul (*anima mundi*), which works within it and keeps it in motion. The stars, being of a fiery nature, are especially 'endowed with divine intelligences'. From them the souls of men are said to be derived. There is a mixture here of Stoicism with the idea of the World Soul in Plato's *Timaeus*.

83 **iniussu** : This prohibition of suicide is expressed by Socrates in the *Apology*, on the ground that a sentry may not desert his post without orders. The Stoics generally allowed suicide as a final means of escape from a hopeless situation *e.g.* the suicide of the Younger Cato in Africa in 46 B.C.

84 **munus** : 'duty'.

87 **cum** . . . **tum** : lit. 'both . . . and'. **in parentibus** : 'in relation to parents'. Trans. 'which, nobly shown in duty towards parents or relatives, reaches its highest point in patriotism'.

89 **qui iam vixerunt** : =*mortui sunt,* lit. 'whose life is over'.

91 **flammas** : 'stars'.

92 **orbem lacteum** : the 'Milky Way,' a faint band of very distant stars stretching across the sky and clearly visible on a dark

night, which we know now to be our own galaxy, as seen in depth through its plane.

    ex quo : =*unde*, 'from this point'.

    94 **eae** : almost =*tales*: 'there were stars such as . . . .' See Note 4(*a*).

    95 **eae magnitudines omnium** : 'and all of such a size'. See Note 3.

    97 **ultima . . . citima** : 'furthest from the heavens, (and) nearest the earth', *i.e.* the Moon. See Note 1(*b*). **aliena** : *i.e.* reflected.

    98 **iam vero** : 'moreover'.

    99 **me . . . paeniteret** : 'I felt dissatisfied with our empire'.

    100 **quo . . . attingimus** : 'with which we cover, as it were, a single point on its surface'. (Loeb)

    9–11 Africanus explains the motions of the stars and planets (9), *and the music of the spheres* (10–11).

    102 **quousque** : 'how much longer?' **defixa . . . erit** : fut. pf. 'will your mind remain intent upon'.

    103 **tibi** : ethic dat., 'you must know'.

    orbibus vel globis : 'circles, or rather spheres'. *Globus* usually = 'globe', like that of the earth, here, 'a hollow sphere'. The universe (see Fig. 1) is supposed to comprise nine inter-connected (*conexa*) spheres. The outermost of these, studded with the fixed stars, is in continual motion, completing a revolution in twenty-four hours from east to west. Encircled by it, but rotating in the opposite direction, come seven planetary spheres, to which are attached Sun and Moon and the five planets known to the ancients, in the following order: Saturn, Jupiter, Mars, then the Sun, and close to it Venus and Mercury, the Moon in the smallest orbit of all, and finally the Earth, a solid sphere, stationary at the centre.

    105 **summus ipse deus** : 'which (the outermost sphere) is itself the supreme God, enfolding and containing all the other spheres'.

    106 **in quo . . . sempiterni** : 'to which are attached the stars revolving in their eternal courses'; *illi qui volvuntur stellarum cursus sempiterni* = *stellae quae sempiterno cursu volvuntur*. For position of rel. clause, see Note 4(*c*).

    108 **contrario . . . atque** : 'opposite to'. **ex quibus . . . nominant** : 'one of which is assigned to that (star), which on earth is called Saturn's'. With *Saturniam* supply *stellam*.

    110 **prosperus et salutaris** : The belief in the 'influence' of the

stars on human affairs, widespread among the ancients, belongs
to astrology rather than astronomy. (See XXVI 17).

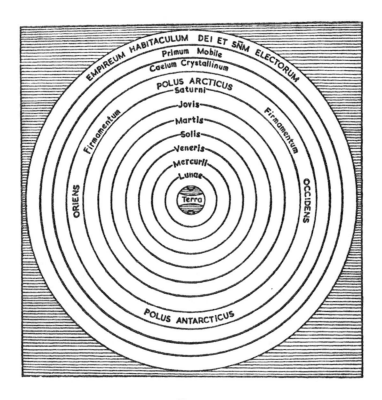

FIG. 1

Aristotle's scheme of the Universe, as developed in the Middle Ages.
In addition to the spheres of sun, moon and five planets, there are:
(1) the firmament, the sphere of fixed stars; (2) the crystalline sphere,
which caused the pole to rotate; (3) the First Mover, which moved all
the rest; and (4) the habitation of God and the elect Saints. (See
sects. 7–10.)

111 **fulgor** : 'brightness';   here concrete, 'that luminosity called
Jupiter'.

112 Martium : sc. *fulgorem*, the planet Mars, the star of the War god, hence 'red and threatening' (*rutilus horribilisque*).

113 mediam fere regionem : 'a middle position', *i.e.* between heaven and earth.

Sol : Cicero appears to be following Cleanthes (see Introduction II 7), who placed the seat of the supreme God in the Sun. *Cp.* Milton: *Paradise Lost*:—

Thou Sun, of this great World both Eye and Soule.

114 mens mundi et temperatio : 'the mind and controlling principle of the universe'. According to the Stoics, 'mind' and 'God' are identical.

115 lustret : 'illuminates'.

117 cursus : 'orbits'. **radiis** : 'rays'.
convertitur : 'revolves'.

118 caducum : 'falling, perishable'.

119 animos : 'souls, lives'.

121 neque . . . et : see Note 8(*c*).

122 nutu suo : 'by their own downward tendency', *i.e.* gravity.

123 ut me recepi : 'when I came to myself'.

125 sonus : The spheres in their revolution were supposed to produce musical notes, whose pitch varied with their speeds of rotation, and these combined formed a perfect harmony or octave. The heavenly sphere, being the fastest (*concitatior*), produced the highest note. The 'music of the spheres' is often mentioned by English poets: *e.g.* Shakespeare (*Merchant of Venice*):

There's not the smallest orb which thou beholdest,
But in his motion like an Angel sings.

and Milton (*Paradise Lost*):

And ye five other wandering fires that move
In mystic dance, not without song, resound
His praise, who out of darkness call'd up light.

hic est . . . : 'The sound you hear is the music caused by the forward motion of the spheres themselves; it is composed (*coniunctus*) of intervals which, though unequal, are systematically (*ratione*) arranged in due proportion (*pro rata parte*), producing by a blend of high and low notes a varied system (*aequabiliter*: lit. uniformly) of harmonies'.

129 neque . . . et : see Note 8 (*c*). **natura fert ut** : 'nature ordains that'.

130 **extrema . . . sonent**: 'the extremes of the octave produce low-pitched notes at one end, and high-pitched at the other'. *Cp.* Milton: (*Hymn on Christ's Nativity*):
>the bass of Heaven's deep organ . . .

131 **summus . . . cursus**: 'the highest of all, the starry sphere'.

135 **octo . . . cursus**: 'eight spheres', *i.e.* not counting the Earth, which is 'ninth' (*nona*).

136 **eadem vis est duorum**: 'two of which have the same velocity', thus producing the same note. Mercury and Venus, the planets nearest the sun, are meant.

137 **nodus**: 'bond', lit. 'knot.' The number seven is, as it were, the foundation number of the universe (*cp.* line 44 note).

138 **quod**: *i.e.* this system of sounds. **nervis . . . cantibus**: There were seven strings (*nervi*) on the lyre and seven notes in the scale. Thus musicians (*docti homines*) might be said to have derived (*imitati*) their system from the heavens.

139 **reditum**: Poets and musicians were supposed to be inspired and nearest of men to the gods.

140 **divina**: contrasts with *humana*. Trans. 'who, while living as men, have devoted themselves to godlike (*i.e.* intellectual and artistic) pursuits'.

141 **obsurduerunt**: from *obsurdescere*, 'I grow deaf'.

142 **hebetior**: 'duller'.

143 **Catadupa**: (neut. plur.), the cataracts of the Nile. Shakespeare (*Merchant of Venice*, V 1 63) gives a genuinely Platonic reason for our not hearing the heavenly music:—
>For whilst this muddy vesture of decay
>Doth close us in, we cannot hear it.

143 **praecipitat**: 'rushes down'.

145 **sensu . . . caret**: 'is without the sense of hearing'.

146 **incitatissima conversione**: abl. of cause; '(produced) by the extremely rapid revolution'.

147 **capere**: 'take in (the sound)'.

148 **intueri solem adversum**: 'to gaze full at the sun'.
nequitis: 'you are unable'. **acies . . . sensusque**: hendiadys; 'the power of sight'. See Note 2.

150 **admirans**: concessive, 'though wondering'.

12–13 *The Insignificance of the Earth*; 14 *Its Geography*

154 **spectato, contemnito**: imperatives, 2nd person sing.

155 **celebritatem . . . hominum** : 'fame upon the lips of men'.

156 **expetendam** : 'worth seeking'. Trans. 'what worth-while fame can you attain?'

FIG. 2

Map of the World according to Pomponius Mela (first century A.D.); based on the ideas of the Greek geographer, Eratosthenes (second century B.C.). (See XXV sects. 12–14.)

157 **vides habitari in terra** : 'you see that the Earth is inhabited' (impers. pass.).

158 **in ipsis quasi maculis . . .** : 'even in the patches where it is inhabited'.

159 **interruptos** : 'separated'.

160 **ut nihil . . . possit** : 'so that there can be absolutely no communication between them'. *mānare*: lit. 'to flow'.

162 **cernis** : This description of the earth dates from the Greek astronomer, Eratosthenes (275–194 B.C.). The earth is a sphere, surrounded by sea (*Oceanus*). Its surface is separated into five bands or zones (*cinguli*), of which the two extreme (*maxime inter se diversos*), lying close (*subnixos*) to the north and south poles (*verticibus*) respectively, are perpetually frozen and uninhabitable, as is the centre or torrid zone (*medium*) which is burnt (*torreri*) up by heat. Lying between these two extremes are two temperate, habitable zones: our own, the northern (*subiectus aquiloni*), and the southern (*australis*), whose inhabitants, the Antichthones walk head downward in relation to us.

eandem terram : 'the earth also, besides'.

163 **redimitam** : 'encircled'.

165 **obriguisse pruina** : 'be hard with frost'.

167 **qui insistunt** : see Note 4(*e*).

adversa . . . vestigia : 'plant their feet the opposite way to you', *i.e.* walk feet uppermost.

168 **nihil ad vestrum genus** (sc. *pertinet*): 'has nothing to do with your zone'.

169 **quam . . . contingat** : 'to how narrow an area of it you are confined'.

171 **angustata . . . latior** : 'narrow from pole to pole (*i.e.* from North to South), and wider from side to side (*i.e.* from East to West)'. The northern zone is compared to an island much broader than long.

172 **circumfusa** : here passive in sense, 'surrounded'.

173 **quem** : attracted into gender of masc. predicate '*Oceanum*'.

174 **tanto nomine** : 'though it is called "Great" '.

175 **nostrum** : genit. of *nos*: 'of us Romans'.

178 **orientis aut obeuntis solis** : 'of East or West'. **aquilo** : 'North'. **auster** : 'South'.

179 **amputo** : 'cut off'.

180 **profecto** : 'really, truly, doubtless'. **angustiae** : 'narrow confines'. **dilatari** : 'spread'.

181 **quam** with **diu** : 'how long?'

15–16 *The shortness of human fame*

182 **si cupiat . . . possumus** : The change of mood corresponds to a change in sense: *i.e.* 'even should (subj.) posterity desire (to

remember us), we cannot (ind.) in fact achieve permanent fame'.
proles illa futurorum hominum : 'the coming generation'.

183 **deinceps** : 'in turn'. **nostrum** : 'of us'.

185 **certo tempore** : 'at fixed times'. The Stoics held that the fixed order of history included disasters by flood and fire (*eluviones exustionesque*).

186 **aeternam** : 'everlasting', contrasted with the weaker *diuturnam*, 'lasting'.

188 **nullus** : sc. *sermo*. Emphatic use, 'non-existent'.

189 **nec . . . et** : see Note 8(*c*).

191 **nemo . . . possit** : 'no one can be sure of being remembered even for one year'.

192 **populariter** : 'according to the common notion', *i.e.* of the solar year. **tantum modo** : 'merely'.

193 **metiuntur** : 'measure, reckon'. **cum autem . . . tum** : see Note 8(*a*).

196 **vere** with **appellari potest** : 'may be properly called'.

vertens annus : This refers to the Great Year, which was supposed to elapse when the planets returned to exactly the same position from which they had started at the beginning of all things (*ad idem unde semel profecta sunt*), and, after thousands of solar years (*longis intervallis*), the original pattern of the sky (*eandem totius caeli descriptionem*) had been restored. Then was to occur a destruction of the world by fire (ἐκπύρωσις), followed by a renewal of all things as at the beginning (ἀποκατάστασις τοῦ παντός), after which history was to be exactly repeated. Thus Vergil, in the *Fourth Eclogue*, speaks of a renewal of the Trojan War, and Shelley begins his Chorus in *Hellas*:—

> The world's great age begins anew,
> The golden years return.

198 **deficere sol** : Romulus was supposed to have ascended into the heavens to the accompaniment of a storm and an eclipse of the sun, to be deified as Quirinus. The date of this event, 716 B.C., 567 years before the *Somnium* (149 B.C.), is here taken as the starting point for reckoning a Great Year, which will thus be more than 20 × 567 = 11,340, *i.e.* approx. 12,000 solar years, since Scipio supposes that, at the time of speaking, only a twentieth part of the circuit is completed.

199 **animus** : 'soul'. **quando** : used here with fut. pf. in sense of

cum 'when', and picked up by *tum*. An early use, occasionally found in Cicero.

202 **habeto** : =*habe*, 'reckon'. **vicesimam partem** : 'one twentieth'.

203 **conversam** : 'completed'.

17–18 *True fame comes after death to those who have preferred virtue to pleasure. Man's body is mortal, but his soul divine.*

205 **in quo omnia . . . viris** : 'which great and distinguished men have made the object of all their striving'. *sunt*=*posita sunt.* **quanti** : =*quam parvi*, 'of how little value'.

206 **ista . . . gloria** : 'the fame you seek among men'. *Iste* has, as often, a contemptuous sense.

209 **dedideris . . . posueris** : fut. pf. in apodosis after *si voles* is used to emphasise the completion or finality of the future action. 'You will never again attend to the talk of the vulgar nor put your confidence in human rewards for your achievements'.

210 **trahat** : depends on *oportet*: 'Virtue herself must draw you'.

211 **videant** : jussive subj. 'Let others see to it what they say of you: they will say it just the same'.

217 **bene meritis de patria** : 'to those who have served their country well'. **limes** : 'path'.

219 **decori vestro non defui** : 'I have never disgraced your names', *i.e.* those of Africanus and Paulus.

220 **enitĕre** : imperat. of *enitor*: 'struggle on'.

221 **nec enim . . .** : 'nor are you the man (*is*) whom your mere outward appearance (*forma ista*) proclaims, but it is the mind of every individual which is the man himself (*is*)'.

224 **deum te esse** : The soul is itself 'god', because, like the Supreme God, it lives, perceives, remembers and foresees, and bears the same relation to the body over which it is set (*praepositus*), as God (*ille princeps deus*) does to the universe which he keeps in motion. As Epictetus, a Stoic of the early Empire, says: σὺ ἀπόσπασμα εἶ τοῦ θεοῦ, 'you are an off-shoot of God'. **deus est qui** : ' "God" is that which lives . . .'

225 **tam . . . quam** : 'just as'.

227 **ex quadam parte mortalem** : 'in part mortal', *i.e.* material. The Stoics distinguished two elements in the universe, matter, and cause or mind. Matter is inert and formless, mind imposes form upon it.

19–20 *Proof of the soul's immortality*

230 The proof here given is a literal translation of Plato's proof, taken from the *Phaedrus* (245 c ff.). It falls into two parts as follows:—

1   (i) What is always in motion is immortal (*aeternum*).

   (ii) Only what moves itself is always in motion (since if it were moved by anything else, it would cease to move with the cessation of the external impulse).

  (iii) What moves itself is the source or first cause (*principium*) of motion in other things, and is therefore without beginning (since it would not be a first cause, if it arose from anything else).

  (iv) What moves itself can never cease to be in motion (*moveri*) (since, if it came to an end (*exstinctum*), all motion would cease, there being no other *principium* to start it).

∴ What moves itself is immortal

2 It is the property of whatever is alive (*animal*) to be moved only by an internal impulse of its own and not by an external cause. Now it is the essential nature of the soul, as the principle of life (*propria natura et vis*), to move itself.

∴ The soul is immortal

The whole argument may be put briefly thus:
Whatever moves itself is immortal
The soul moves itself
∴ The soul is immortal

The weakness of the argument is that the minor premiss, 'The soul moves itself', is assumed, but not proved. Even if it were granted that whatever moves itself is immortal, the question would remain: Does there actually exist such a thing in the world? Plato seems to assume that the answer is too self-evident to need proving. It is noteworthy that the first part of the argument is given by Plato himself in the *Laws* in a different form as a proof of the existence of God. There is no inconsistency here, since to the Greeks, 'immortal' meant 'divine'.

231 **aliunde :** 'from elsewhere, by something else'.

232 **quando :** =*cum*, see note on line 199.

234 **ne moveri quidem desinit :** 'never ceases to move either'.

235 **hic . . hoc :** attracted into the gender of the predicates.

238 **gigneretur :** see Note 6(*a*).

239 **ne occīdit quidem** : 'does not perish either'.

242 **ex eo sit quod** : 'springs from that which'.

244 **vel** : 'or else'. **concĭdat** : dep. on *necesse est* = 'must collapse'. **natura** : 'the universe'.

245 **consistat** : 'come to a standstill'. **a primo** : 'at first'.

247 **pateat** : 'it is clear'.

248 **naturam** : 'essential nature'. Cicero is translating Greek οὐσία. Lower down, *natura animi atque vis* is Greek φύσις, 'the natural constitution of a thing'.

250 **cietur** : 'is put in motion'.

253 **neque . . . et** : see Note 8(*c*).

21 *Africanus' final exhortation*

255 **agitatus** : 'occupied, exercised'.

257 **eminebit foras** : 'will come forth'.

262 **circum . . . volutantur** : Plato (*Phaedo* 81 c) describes how earth-bound souls, contaminated by the pleasures of the body, cannot enter Hades, but flit like phantoms around tombs. They remain in this condition for many ages (*multis saeculis*), until finally released from the earth.

264 **agitati** : here lit., 'driven about'.

XXVI

1 **iam usque . . . temporibus** : 'dating back to the Heroic Age'. According to the early Greek poet Hesiod (8th century B.C.), in his *Works and Days*, the gods created four races of men before the present race. First came the Golden Age, when Cronos (Saturn) ruled on earth and all was perfect, including mankind; then the men of the Silver Age, who became corrupt and were destroyed by Zeus; third the race of the Bronze Age, which destroyed itself in civil war; fourth came the Age of Heroes, demi-gods and warriors, who fought in the legendary wars against Thebes and Troy, and went after death to the Isles of the Blest. Finally, came the Iron Age, the most degenerate of all. This is, of course, a poetical account and Cicero probably means merely the earliest age of which he has heard, the pre-historic, half legendary era of the Trojan War about 1100 B.C. He is perhaps

thinking of the seers and prophets who appear in Homer and Greek Tragedy, such as Calchas and Tiresias.

2 **eaque** : 'and one which'. See Note 4(*f*).

3 **versari . . . divinationem** : acc. and inf. dependent on *opinio*, 'that there exists among men some faculty of divination'.

5 **magnifica . . . salutaris** : 'a power indeed wonderful and beneficial'; *quaedam*, by making the adjs. more indefinite, has the effect of strengthening them.

5 **si modo est ulla** : supply *divinatio*, 'if only such a thing exists'. After *si*, *ullus* is used instead of *qui* (indef. adj.) in the emphatic sense of 'any at all'.

6 **quaque . . . possit accedere** : 'and such as would enable mortal man (*natura mortalis*) to approach closest to the divinity of the gods'. See Note 6(*a*).

7 **quidem** : 'at any rate'. See Note 8(*e*).

8 **humanam** : 'civilised'. **immanem** : 'savage'.

9 **barbaram** : 'outlandish'.

10 **censeat** : see Note 6(*a*). **principio** : 'first of all'. **Assyrii** : Assyria proper was an ancient kingdom on the Upper Tigris, whose capital was at Nineveh, but the name is also used loosely, as here, to include Babylonia and Chaldaea.

11 **ut . . . repetam** : 'to go back to the earliest peoples for my warrant'. **planitiam** : 1st decl. form for *planitiem*.

13 **traiectiones** : 'transits'.

14 **observitaverunt** : frequentative, 'kept under observation'.

15 **quid cuique significaretur** : 'what was portended in every case'.

17 **scientiam . . . ut** : 'are believed to have attained such knowledge that . . .'

Astrology, the study of the effect of the heavenly bodies on human behaviour, originated in Mesopotamia, was taken over by the Greeks and Romans, and had a profound influence on ancient thought, appealing to the superstitious and philosophers alike. Tradition held that the Chaldaei, about 2800 B.C., mapped out the heavens in the belief that they contained a message to mankind. Their doctrine was a mixture of scientific observation and a primitive philosophy, based on the idea of an interdependence between heaven and earth. Their claim to foretell the future and their belief in a fixed and unalterable fate (*fatum*) reappear in the Stoic philosophy. (See E. V. Arnold: *Roman Stoicism*, p. 5.)

20 **Cilicum** : nom. *Cilix*, 'of the Cilicians'.

21 **Pisidarum** : nom. *Pisida*, 'of the Pisidians'. Cilicia, Pisidia, and Pamphylia were districts in Asia Minor.

22 **praefuimus** : Cicero was appointed governor of Cilicia in 51 B.C. Note that he often refers to himself in the first pers. plur., especially in his letters. It is possible here that he is including his brother Quintus who had been governor of Asia.

24 **Aeoliam** , etc. : Cicero mentions the areas of Greek colonisation from east to west, from Aeolia on the N.W. coast of Asia Minor and Ionia and Asia to the S., to Sicily and Italy.

25 **Pythio** : the Pythian oracle was that of Apollo at Delphi.
Dodonaeo : oracle of Zeus at Dodona in Acarnania.
Hammonis : oracle of Zeus Ammon in Libya, visited by Alexander the Great. Ammon was an Egyptian god identified with the Greek Zeus.

27 **unum** : *i.e.* not one only.

30 **auspicato** : impersonal abl. abs. = 'after taking the auspices'. The legend tells how Romulus decided by observing a flight of birds from the Palatine, whether he or his brother Remus should be founder of Rome.

32 **usi** : sc. *sunt*. **exactis regibus** : 'after the expulsion of the kings'.

33 **auspiciis** : Nothing, Cicero says, was ever done at home or abroad without taking the auspices (*auspicia*), that is ascertaining the will of the gods about a proposed action by observing especially the flight of birds, wild or domestic. This was done by the *augurs*, who belonged to a special college and were responsible for maintaining the whole tradition of augury, ranking next to the *pontifices* in importance.

34 **monstris interpretandis** : dat. of purpose after *vis*. Trans. 'since there was considered to be great efficacy for the interpretation of omens in the art of the *haruspices*'.

35 **haruspicum disciplina** : The *haruspices* were introduced by the Romans from Etruria, and, from the time of the Second Punic War, gradually encroached on the sphere of the augurs. Their art or lore (*disciplina*) was concerned with interpreting *exta*, omens observed in the spots and markings on the livers of sacrificed animals; *monstra*, out of the way phenomena, such as monstrous births; and *fulgura*, lightning.

36 **adhibebant** : 'they took over'.

38 **animi** : 'souls'. **motu . . . libero** : 'by their own free and unimpeded activity'.

39 **furente . . . somniante** : the adjs. agree with *modo*, understood from *modis*. *Furentium . . . somniantium* would have been more
usual. Trans. 'the one by inspiration, the other through dreams'.

40 **furoris** : 'inspiration'. **Sibyllinis versibus** : The Sibylline
Oracles were a collection of prophecies in Greek hexameter verse
preserved at Rome, according to tradition, from the time of
Tarquinius Superbus, to whom they were sold by the Sibyl
(prophetess) of Cumae. They were consulted by a board of ten,
later fifteen (*quindecimviri sacris faciundis*), in times of crisis, and
played a great part in Roman history. In course of time they
were replaced and added to; for example, the early collection
was destroyed in the burning of the Capitol in 83 B.C. They
continued to be consulted until the fall of the Empire, and so
might be said to be coextensive with Rome. They were finally
burnt by order of the Emperor Honorius between 404 and 408
A.D. It is interesting to note that there were current also Sibylline
Oracles of Jewish origin, containing apocalyptic passages from the
Old Testament, but these are to be distinguished from the official
collection. It is the Jewish 'Sibyl' who is referred to in the well-
known lines of the Christian hymn:—

Dies irae, dies illa
Solvet saeclum in favilla,
Teste David ac Sibylla.

41 **delectos esse** : acc. and inf. after *voluerunt*, 'they determined'.

43 **summo concilio** : 'supreme council', *i.e.* the Senate.

XXVII

1 **quiddam . . . divinans** : 'a certain faculty of foresight and
prophecy'.

2 **si quidem** : see Note 8(*e*). Almost 'for example' here.

3 **Callanus** : a famous Indian gymnosophist or fakir, who
astonished Alexander the Great by ascending his own funeral
pyre at the age of 83.

4 **o . . . discessum** : acc. of exclamation. 'How glorious will
be my departure from life . . .'
Herculi : Hercules died in agony after putting on a poisoned
robe unwittingly sent him by his wife Deianira, and is said to
have ascended into heaven from his funeral pyre.

5 **lucem** : *i.e.* the light of glory or immortality. **animus** : as
often, 'soul'. **excesserit** : fut. perf.

6 ut . . . diceret : take directly after *rogaret*.

7 optime : sc. *rogas*, an expression of gratitude, here slightly ironical, 'Much obliged to you'. **propediem** : 'very shortly'.

8 Alexander : died in 323 B.C., at the age of 32.

10 apud Platonem : the reference is to Plato's dialogue *Crito*, in which Socrates appears conversing with his friends the day before his death.

13 Homericum . . . versum : the line is:—

ἤματί κεν τριτάτῳ Φθίην ἐρίβωλον ἵκοιο.

'On the third day you will come to fertile Phthia', *i.e.* your home in Thessaly. As quoted by Socrates, it is a modification of *Iliad* IX 363, where Achilles rejects Agamemnon's offer of reconciliation and threatens to sail home again to Greece. For Socrates, death was a 'home-coming'.

15 In Cicero's translation of the line, *Phthiae* is locative, 'in Phthia'. **tempestas** : 'season, day'.

18 quidem : emphatic 'indeed'. See Note 8(*e*).

Sophocles : second of the three famous tragic dramatists of fifth century Athens, between Aeschylus and Euripides.

19 patera : 'sacrificial dish'.

20 semel iterumque : 'again and again'.

21 ubi idem saepius : sc. *accidit.*
Areum Pagum : the Areopagus (Mars' Hill) was west of the Acropolis and was the site of the highest court of Athens, before which Orestes was traditionally tried for the murder of his mother Clytemnestra.

23 quaestione adhibita : 'when interrogated'.

26 pro cos : *pro consule.* Quintus Cicero was proconsul (pro-vincial governor) of Asia from 61–58 B.C.
me . . . vidisse . . ., cum . . . apparuisses, me contremuisse : The construction is awkward. It is probably simplest to take *vidisse in quiete* as one phrase, 'to have dreamt', and trans. 'I have often told you how I dreamt that, when you . . . had disappeared, I trembled . . .'

31 coniectura : 'interpretation'.

32 eos eventus, qui acciderunt : 'those events which did actually happen'. Quintus seems to have understood Cicero's disappearance and re-appearance in the dream as a symbolic prophecy of his exile in 58 B.C. and his sudden restoration in 57 B.C. This would agree well with the dates of Quintus' proconsulship.

34 **quid?** : 'again'.

The story of Flaminius' rashness before the battle of Lake Trasimene in 217 B.C., when the Roman armies were trapped between the mountains and the lake and disastrously defeated by Hannibal, is also told by Livy (XXII 3).

consul iterum : 'when consul for the second time'. ,

35 **cum clade** : 'thus bringing disaster on his country'.

36 **lustrato** : 'reviewed'. **versus** : prep. 'towards', after its case. **Arretium** : a town in Etruria.

38 **signum** : 'statue'. **Iovis Statoris** : Jupiter, 'the stayer of rout', traditionally supported the armies in battle.

39 **nec habuit religioni** : 'did not treat it as a religious prohibition'. *religioni*: predicative dat. *Religio* is a scruple against violating conscience or the law of the gods, mingled with a strong element of religious fear or awe.

obiecto signo . . . ne : concessive, 'though he had been given a warning not to . . .' N.B. *signum* used in two different senses, 'statue' and 'omen', within two lines.

41 **idem** : 'again'. *Cp.* Note 4(*f*). **tripudio auspicaretur** : 'he was taking the auspices by consulting the sacred chickens'. *Tripudium* was a method of augury from the observations of sacred chickens, specially kept for the purpose in charge of a *pullarius* (keeper). If the birds ate greedily, the omen was good, and vice versa. As well as the story told here, it is also recorded that, at the naval battle of Drepanum in the First Punic War (249 B.C.), the Roman commander, P. Claudius Pulcher, on being informed of the refusal of the chickens to eat, ignored the omen, and ordered them to be thrown overboard, remarking that, if they would not eat, at least they could drink. Like Flaminius, he lost the battle. This story well illustrates the old Roman conservatism, which regarded an offence against *pietas* as more serious than incompetence.

42 **differebat** : N.B. tense, 'he was for putting off'.

45 **esurientibus . . . saturis** : antithesis and asyndeton. See Note 1(*b*). *satur*: 'full, satisfied'. *esurio*: 'be hungry'.

48 **nec quicquam proficeretur** : 'no success was achieved'.

50 **tribus iis horis** : 'within three hours'.

XXVIII

1 **cum . . . tum** : see Note 8(*a*).

animus : 'soul', the rational element in man, not always distinguished from *anima*, properly 'the breath, the physical life'.

a societate . . . corporis : 'from defiling association with the body'. See Note 2.

2 **meminit . . .** : asyndeton. See Note 1(*a*).

4 **viget** : 'is vigorous'. **autem** : see Note 8(*d* ii).

quod . . . faciet : 'This it will be able to do much more effectively', *i.e.* transcend the body.

6 **divinior** : 'more inspired, prophetic'.

id ipsum : refers forward to acc. and inf. *instare mortem*. *Cp.* Note 5. **et** : emphatic. Trans. 'are aware of this very thing', *i.e.* the approach of death.

7 **qui** : i.e. *ii qui*. See Note 4(*e*).

9 **tum vel maxime** : emphatic *vel* with superlative, 'then most of all', 'it is then that'.

laudi student : 'they are anxious for their reputation'.

10 **secus quam** : 'otherwise than they ought to have done'.

11 **illo . . . quod** : 'in the well-known case which he quotes', followed by acc. and inf. *Rhodium . . . nominasse*. See Note 5.

12 **Posidonius** : Introduction II 8. His system was mainly Stoic, but he took over from Plato much of his doctrine of the soul.

13 **aequales** : 'of the same age'.

13 **qui . . . qui . . . qui** : interrog. adjs. instead of pron. *quis*. Not infrequent in Cicero.

15 **appulsu** : 'impulse, inspiration'.

16 **quod** : ' in that; namely that'. Explanatory of *uno*. Trans. 'the first of which consists in the soul's foreseeing'.

ipse per se : 'of its own powers, unaided'.

quippe qui : with subj., has a causal sense, 'inasmuch as'. Trans. 'since it is bound by affinity to the gods'.

18 **in quibus . . . appareant** : 'upon which records (*nŏtae*) of truth are to be seen, as it were, clearly imprinted (*insignitae*).

The immortal spirits which fill the air are the δαίμονες (daemons) of Greek thought, beings intermediate between men and gods. According to Plato (*Sym.* 203a), they are the sole means of contact between men and gods, and the source of all prophecy.

20 **id** (*que*) : anticipates *ut . . . augurentur. Cp.* Note 5.

21 **ex quo** : supply some verb like *oritur*, 'this is the source of'.
et : 'also'.

22 **illud** : sc. *dictum*, 'the well-known saying of Homer's Hector'.
    Hectoris : the reference is to *Iliad* XXII 356 ff., where the
dying Hector foretells Achilles' death at the hands of Paris.

XXIX

1 **explodatur** : 'let us rule out of court'. *Explodo*, lit. 'to hiss
off the stage'.

2 **superstitio** : excessive fear of the gods, as opposed to *religio*,
due reverence.

3 **oppressit . . . occupavit** : Note the military metaphor, 'has
vanquished the minds of men and taken possession of their
weakness'.

5 **de natura deorum** : the reference is to Cicero's work of this
title, in which he had already discussed the existence and character
of the gods.
    hac disputatione : 'the present discussion'.
    id maxime egimus : 'it has been my chief contention'.

7 **eam** : i.e. *superstitionem*. In advocating enlightened belief in
a religion which is consistent with science (*iuncta cum cognitione
naturae*) and purged of superstition, Cicero is at the same time
aware of the value of an established religion and ancestral customs.
Like Plato, he makes provision for this in his ideal state, described
in *De Legibus* II.
    sustulissemus : represents fut. perf. of the direct speech.

10 **sapientis est** : 'it is but wisdom', lit. 'the mark of a wise man'.
    esse . . . generi : acc. and inf. dependent on *cogit* (*nos*) . . .
confiteri.

11 **naturam** : here 'substance, being' (Gk. οὐσία), *i.e.* God.
    suspiciendam : 'to be reverenced'. N.B. No part of this
verb, except *suspectus* (suspected), means 'to suspect' in Ciceronian
Latin.

12 **hominum generi** : dat. of agent with gerundive.

14 **ut . . . sic** : adversative sense, 'while . . . yet'.

15 **naturae** : here = 'the universe'.

eligendae : here 'uproot'. The metaphor here and in *propaganda* (lit. spread by slips) is from horticulture.

16 **proprium** : 'characteristic of'.

Academiae : the New Academy, or later Platonic school, headed by Carneades (214–129 B.C.) held that knowledge is only probable, not certain. Cicero often, as here, adhered to this view, refusing to dogmatise in disputed questions. At other times he is quite positive that God exists, that good is better than evil, and that the soul is immortal.

iudicium . . . interponere : 'put forward no opinion of one's own as final'. N.B. Asyndeton between the infs. in this sentence. See Note 1(*a*).

18 **conferre causas** : 'adduce all (possible) reasons'.

in quamque sententiam : 'for every conclusion'.

20 **integrum** : 'unprejudiced'.

21 **consuetudinem . . . traditam** : 'the procedure we have learnt from Socrates', whose method of discussion was to profess ignorance himself (irony, εἰρωνεία), and by question and answer to prove to his companions that they themselves knew no more. Then, by further questioning, he would lead them to a more positive conclusion apparently elicited from their own minds. The sceptical and tentative side of Socrates' thought is emphasised by Cicero here.

XXX

In Book I of the *De Natura Deorum* (see Introduction III v), Gaius Velleius expounds the Epicurean view that the gods indeed exist, but live a blissful life, 'careless of mankind'. After this has been criticised by Cotta, Q. Lucilius Balbus, '*homo doctus et eruditus*', as Cicero elsewhere calls him, proceeds in Book II to explain the Stoic theory of a divine providence. For proof of the existence of the gods, he appeals first to the argument based on the *consensus hominum* (the general agreement of mankind), then adds four popular arguments as formulated by the Stoic Cleanthes:

1 Argument from divination. 2 Argument from the accommodation of the world to the needs of man. 3 Argument from the fear of natural events and omens. 4 Argument from the order and beauty of the heavenly bodies.

1 **summa constat** : 'there is agreement on the main point'.

2 omnibus . . . deos : 'the conviction is born with us and imprinted on our souls that the gods exist (*esse*)'.

3 quales . . . negat : for the asyndeton, see Note 1(*b*).

4 Cleanthes quidem noster : 'our own (Stoic) Cleanthes'. Cleanthes (see Introduction II 7) was successor to Zeno as head of the Stoic school. His famous Hymn to Zeus, in Greek hexameter verse, is addressed, not to the Zeus of mythology, but to the one Divine Spirit pervading the universe. It begins:

> Κύδιστ' ἀθανάτων, πολυώνυμε, παγκρατὲς ἀεί,
> Ζεῦ, φύσεως ἀρχηγέ, νόμου μέτα πάντα κυβερνῶν,
> χαῖρε· σὲ γὰρ πάντεσσι θέμις θνητοῖσι προσαυδᾶν,
> ἐκ σοῦ γὰρ γένος ἐσμέν . . .

> Lord of Immortals, God of many names, Zeus ever omnipotent, ruler of Nature, piloting all things in accordance with Law,—all Hail! It is right for all mortals to call upon Thee; for we are sprung from Thee . . .

The last phrase became so well known that it is quoted in St. Paul's address to the Athenians in the form, 'for we are also his offspring'. (*Acts* XVII 28.)

5 informatas . . . notiones : 'ideas of the gods have been formed'.

7 ceperimus : 'we have derived'. The sudden change of sequence appears to be due to the change of subject, the argument being stated now from the point of view of the speaker instead of quoted from Cleanthes. But the indicative would have been more logical in this case.

8 caeli temperatio : 'the due ordering of the climate'.

9 fecunditas : 'fertility'.

10 quae terreret : *quae*, antecedent *causa*, is illogically made the subject. Trans. 'The third cause he found in the fear inspired by . . .' The list of natural phenomena recalls the catalogues of omens given by Livy, *e.g.* in Books XXI and XXII, at the crises of the Second Punic War.

fulmen : 'lightning'.

11 nimbus : 'rain-cloud'. **grando** : 'hail'. **vastitas** : 'desolation'.

12 terrae motus : 'earthquake'. **fremitus** : 'noise'. **lapidei imbres** : 'showers of stones'.

13 guttis: 'with drops'. **quasi cruentis** : lit. 'as it were, bloody'; tr. 'the colour of blood'.

tum . . . tum . . . : 'now . . . now', used in long enumerations.
lābes : 'land-slide'.

14 **hiatus :** 'gap, fissure (in the ground)'.

15 **portentum :** 'prodigy, omen'. **faces :** 'shooting stars'.

16 **cincinnatas :** lit. 'with curled hair', Latin equivalent for the Greek κομήτης (long-haired). Comets were thus called from the appearance of their tails.

17 **bello Octaviano :** the civil conflict of 87 B.C., when Marius and Cinna took Rome by violence against the opposition of the consul C. Octavius. This was still recent (*nuper*) at the time of the dialogue (76 B.C.).

18 **praenuntiae :** 'harbingers of disasters'. **sole geminato :** 'a doubled, twin sun'.

19 **Tuditano . . . consulibus :** The year was 129 B.C., when P. Scipio Aemilianus died mysteriously in the middle of a dispute about assigning land to the Italians.

20 **sol alter :** in apposition to Africanus, 'our second sun'. **quibus :** refers to all the preceding omens.

22 **quartam causam esse :** the construction is changed. Supply *dixit.*

eamque vel maximam : 'and that the most important'. See Note 4(*f*).

23 **aequabilitatem :** 'regularity'. **conversionum :** 'revolutions (of heavenly bodies)'. **caeli :** notice asyndeton here and in following nouns. See Note 1(*a*).

24 **distinctionem :** 'orderly arrangement (of stars)'.

25 **aspectus ipse :** 'the mere sight'.

26 **indicaret :** 'should of itself proclaim'. See Note 6(*a*).

ut . . . intellegat : a long comparative clause answered by *multo magis* (instead of the usual *ita*) . . . *statuat necesse est*. The *ut*–clause is complicated by having a *si*–clause subordinated to it. The outline of the sentence is: 'just as, if anyone were to have entered a house . . . he would realise (*intellegat*) . . . so much more . . . must one conclude. . . '

27 **venerit :** the perf. subj. replaces the pres. subj. in ideal conditions, when the supposed action is viewed as completed. Trans. 'suppose someone to *have* entered a house'. *Veniat* would mean, 'suppose he were to enter'.

28 **rationem, modum, disciplinam :** 'arrangement, proportion and order'. See Note 1(*a*).

33 **vetustas** : 'period of past time'. **mentita sit** : 'disappointed expectation, shown variation'.

aliqua mente : the Divine Intelligence of the Stoics, referred to above (line 21), as '*vim caelestem et divinam*'. Yet earlier (line 3), Cicero speaks not of 'God', but of 'gods'. The explanation of this apparent inconsistency is that, although the Stoics held that there existed one divine spirit, they also tried to reconcile their belief with the current mythology, by supposing that the cult of the many popular gods was really the worship of the one God under different names. Thus Cleanthes (see note on line 4) calls the Ruler of the Universe 'Zeus'. The clearest expression of an analogous attitude in English is Pope's 'Universal Prayer', which begins:—

DEO OPT. MAX.

Father of all! in every age,
In every clime adored,
By saint, by savage and by sage,
Jehovah, Jove or Lord!

XXXI

1 **qui** : archaic abl. = 'how'. **convenit** : 'is it consistent?' **tabulam pictam** : 'picture'.

4 **solarium** : Sundials became known to the Romans from the Greeks during the third century B.C. The first actually to be set up in Rome was presented to the state by Q. Marcius Philippus, censor in 164 B.C. The face of a sundial is shown in Fig. 3. In the middle was a gnomon, a metal stylus which cast the sun's shadow on the concave stone dial. This was marked out (*discriptum*) so as to show the hours of the day, as well as certain fixed points, the shortest and longest days, the spring and autumn equinoxes.

Another type was the *solarium ex aqua* or water-clock. In 159 B.C., Scipio set up the first one at Rome, as Varro (*de Lingua Latina* VI 4) tells us, in the shadow of the Basilica Aemilia, to supplement the sundial on sunless days. By our standards not very accurate, these instruments at least brought the Romans beyond the stage of merely dividing the day into two halves, before mid-day and after. Some no doubt felt like the character in Plautus :

> *Ut illum di perdant, qui horas repperit,*
> *Quique adeo primus statuit hic solarium.* (Frag.)

5 **contemplēre** : i.e. *contempleris*, 2nd sing. pres. subj. dep.

6 **autem** : The whole sentence beginning *Qui convenit* . . . is a long question, falling into two contrasting parts. *Autem* serves to mark the beginning of the second and bring out the antithesis. See Note 8(*d*). The sense is: How is it consistent to admit a statue, a picture or a ship to be products of skill, and yet (*autem*) suppose that the universe is devoid of design?

artes . . . artifices : 'all these skills and the masters of them'.

8 **Scythia** : country north of the Black Sea, coupled with Britain as unknown and barbarous land.

9 **sphaeram** : a celestial globe, representing the planets and constellations and their movements. Such globes are said to have been current among the Greeks from early times.

tulerit : perf. subj. instead of pres. subj. emphasises the completion of the supposed action. (See Note on XXX 27.) Trans. 'suppose someone to *have* brought'.

10 **Posidonius** : Introduction II 8 and XXVIII 12. He wrote a work on astronomy and calculated the diameters of the earth and the sun.

singulae conversiones : 'every complete revolution'.

idem efficiunt . . . quod : 'exhibits the same movements of (lit. 'in regard to') sun, moon, and five planets as actually take place in the heavens every day and night'.

11 **quinque** : Only the five planets visible to the naked eye were known to the ancients, Mercury, Venus, Mars, Jupiter, and Saturn.

13 **barbaria** : 'foreign parts'.

14 **hi autem** : *i.e.* the Epicureans, who denied the existence of a divine reason. **de mundo . . . casune** : N.B. proleptic order. See Note 7.

16 **Archimedem** : Cicero elsewhere mentions Archimedes as the constructor of a globe (see V 68). **plus valuisse** : 'showed greater ability'.

18 **efficiendis** : 'creating'. **praesertim cum** : 'especially when', with an adversative sense, almost 'even though'.

multis partibus : with *sollertius*, 'many times, much (*multo*)'.

19 **illa** : *i.e.* the originals in nature. **haec** : Archimedes' model. Trans. 'even though the natural originals show a far greater perfection of design than the human imitations'.

XXXII

1 **cernatur** : 'Behold !'. **universa** : 'as a whole'. **media sede** : the central point of the universe, occupied by the earth.

2 **globosa** : 'spherical'. **nutibus** : downward pull, gravity, causing earth, the heaviest of the four elements, to sink downwards into one mass.

undique . . . **globata** : Mayor translates, 'gathered into a ball by the natural gravitation of all its parts'.

4 **quorum** : neut. since the antecedents, though of different genders, all refer to things.

insatiabili : active sense, 'never producing satiety'. Trans. 'are resplendent in their inexhaustible profusion'.

5 **adde huc** : 'add to these'. **fontium** . . . **perennitates** : for this and the following phrases, see Note 3, and observe that the use of abstract nouns is in keeping with the poetical style of the passage. They may all be translated on similar lines, e.g. 'fountains of unfailing coolness', 'caves with their vast spaces', the 'frowning heights of the mountains', etc.

9 **venas** : 'seams'.

10 **vim marmoris** : 'abundance of marble'.

11 **cicurum** : from *cicur-uris*, 'tame, domestic'.

12 **lapsus** : 'flight'. **pastus** : 'pasture, grazing'.
vita silvestrium : 'wild life of the woodlands'.

15 **immanitate** . . . **efferari** : 'to be turned into a wilderness by wild beasts'. **asperitate stirpium** : 'wild growth'.

16 **collucent** . . . : 'shine resplendent with houses'.

17 **quae** . . . **si dubitaret** : 'If we men could behold them in thought as vividly as we see them with the eye, no one could doubt the existence of a supreme Mind'.

19 **at vero** : 'again'.

20 **quae species universi (maris)** : 'how glorious the general view of it'.

22 **submersarum** : 'under-water'.

24 **nativis testis** : 'with the shells nature has given them', *i.e.* not artificial. *testa –ae*, f.

25 **appetens** : 'yearning for (the land)'. **alludit** : 'playfully dashes upon its shores'. This ascription of human joy to nature recalls Vergil's *Georgics*.

una : sc. *natura.* **naturis** : 'elements'.

26 **conflata** : 'fused together, composed'.

aer : the lower atmosphere near the earth as distinct from *aether*, the celestial ether, in which the stars and planets move.

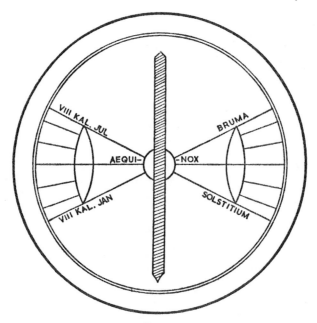

FIG. 3

Face of a portable sun-dial (*solarium discriptum*), found in France.   The dates for the shortest day (*bruma*) and for the longest (*solstitium*), Dec. 23rd, and June 22nd, are reasonably accurate.   (See XXXI 4 and XXXII 38.)

die et nocte distinguitur : 'exhibits the alternations of day and night'.

27 **tum . . . tum autem . . . tum** : 'at one time . . . at another . . . at yet another'. **fusus** : 'diffused'. **extenuatus** : 'rarefied'.

sublime fertur : 'is borne aloft, streams upwards'.

28 **concretus . . . cogitur** : 'condenses into clouds'.

umorem colligens : 'forming moisture'.

29 **effluens** : 'dispersing'.

31 **alitum** : from *ales –itis,* 'bird'. **spiritu ductus** : 'drawn in by breathing'.

33 **restat** : We now pass to the celestial sphere.

omnia . . . complexus : 'the sweep of the heavens enfolding and embracing all'.

34 **qui idem aether vocatur** : 'which is also called the "aether".'

35 **extrema . . . mundi** : 'the furthest bound and frontier of the universe'. **in quo** : antecedent *aether.*

36 **igneae formae** : the stars, which are composed, according to Stoicism, of elemental fire, and are themselves gods.

cursus . . . definiunt : 'trace out their ordered courses'.

37 **multis partibus** : 'many times'.

38 **oriens et occidens** : There are two apparent motions of the sun: (1). Its daily course across the sky from rising to setting. (2). Its yearly movement, by which, sometimes approaching (*accedens*) and sometimes withdrawing (*recedens*), it alternates between its furthest and closest points of rising and setting, between the longest and shortest days respectively. When it reaches these extremities, it appears to stand still before turning back; hence *solstitium,* the 'standing-still of the sun', the longest day. On the diagram of the sundial (see Fig. 3), the date of the shortest day is given as VIII. Kal. Ian.=23rd December, and the longest as VIII. Kal. Iul.=22nd June.

The meaning here is: from the furthest points of his course (*ab extremo*) the sun completes two movements every year (*binas reversiones*) in opposite directions (*contrarias*) from the winter solstice (*bruma*) to the summer solstice (*solstitium*) and back again.

39 **modo** :=*tum,* balancing *tum autem.*

41 **quarum in intervallo** : 'in the course of which', *i.e.* between the shortest and longest day.

42 **tristitiā . . . contrahit** : (sc. *sol*), 'spreads a frown of wintry gloom over the earth'. *Cp. frontem contrahere,* 'to frown'. **laetificat** : 'gladdens'.

43 **ut . . . videatur** : 'so that it seems to share the joy of the heavens'.

44 **mathematici** : 'mathematicians, scientists'. Anaxagoras (see Introduction II 1) first explained the phases of the moon and eclipses. Aristarchus of Samos (third cent. B.C.), using trigonometry, calculated that the sun was nineteen times as distant from the earth as the moon, and that the diameter of the earth was seven

times that of the moon. The first of these is twenty times too little, and the true figure for the second is four. **dimidia pars :** 'half'.

45 **spatiis** : 'track', *i.e.* the Zodiac, to which the apparent courses of the sun, moon, and planets, except occasionally Venus, are confined. The twelve constellations lying along this path, or twelve signs of the Zodiac, were known to the earliest Babylonian astronomers.

47 **mutationes** : 'phases'.

48 **atque etiam tum . . .** : An eclipse of the sun takes place when the moon is brought into conjunction with it (*subiecta*), and is directly between it and the earth (*opposita*).

50 **e regione** : 'in line with'. **interpositu . . . terrae** : 'by the interposition of the earth', *i.e.* between the sun and moon, thus causing an eclipse of the moon.

51 **deficit** : 'is eclipsed'. **iisdem spatiis** : see Note on line 45 above.

52 **vagas** : wandering stars, *i.e.* planets.

53 **incitantur** : the planets appear to follow irregular courses, sometimes accelerating (*incitantur*), sometimes slowing down (*retardantur*), sometimes stopping before turning back (*insistunt*). Instead of following a uniform forward course, they often form loops and spirals, which are actually combinations of their own motions with that of the earth. The ancients, regarding the earth as stationary, tried to explain this by a complicated system of epicycles (circles described round centres themselves moving round the circumference of other circles), systematised by the astronomer Ptolemy of Alexandria (second century A.D.). See Fig. 4.

56 **discripta . . . est** : 'arranged in such clearly marked patterns'.

57 **notarum figurarum** : The classification of the stars into constellations, and their association with 'well-known figures' from nature or mythology was due to the Greeks under Babylonian influence. Homer mentions Orion, the Pleiades, and the Great Bear, but the total number comprised over forty. Ptolemy grouped 1022 stars into forty-eight constellations.

59 **haec omnis discriptio** : This sentence summarises the argument: the order and beauty of the heavens point to a designer.

60 **corporibus** : 'atoms', according to Epicurean physics, the constituent elements of the universe, whose accidental collisions (*casu et temere cursantibus*) produced the visible world.

61 **aut alia quae** : *quae*, indefinite adj.=*aliqua*. Trans. 'or is there any other'.

62 **natura** : 'being', or 'natural power'.

63 **eguerunt** : 'needed an intelligent being to produce them'.

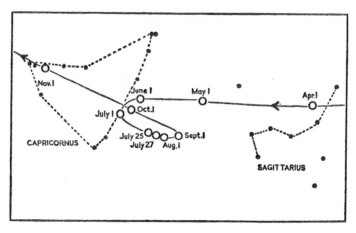

FIG. 4

The path of the planet Mars among the stars in 1939, showing its retrograde motion. (See XXXII 53)

XXXIII

1 **age** : orig. imperative of *ago*, used as an exclamation 'come, now', or as a particle of transition to a new subject, 'well, now', as here.

2 **naturae ratio intellegentis** : 'the design of an intelligent being.'

    appareat : see Note 6(*a*).

3 **stirpes** : includes both stems and root.

4 **sucum** : 'moisture, sap'. **obducuntur** : 'are drawn over, covered'.

    libro : 'bark' or 'rind' (hence parchment, papyrus, book).

6 **iam vero** : 'again'. **vites** : 'vines'. **claviculis** : 'tendrils'. **adminicula** : 'supports'.

7 **animantes :** living things in general, here animals, as distinct from plants. **quin etiam :** 'moreover'.

8 **caulibus :** 'cabbages'. **propter :** 'near' (adv.). **sati :** sc. *caules*. **pestifer :** 'deadly'.

9 **nocens :** 'injurious'. **dicuntur :** sc. *vites*.

10 **ad eam rem . . . ut :** 'to the end that'.

quanta . . . permaneat : 'what capacity (*vis*) does each possess of remaining true to type'.

12 **eum** with **pastum :** Note emphatic position, see Note 4(*a*).

14 **sensum :** 'sensation'. **appetitum :** 'desire, appetite'.

altero . . . altero : note chiastic order: the first *altero* refers to *appetitum*, the second to *sensum*. See Note 1(*c*). **conatum :** 'impulse'.

16 **gradiendo :** 'by walking, on foot'. N.B. abl. of gerund= pres. participle.

17 **serpendo :** 'by crawling'.

19 **unguis :** 'claw, talon'. **tenacitas :** 'grip'. **aduncitas rostrorum :** 'hooked beak'.

20 **sugunt :** 'suck'. **carpunt :** 'tear'. **vorant :** 'swallow whole'.

21 **mandunt :** 'chew'; from *mandĕre*. Distinguish from *mandare*, 'entrust'. **ea** with **ut :** = *talis*. See Note 4(*a*). **humilitas :** 'lowness of stature'.

22 **quae :** see Note 4(*e*).

23 **anser :** 'goose'. **cygnus :** 'swan'. **grus :** 'crane'. **camelus :** 'camel'.

24 **proceritate collorum :** 'by the length of their necks'. **manus :** *i.e.* trunk.

25 **difficiles :** predicative, 'found access to food difficult'.

26 **at quibus bestiis . . . :** The construction is: '*natura aut vires aut celeritatem dedit (eis) bestiis quibus . . .*' Note 4(*b*). N.B. pronoun antecedent here omitted.

is with **ut :**=*talis*. See Note 4(*d*). Trans. 'to those animals whose diet involved feeding upon animals of another species, nature gave either strength or speed'.

28 **machinatio :** 'craft'.

29 **sollertia :** 'skill'. **ut :** 'as, for example'. **in :** 'among'. **araneola :** 'spider'. **rete texunt :** 'weave a web'.

30 **conficiant :** 'despatch, kill'. The distinction is between the web-spinning spider and the hunting spider, which lies in wait to leap upon its prey.

XXXIV

1 **providentiam** : 'foresight'.

2 **e quibus** : see Note 6(*a*).

3 **res** : 'powers'.

4 **excitatos** : 'raised up, erect'.

5 **intuentes** : 'by the contemplation of the heavens'. For the idea that man is distinguished from animals by standing erect and looking upward *cp.* Ovid. *Met.* I 85:—

> *Os homini sublime dedit: coelumque tueri*
> *Iussit et erectos ad sidera tollere vultus.*

7 **ut habitatores** : 'as inhabitants (merely)'. Cicero is fond of nouns ending in –*tor* as predicates: *cp. spectatores* and *speculatores* (line 12).

superarum rerum : 'things above', *i.e.* the heavens.

9 **sensus . . . rerum** : 'the senses which convey information from the outside world'.

10 **ad usus necessarios** : 'to fulfil the essential wants (of man)'.

11 **tamquam speculatores** : 'like watchmen'.

12 **ex quo** : see Note 6(*a*).

14 **qui . . . fertur** : 'whose property is to rise': *naturā:* abl.

16 **qua . . . potest** : 'unsurpassable in her skill'; *quā:* abl. of comparison.

17 **sollertiam** : 'intricate design'. **persequi** : 'achieve, produce'.

18 **saepsit** : 'has guarded, enclosed'.

19 **firmas . . . continerentur** : 'strong enough to retain their shape.' **autem** : see Note 8(*d*).

20 **lubricos . . . mobiles** : 'quick . . . active'.

22 **acies . . . vocatur** : 'the seeing part of the eye, which is termed the pupil'.

24 **palpebrae** : 'eye-lids'. **tegmenta** : 'protective covering'.

25 **laederent** : Cicero apparently reverts to secondary sequence, forgetting that *possint* has preceded. Such variations occur occasionally.

27 **idque providit ut . . . posset** : '(nature) has made provision that this should occur'. *id* is not obj. of *providit*, but subj. of *posset*. Note proleptic order, and *cp.* Note 7.

29 **domina rerum** : 'mistress of human affairs'. *Cp.* Note 7.
vos : *i.e.* the Academics. **eloquendi vis** : 'gift of speech'.

34 **gestientes** 'the exultant'. **comprimimus** : 'we restrain'.

37 **ad usum orationis** : 'for the production of speech'. **autem** :
see Note 8(*d*).

38 **attenderis** : sc. *animum*='observe'. **quanta opera** : acc. plur.

39 **pulmonibus** : 'lungs'. **arteria** : 'wind-pipe'. **usque** . . .
pertinet : 'reaches as far as the back of the mouth'.

40 **principium** . . . **funditur** : 'originating in the mind, is taken
up and uttered'.

42 **immoderate** : 'without restraint, inarticulately'.
fingit et terminat : 'gives form and precision to'.

43 **distinctos et pressos** : 'sharp and well-defined'.

45 **aptas** . . . **ministras** : used predicatively. 'How capable are
the hands nature has given to man, how varied the purposes to
which they can be applied'.

46 **contractio** . . . **porrectio** : note chiastic order. See Note 1(*c*).

47 **propter** . . . **artus** : 'owing to the flexibility of joints and
limbs'.

48 **nullo in modo laborat** : 'is accomplished with the greatest
ease'. **ad pingendum** : 'for painting'.

49 **fingendum** : 'moulding'. **scalpendum** : 'carving'. **ad** . . .
tibiarum : 'for drawing out notes from strings and pipes'.

51 **haec** : supply *sunt*: 'these (just mentioned) are (matters) of
pleasure'. **illa** : 'the following'. **dico** : 'I mean'.

52 **texta vel suta** : 'woven or stitched'.

53 **fabricam** : 'art of forging bronze and iron'.

54 **inventa** . . . **percepta** : asyndeton. See Note 1(*b*). *adhibitis* with *manibus*, abl. abs. Trans. 'that all our progress has
been achieved by the application of the hands of craftsmen to the
inventions of the mind and the observations of the senses'.

59 **quaesita** : emphatic. 'It is the hand which gathers the
many products (*efferunt*) of the land'.
quae vel statim . . . **vetustati** : 'either for immediate con-
sumption or to be stored up for future use'. See Note 6(*a*).

62 **domitu** . . . **vectiones** : abstract nouns in –*us* and –*io* derived
from supine stems may often be translated by verbs, *e.g.* 'we train
four-footed beasts to convey us'.

63 **celeritas . . . celeritatem** : a good example of chiasmus. See Note 1 (*c*).

66 **abutimur** : 'we make full use of'.

67 **rem . . . necessariam** : in apposition to *ferrum*.

71 **calficio** : 'to heat'.

72 **mitigandum** : 'softening', *i.e.* cooking.

74 **affert** : subject *materia*. **cursibus** : 'voyages'. **suppeditantur** : 'are supplied'.

75 **quasque res . . . earum** : inversion of antecedent and relative. See Note 4 (*b*).

77 **maris atque ventorum** : in apposition to *earum*.

83 **arcemus, derigimus, avertimus** : 'dam, direct, and divert'. See Note 1 (*a*).

84 **alteram naturam** : 'a second "nature" within nature'.

XXXV

The main points in this passage are as follows:
1. Man alone is possessed of reason. 2. He alone of all creatures observes the heavenly bodies. 3. The study of astronomy leads to knowledge of the gods. 4. Knowledge of the gods is the foundation of right living (*virtus*). 5. The life of virtue (*vita beata*) makes man equal to the gods in everything except eternity. 6. The universe was created for the benefit of gods and men: it is a community of gods and men, a universal family or state (*cosmopolis*).

1 **quid vero?** 'again'.

3 **finitus** : 'determined'; agrees with the first of the three subjects, *dies*. See Note 1 (*a*).

4 **defectiones . . . sint** : for construction see Note 7.

7 **qua . . . cui . . . quibus** : a 'chain' of relatives, each with a different antecedent. **pietas** : 'religion'.

8 **reliquaeque virtutes** : Virtue, being a disposition of the whole man, is one, but expresses itself in particular virtues (*virtutes*). Plato, in the *Republic*, distinguishes four, which came to be generally recognised as 'cardinal virtues', from which the rest could be derived: σοφία, *sapientia*, wisdom: ἀνδρεία, *fortitudo*, courage: δικαιοσύνη, *iustitia*, justice: σωφροσύνη, *temperantia*,

temperance or self-control. According to Cicero (*de Fin.* V 67) wisdom is shown in the choice between good and evil, courage in facing hardship or danger, justice in giving every man his due, and self-control in refraining from pleasures.

9 **deorum** : sc. *vitae*.

immortalitate : Stoic teachers differed about the immortality of the soul. Some held the soul to be deathless, because divine, others, like Panaetius and Cicero here, thought that the individual soul could not survive final absorption into the divine essence. On the other hand, personal survival is implied in the *Somnium Scipionis* (XXV).

quae . . . pertinet : the Stoics held that duration did not increase the happiness of the wise men. Since virtue in itself was perfect, immortality could add nothing to it. Yet most thinkers have agreed with the lines of Tennyson, *Locksley Hall Sixty Years After*:

> . . . the Good, the True, the Pure, the Just—
> Take the charm 'for ever' from them, and
>   they crumble into dust.

10 **cedens caelestibus** : 'inferior to the gods'.

11 **hominis natura** : proleptic order. See Note 7.

13 **figuram situmque** : 'structure and design'.

14 **fortuna** : abl. 'by chance'.

restat ut . . . : 'it remains for me to conclude my argument (*perorem*) by showing that . . .'

19 **quaeque . . . ea** : see Note 4(*b*).

20 **communis . . . urbs** : the idea of *cosmopolis*, or world-state, is said to go back at least to Socrates, who, being asked, 'Of what city are you?' answered, 'Of the Universe'. (κοσμοπολίτης) After the conquests of Alexander and with the spread of Hellenistic civilisation, it was developed by the Greek Stoics, as an inevitable deduction from 'Natural Law', and in turn by the Romans, who found in it a philosophical basis of the *ius gentium*. From this, it was a natural step to identify Cosmopolis with the *Imperium Romanum*, as was done by Posidonius. Perhaps the noblest expression of the ideal of one world comes from a later time, from the *Meditations* of the Stoic 'philosopher on the throne', the Emperor Marcus Aurelius (169–180 A.D.): πόλις καὶ πατρὶς ὡς μὲν Ἀντωνίνῳ μοι ἡ ‘Ρώμη, ὡς δὲ ἀνθρώπῳ ὁ κόσμος. (*Med.* VI 44). 'For me, as Emperor, Rome is my city and country, as a human being, the world'.

25 **populorum** : possessive genit. with *esse*.

XXXVI

In this concluding passage from *De Legibus* I, Cicero treats of the destiny of the human soul in the individual and in society, a theme inspired by Plato, for whom the doctrine of the ψυχή was the central point of philosophy. Many philosophical themes are summed up: the pursuit of virtue; the liberation of the soul from the body, and contempt of death; the union of the individual with kindred souls; true religion; the distinction between good and evil; true happiness; knowledge of the universe, its beginning and end; the being of God; internationalism; the use of logic as the safeguard of truth; and the use of eloquence in the propagation of truth, this last typically Roman. The whole passage is a fine example of the eloquence its author recommends.

1 **animus** : 'soul'. **virtutibus** : see Note on XXXV 8.

2 **discesserit** : fut. perf.

voluptatem : that pleasure contaminates the soul is a Platonic doctrine: *e.g.* in *Phaedo* 65 c, Socrates says: ἡ τοῦ φιλοσόφου ψυχὴ μάλιστα ἀτιμάζει τὸ σῶμα καὶ φεύγει ἀπ' αὐτοῦ. 'The soul of the philosopher treats the body with contempt and seeks to escape from it'.

3 **oppresserit** : 'subdued, mastered'.

4 **societatem caritatis** : 'bond of affection'.

5 **suis** : *i.e.* members of family, city, or nation.

omnesque . . . **duxerit** : 'considers as its kin (*suos*—predicative) all with whom it is associated by nature'.

6 **puram** : 'without superstition'. *Cp.* XXIX 7.

7 **exacuerit**...**aciem** : 'sharpens its (moral) perception, which is the eye of the mind'.

8 **ex providendo**; *prudentia*, orig. *providentia*, 'foresight,' is derived from *providere*.

9 **eo** : 'than such a (state).' Abl. of comparison after *beatius*.

10 **idemque**; 'again.' (cp. Note 4 (*f*).

11 **eaque**; see Note 7.

unde . . . **obitura** : 'whence they originated, whither they will return, when and in what manner they will cease to exist'. *Recursura* seems to imply that history repeats itself in a succession of cycles. (Introduction II 7 (i)).

13 **ipsum** : *i.e.* God.

14 **paene prehenderit** : 'has almost grasped'.

15 **unis** : . . **moenibus**=*unius urbis moenibus.* MSS. are corrupt:
unis makes tolerable sense.

popularem . . . : 'a native of one fixed place'.

16 **civem totius mundi** : see Note on XXXV 20.

17 **ille** : picks up *animus* (line 1).

18 **quam se ipse noscet** : 'how it will come to know itself'.

19 **quod** : the clause is parenthetical. The antecedent, sc. *id*,
refers to the preceding clause. Trans. '(the duty) which the
oracle of Apollo (Pythius) enjoins'. The reference is to the
famous precept inscribed on the temple of Apollo at Delphi,
γνῶθι σεαυτόν (know thyself).

21 **haec omnia** : 'all these truths'.

quasi . . . **vallabit** : 'will hedge round as with a fence'. The
Stoics compared philosophy with a fertile field, of which the
produce was ethics, the land and trees physics, and the hedge
logic.

22 **disserendi ratione** : 'the theory of argument', 'logic', which
deals with the means by which the mind attains truth.

veri . . . **scientia** : 'the science of distinguishing truth from
falsehood'.

23 **arte** . . . **contrarium** : 'the art of deducing what follows from
a given premiss and what is contrary to it'.

24 **civilem societatem** : 'the life of society'.

25 **illa subtili disputatione** : 'the precise method of logical
argument'.

26 **fusa** . . . **oratione** : 'the more expansive (*fusa latius*) style of
continuous (*perpetua*) speech'. The contrast is between dialectic,
or 'question and answer' argument, common in Plato's dialogues,
and oratory with its continuous exposition.

27 **qua regat populos** : lit. 'by means of which (eloquence) it
(the mind) may rule nations'.

The argument is that, to be effective in the world of affairs,
the mind which is in possession of the truth needs the support of
eloquence, which will enable it to govern (*qua regat populos*),
legislate (*stabiliat leges*), penalise vice and protect virtue (*castiget
improbos, tueatur bonos*), and 'praise famous men', *i.e.* pronounce
laudatory orations: *cp.* Cicero's panegyric on Sulpicius (VII).

29 **praecepta salutis et laudis** : 'advice advantageous to their welfare and good name'.

apte ad persuadendum : 'in a manner designed to convince'.

edat : 'publish, issue'.

30 **decus** : 'personal honour'.

32 **cum . . . ignominia** : 'as well as the disgrace of the wicked'.

monumentis : 'literary records'.

XXXVII

1 **ingeniis** : 'dispositions', 'natures'.

quae : belongs only to the *si*– clause, *natura* being subject of *perduceret. quae . . . adolescere*: acc. and inf. after *liceret*, a normal construction.

2 **natura** : *i.e.* the natural constitution of man, which is assumed to be good. The question Cicero is trying to answer is why, assuming the natural goodness of men, the majority become corrupt. It is the same question which Plato asks in *Rep.* 490 d, τί ποθ' οἱ πολλοὶ κακοί; 'Why are most men bad?' Like Plato, Cicero blames environment, teachers, poets and society.

3 **nunc autem** : after an unreal condition, this formula signifies what is, as opposed to what might have been: 'But as things are'. **editi in lucem** : 'have seen the light', *i.e.* been born.

4 **suscepti** : sc. *a patribus*. When the father 'took up' a newly born child, he acknowledged it as a member of the family.

continuo : 'at once'.

5 **versamur** : 'find ourselves amid'.

6 **suxisse** : 'to have imbibed'.

cum . . . tum : 'no sooner than'. See Note 8(*a*).

7 **imbuimur** : 'we are infected'.

8 **vanitati** : 'falsehood'.

opinioni confirmatae : 'established prejudices'.

9 **cedat** : 'gives way to'.

poetae : This recalls Plato's attack on the poets, among them Homer, as teachers of immorality, and his exclusion of inferior poets from his ideal state (*Rep.* III 398).

magnam . . . tulerunt : 'make a great show'.

12 **eodem** : lit. 'to the same place', 'also'.

quasi . . . populus . 'the multitude, like some great professor'. In Plato (*Rep.* 492 b.), the false teacher is, above all, the people gathered in assembly, court, and theatre, where everything is done in clamour and excess, so that the individual is overwhelmed and cannot help accepting the false opinions of the majority. The problem, and it is a modern one, is: How far must the man of principle, if he is to be true to himself, be anti-democratic?

15 **naturae . . . videantur** : 'we think the true meaning of nature has been best understood by those who . . .'

16 **qui** : see Note 4(*e*).

17 **honoribus . . . gloria** : 'civil offices, military commands, and popular acclaim', *e.g.* demagogues, like Clodius, and *imperatores*, like Marius and Caesar are no doubt meant.

18 **ad quam** (sc. *gloriam*) **fertur** : 'to this the best among us are attracted'.

19 **honestatem** : 'virtue'. **expetens** : concessive, 'although they aim at'.

quam unam natura anquirit : 'which is the one thing nature above all pursues'.

20 **in summa inanitate versatur** : 'find the search completely futile'. *inanitas*: 'emptiness, futility'.

21 **effigiem** : In this sentence and the beginning of the next, there is a metaphor drawn from art, in which a marble or bronze statue is contrasted with a drawing or sketch. The former is an *effigies* (a moulded form), *solida* (substantial or tangible), and *expressa* (sharply delineated or chiselled), whereas the latter is a mere *imago* (sketch or outline), *adumbrata* (roughly or obscurely 'shadowed forth'). Trans. 'pursue no lofty model of virtue, but a mere counterfeit image of glory. For (true) glory is no mere shadowy sketch, but a real lifelike figure'.

23 **consentiens laus bonorum** : 'the general approbation of good men'.

24 **excellenti virtute** : 'outstanding merit'.

ea virtuti . . . imago : lit. 'answers to virtue as an echo (to the voice)'. Trans. 'it is, as it were, virtue's echo'.

25 **quae** : *i.e.* true fame.

26 **illa** : with *fama popularis* below, *i.e.* counterfeit fame.

27 **quae . . . vult** : 'which attempts to counterfeit true fame. See Note 4(*c*).

imitatricem : The termination –*trix*, fem. of –*tor*, is confined to a few nouns in Latin prose. Cicero uses it several times in this and the next passage.

29 **simulatione honestatis** : 'by a false assumption of honour'.

30 **qua caecitate** : 'blinded by this'.   Probably a causal abl.

31 **cum . . . cuperent . . . nescirent** : 'aiming at noble objects, but not knowing . . .'   **eaque** : see Note 7.

33 **occiderunt** : N.B. quantity: lit. 'have fallen'.   Trans. 'have brought about their own ruin'.

   atque hi quidem : 'these, it is true', contrasts with *qui* in next sentence.   See Note 8(*e*).

34 **nom tam voluntate quam cursus errore** : 'not so much by intention as by an error in direction'.

35 **qui** : antecedent *his* below *Cp.* Note 4(*b*).

38 **noceant . . . possint . . . sit** : the subjs. are due to the fact that the *quod*–clauses give alternative reasons, which are both rejected.

39 **corpora . . . possint, animorum . . . sit** : for asyndeton see Note 1(*b*).   Trans. 'because, while the body can be cured, there is no medicine for the mind'.   A similar thought appears in the Greek poet, Theognis, about 550 B.C.:

εἰ δ' Ἀσκληπιάδαις τοῦτό γ' ἔδωκε θεός,
ἰᾶσθαι κακότητα καὶ ἀτηρὰς Φρένας ἀνδρῶν,
πολλοὺς ἂν μίσθους καὶ μεγάλους ἔφερον.

If God had given the sons of Asclepius the power to heal the wickedness and perverse minds of men, many and great would have been their rewards.

42 **foris** : 'outside ourselves'.

43 **ut . . . possimus** : governed by *elaborandum est* below.

XXXVIII

1 **indagatrix, expultrix** : only here in Cicero.   N.B. feminine forms in *–trix*.   Trans. 'thou that searchest out virtue, and banishest vice'.

5 **litterarum et vocum communione** : 'by mutual sharing in the written and the spoken word'.

7 **disciplinae** : 'morality'.

9 **est autem unus dies . . .** : the tone of religious veneration in which philosophy is addressed is remarkable.   *Cp. Psalm* LXXXIV 10:—

A day in Thy courts is better than a thousand. I had rather be a door-keeper in the house of my God than to dwell in the tents of wickedness.

ex praeceptis tuis : 'in accordance with thy teaching'.

10 **peccanti immortalitati** : 'an eternity of wrong-doing'.

11 **utamur** : deliberative subj., 'should we use?'
quae : antecedent *tu*, understood from *tuis*.

XXXIX

1 **libri nostri** : *i.e.* his philosophical works.

3 **bonis viris** : 'worthy persons', practical Romans, who have more regard for action than for speculation and fear that Greek thought may corrupt the Roman character. This attitude was traditional. As late as 155 B.C., three Greek philosophers, Carneades, Diogenes and Critolaus, who had come to Rome on an embassy, were not allowed to lecture and were expelled by a decree of the Senate. Cicero feels the need to defend himself against the charge of being un-Roman.

5 **quam diu . . . commiserat** : 'as long as the state was governed by rulers appointed by itself', *i.e.* while the republican constitution lasted.

7 **dominatu unius** : the dictatorship of Julius Caesar, dead at the time Cicero was writing in the latter half of 44 B.C. Elsewhere in the *De Officiis* Cicero openly condemns Caesar as a tyrant (XVI 16).

8 **consilio aut auctoritati** : 'public debate or free decision', *i.e.* in the Senate.

9 **socios tuendae rei publicae** : 'associates in the defence of the constitution', *i.e.* the Republic.

10 **angoribus** : note plur. 'fits of depression'.

11 **rursum** : 'on the other hand'.

13 **homines** : Cicero is thinking not only of Caesar and the whole Civil War period, but especially of Marcus Antonius who, now, after Caesar's death, has emerged as the enemy of the constitution.
tam . . . quam : 'so much . . . as'.

16 **poneremus** : 'I should now have been devoting'. The imp.

subj. in an unreal condition often denotes continuance of the action into the present.

17 **ipsis scriptis** : dat. after *mandaremus*. With *ea quae nunc* supply *mando*. Trans. 'the theme of such writings as I did produce would not have been philosophy, as it now is, but, as so often in the past, my own political activities (*actiones*)', *i.e.* he would have been writing speeches, not philosophical works.

18 **res publica** : the common interest of all the citizens, the state as a political body, may also mean the form of government or constitution of a state, or simply politics.

For Cicero, the *res publica*, to which he had devoted his life, meant the Roman republican constitution, in which political power was harmoniously divided between senate, magistrates and people, and which could only be maintained by agreement between all parties. But this *concordia ordinum*, which was Cicero's ideal, had been made impossible by the rise of great military commanders, like Caesar and Pompey, resulting in civil war and the despotism of one man. The dictatorship of Caesar had prevented all normal political life, the *res publica* had been destroyed, speech had been silenced, and there was nothing left but retirement into the study of philosophy.

19 **cura, cogitatio, opera** : 'all my ambitions, thoughts, and efforts'. For asyndeton, see Note 1(*a*).

20 **nulla esset omnino** : 'had altogether ceased to exist'. Note emphatic *nulla*, used as predicate.

illae scilicet litterae . . . senatoriae : 'silence naturally (*scilicet*) fell upon all our (*illae*) eloquence, whether in the courts or in the House'.

21 **nihil agere** : 'be inactive'.

22 **animus** : 'disposition, inclination'.

in his studiis : *i.e.* the study of philosophy.

ab initio . . . aetatis : Cicero had begun his career as a student of Greek thought. (See Introduction III.)

25 **honoribus inservire** : 'to be tied to the duties of office'.

26 **meque . . . tradidi** : 'devoted myself entirely to a political career'.

tantum . . . temporibus : 'there was only as much time for philosophy as was left over from the needs of my friends and the state', *i.e.* from the defence of his friends in court, and from politics. *tempora* often means 'times of distress or necessity'.

28 **id autem . . . non erat** : for chiasmus. see Note 1(*c*).

30 **hoc . . . boni** (partitive gen.) . . . **ut** : 'this much good that'.

31 **nec . . . et** : see Note 8(c).

nostris : 'to our people'. Cicero claims that he is doing a public service in making Greek philosophy known to his contemporaries.

34 **qui** : = (ii) *qui*. See Note 4(e).

36 **interpretari** : 'translate'. *Studium sapientiae* is given as the Latin equivalent for the Greek φιλοσοφία, which etymologically means 'love of wisdom'.

37 **veteribus philosophis** : used rather loosely. The definition actually given probably comes from Posidonius (Introduction II 8). σοφία (*sapientia*), speculative wisdom, defined here as the knowledge of all things and their causes, was distinguished by Aristotle and the Stoics from φρόνησις (*prudentia*), practical wisdom, knowledge of what is useful in life.

39 **continentur** : 'depend'.

qui : antecedent, *is* understood, subj. of *putet*. See Notes 4(e) and 7.

XL

1 **munus** : 'a present from me', *i.e.* the three books of the *De Officiis*, which Cicero is sending to Marcus.

2 **perinde . . . acceperis** : 'it will be just as great as your use of it makes it'; *acceperis*: fut. perf.

quamquam : co-ordinating, 'and yet'.

3 **Cratippi commentarios** : 'your notes of Cratippus' lectures'. Cratippus was then head of the Peripatetic school at Athens.

4 **ut** : 'as', answered by *sic* below. The subjs. are conditional.

5 **e medio cursu** : After the murder of Caesar, Cicero was uncertain as to his course. In July, 44 B.C., he left Rome for Greece, but, on his ship being driven back, he decided to return and take sides against Antony.

6 **aliquando** : 'by now'. **audires** : 'you would have been hearing me in person (*me quoque*)'.

7 **his voluminibus** : 'through these rolls (books)'.

9 **cum vero intellexero** : 'as soon as I hear from you'.

hoc scientiae genere : Cicero is anxious about Marcus'

behaviour, and thinks that a treatise on morals will do him good.

10 **gaudere** : 'are interested'. **propediem** : 'very shortly'.

12 **tibi persuade** : 'be assured'. **te quidem** : see Note 8(*e*).

XLI

1 **id quod erat** : 'as was indeed the fact'.

2 **Tusculanum** : sc. *agrum*, his estate at Tusculum, about 15 miles south of Rome.

3 **Formianum** : the town of Formiae was on the Via Appia, about 70 miles south of Rome, near the mouth of the river Liris. Close by was the harbour of Caieta.

   ut . . . conscensurus : 'with the intention of taking ship'. An imitation of the Greek ὡς with the fut. participle, not used by Cicero.

4 **modo . . . modo** : 'at one time . . . at another'.

5 **iactationem** : 'tossing'.

7 **superiorem** : 'previous', *i.e.* the villa he had just left.

10 **quod** : sc. *id*.

11 **prominenti** : sc. *ei*, dat. of disadvantage.

13 **scripsisse** : sc. *eas*. **in Antonium** : refers to the *Philippic Orations*.

14 **exprobrantes** : 'reproaching'.

16 **consularis** : 'as ex-consul'.

17 **quanta . . . vox** : Rather loosely constructed: supply *audita fuerat* with *vox*. Trans. 'he had been heard, as no other human voice had ever been, speaking with an eloquence that astonished his hearers'.

EPILOGUE

This piece is by Velleius Paterculus, who lived in the reign of Tiberius (14–36 A.D.), and wrote two books of a history of Rome up to his own time. The context is an attack on Antony.

1 **rapuisti** : subject M. Antonius. The simple verb is constructed like *eripio*, with acc. and dat.

2 **vitam** . . . **mortem** : 'a life more unhappy under your sole rule than death under your triumvirate'.

4 **adeo non** . . . **ut** : 'so far from . . . that'.

6 **utcumque** : adv., 'in whatever way'.   A post-Ciceronian use.

8 **quod** . . . **illuminavit** : see Note 1(*a*).

9 **comitem aevi sui** : 'as long as it exists'.

10 **trahet** : 'will prolong'.   **illius** . . . **tuum** : see Note 1(*b*).

12 **cedet** : 'will disappear'.

NOTES ON
SOME POINTS OF CICERONIAN STYLE

1. ASYNDETON. This is the absence of conjunctions between co-ordinate clauses, phrases, or words, the precise connection being inferred from the order of words and the general sense. This is one of the most marked features of Cicero's style and a knowledge of it is essential for the understanding of many sentences. It is of two main types:

(a) *Copulative:* —*que* or *et* are omitted between nouns, adjectives, and verbs.

    e.g. *Nos flumina arcemus, derigimus, avertimus.* (XXXIV 83)
    We dam, direct, *and* divert rivers.

(b) *Adversative:* *sed, autem, vero,* etc., are omitted between contrasting clauses, the antithesis being indicated only by the contrasting words.

    e.g. *Quales sint, varium est, esse nemo negat.* (XXX 3)
    The nature of the gods is disputed,
    but no one denies their existence.

    or

    Although the nature of the gods is
    disputed, no one denies their existence.

    Observe the balance: *quales sint* is contrasted with *esse, varium est* with *nemo negat.*

    Tribuo illis litteras, do multarum artium disciplinam, non adimo sermonis leporem, ingeniorum acumen, dicendi copiam . . . testimoniorum religionem et fidem nunquam ista natio coluit. . . . (XII 11–15)

    Literature I grant them, I concede them distinction in many branches of learning, I do not refuse them charm of language, acuteness of intellect, and eloquence . . . *but,* as a nation they have never regarded the sacred and binding obligation of sworn evidence. . . .

N.B. Both types of asyndeton are illustrated in this sentence.

(c) *Chiasmus* (from the Greek letter Chi), is a type of balance between two clauses, often combined with Asyndeton, in which the order of words of the second clause reverses that of the first.

e.g.   *Id autem omne consumebatur in legendo,*
        scribendi otium non erat. (XXXIX 28–29)

   All this time was spent in reading;
   for writing I had no leisure.

N.B.   Observe that in asyndeton generally, the place of the omitted conjunction is often indicated in modern texts by a comma, colon or semi-colon.

2. HENDIADYS.   This figure consists in using a pair of words to represent a complex idea.   A pair of nouns may stand for a noun and an adjective in English, or a pair of verbs for a verb and an adverb;   e.g. *vi et armis*, 'by armed force'; *orare et obsecrare*, 'to beg earnestly'; *alia vita et natura*, 'another sphere of existence'. (II 18.)

   Notice how often Cicero uses double verbs.   This is sometimes not true hendiadys, but due to a fondness for repetition.

3. USE OF ABSTRACT NOUNS.   An abstract noun with a genitive is sometimes used for a noun and an adjective.

e.g.   *novitatem nominis* = *nomen novum.* (II 6)
        the novel name.

        fontium gelidas perennitates = *fontes gelidos perennes.*
                                                         (XXXII 5)
        cool, unfailing springs
               or
        fountains with unfailing coolness.

   In the last example, there is also a transfer of the epithet (hypallage): *gelidas* is made to agree with *perennitates* instead of the noun to which it properly belongs (*fontium*).

4. USE OF THE PRONOUN *IS*

(a)   *Is* is often emphatic when it anticipates a relative clause.

   e.g.   *Solitudo erat ea quam volueramus.* (XI 9–10)
           There was just that seclusion we had wanted.

(b)   *Is* is also emphatic when it resumes a preceding relative clause.

   e.g.   *Qui ingenuis studiis delectantur, nonne videmus* eos *nec valetudinis nec rei familiaris habere rationem?* (I 9–10)

           Do we not observe that it is those who have a real interest in the higher learning who have no regard for health or private affairs?

Quasque res violentissimas *natura genuit,* earum *moderationem nos soli habemus.*   (XXXIV 75–77)

We alone have control of the most violent forces nature has created.

N.B. The noun antecedent is incorporated in the relative clause itself.   The normal order would be: earum rerum violentissimarum, quas. . . .

   (*c*) *Is* is sometimes separated from its noun by an intervening relative clause.

     e.g. . . . *propter* eum, *quem sibi ipse opinionis errore finxerat,* principatum. . . .   (XV 15–16)

     . . . for the sake of that ascendancy which he had mistakenly made his ideal. . . .

   (*d*) *Is* introducing a Relative or *ut* Clause with the Subjunctive = *talis.*

     e.g. *Aliorum* ea *est humilitas, ut cibum terrestrem rostris facile contingant.*   (XXXIII 21)

     So low is the stature of others, that they can easily reach food at ground level with their beaks.

   (*e*) Antecedent *is* is sometimes omitted, especially when it has the same case as the Relative.

     e.g. *Hanc igitur qui expetunt* (*ii*) *philosophi nominantur.*
                            (XXXIX 34)
     Therefore those who seek this wisdom are called philosophers.

   (*f*) Emphatic *et is, isque* (*idemque, et idem*), add a quality or a qualification.

     e.g. *Vetus opinio est iam usque ab heroicis ducta temporibus, eaque et populi Romani et omnium gentium firmata consensu.* . . .
                            (XXVI 1–3)
     It is an ancient tradition dating from the Heroic Age, and one which is confirmed by the agreement of the Roman People and of all mankind.

   5. *HOC, ILLUD* often resume or anticipate a dependent clause, especially *quod* with Indicative or Acc. and Inf.

     e.g. *Sed inter hominem ac beluam* hoc *maxime interest quod* . . .
                            (III 7–8)
     Between man and animals there is this great difference that . . .

6. *QUI* WITH THE SUBJUNCTIVE

(*a*) Expressing a *characteristic or quality* of the antecedent, or the class to which it belongs. The antecedent itself is often negative. The Subjunctive is usually Consecutive, but sometimes approaches a Final meaning.

> e.g. *Nemo est tam stultus qui non intellegat.* (XVIII 6–7)
>
> There is no one so foolish as not to understand.
>
> *Nihil est quod moneam vos.* (XVIII 6)
>
> There is no exhortation I can give you, no need for me to warn you.

(*b*) Causal

> e.g. *Noli ex me quaerere, qui in Phalericum etiam descenderim.*
>
> (XI 31–32)
>
> Do not ask me, as I have actually been down to Phalerum.

7. PROLEPTIC ORDER IN INDIRECT QUESTIONS. The subject of the Indirect Question is taken out and put before the interrogative either remaining in the Nominative or being made object of the main verb.

> e.g. *Satis docuisse videor, hominis natura quanto omnes anteiret animantes.* (XXXV 11–12)
>
> I think I have made clear as regards human beings, how far they surpass all creatures.

A similar order is found also with relative clauses, e.g. *cuius studium qui vituperat.* (XXXIX 39)

8. VARIOUS CONJUNCTIONS

(*a*) *cum . . . tum* with Ind., when the verbs are different ='at the time when.' (N.B. *tum* often precedes *cum*.)

> e.g. *Cum ergo est somno sevocatus animus a societate corporis, tum meminit praeteritorum.* (XXVIII 1, 2)
>
> It is when the soul is dissociated from the body in sleep that it remembers the past.

Sometimes there is more or less adversative force.

> e.g. *Colles enim sunt, qui cum perflantur ipsi, tum afferunt umbram vallibus.* (XIV 64–65)
>
> There are hills, which, while windswept themselves, provide shelter for the valleys.

(b) *cum . . . tum (etiam, vero)* followed by the same verb = 'both
  . . . and, not only . . . but also.'

> e.g.   *. . . cum Romuli tum etiam reliquorum regum sapientia
> definitus.* (XIV 55)
> . . . . marked out by the wisdom of Romulus as well as
> of the other kings.

This meaning may also occur when the verbs are different.

(c) *nec . . . et (–que)* 'on the one hand not . . . but on the other;
  not only not . . . but also.'   Note that the second clause
  has an adversative sense.   Fairly frequent in Cicero.

> e.g.   *. . . quae nec erant satis nota nostris et erant cognitione
> dignissima.* (XXXIX 31–32)
> . . . matters comparatively unknown to our people, yet
> eminently worth knowing.

(d) *autem.*   Common in Cicero.

  (i) Carries on the narrative or introduces an explanation.

> e.g.   *Pythagoram autem Phliuntem ferunt venisse.* (II 1)
> Now they say that P. came to Phlius.

  (ii) More or less adversative, sometimes no more than a weak
    'but', 'whereas', 'while', etc.

> e.g.   *. . . ut alii . . . gloriam . . . peterent, alii emendi quaestu . . .
> ducerentur, esset autem quoddam genus. . . .* (II 11–13)
> Just as some sought fame, and others were attracted by
> profit, *while* there was another class . . .

(e) *quidem.*

  (i) Emphasises or modifies the preceding word, *e.g.* in such
    combinations as *cum quidem*, 'when indeed'; *qui quidem*,
    'who indeed, at any rate'; *si quidem*, 'if indeed'; almost
    'since'.

  (ii) Often concessive, 'indeed'. 'it is true', balanced by *autem*,
    vero, sed . . .

> e.g.   *. . . tibi persuade esse te quidem mihi carissimum, sed multo fore
> cariorem, si talibus monitis praeceptisque laetabere.*
>   (XL 12–13)
> Be assured that, you are indeed most dear to me, but
> that you will be still dearer, if you accept the moral
> principles I advocate.

SELECT VOCABULARY

(1) Note that this vocabulary gives a selected number of useful abstract or philosophical terms of frequent occurrence. The more unusual words are explained in the Notes.

(2) References to Text and Notes are by number of extract and line.

(3) Only such quantities as are especially useful or liable to confusion are marked.

(4) The meaning of many derived nouns may be inferred from the verb or adj. from which they are formed; *e.g.* from the supine stem:

Nouns in –TOR and –SOR (3.m.), –TRIX (f.), denoting the doer of the action: *victor, victrix* (*vinco*), conqueror; *laudatrix* (*laudo*), she who praises.

Nouns in –TUS, –SUS, (4.m.), denoting the action itself: *mōtus* (*mŏveo*), a movement; *cursus* (*curro*), a running, race.

Nouns in –TIO, –SIO (3.f.), abstract, denoting the action itself apart from the doer: *vectio* (*veho*), transport; *mōtio* (*mŏveo*), motion.

Nouns in –TAS, –TUDO (3.f.), abstract, denoting a quality apart from its possessor: *lībertas* (*lĭber*), freedom; *multitūdo* (*multi*), large number.

abrŏgo (1) : annul (a law) (XXI 5 Note).

aciēs, -ei (*f*) : sharp edge; piercing look, power of vision (XXXIV 22).

actio, -onis(*f*) : action; public action; legal action; *litium actiones*, law suits (VII 41); way of life (V 91); *actiones nostras*, my political activities (XXXIX 17).

actus, -ūs (*m*) : act (of a play).

acūmen, -inis (*n*) : acuteness of intellect, shrewdness (XII 12).

adumbratus, -a, -um : sketched; vague, dim (XXXVII 21 Note).

aegrōtatio, -onis (*f*) : sickness, disease (of body or mind) (XXXVII 38).

aemulus, -i (*m*): rival; imitator (IX 5).

aequābilis, -e : uniform, regular; of a river (XIV 44).

aequabilitas, -atis (*f*) : regularity; of the revolutions of the heavenly bodies (XXX 23).

aequālis, -e : equal, of the same age, contemporary (V 13).

aequĭtas, -atis (*f*) : 1. justice, in the sense of fairness; justice governed by benevolence, as opposed to strict *iustitia*, which grants only what is due (VII 41); coupled with *fides* (XVI 7).

2. sometimes used for *iustitia*, e.g. *belli aequitas*, the rules of war (XIX 22).

āēr, -is (*m*) (*acc. sing.* āĕrā) : air, atmosphere close to the earth (XXXII 26).

aeternus, -a, -um : eternal, without beginning or end, beyond time; (of the soul) immortal (XXV 247).

aethĕr, -is (*m*) (*acc. sing.* aethĕra) : upper air; realm of the heavenly bodies (XXXII 34).

aevum, -i (*n*) : age, lifetime, generation; *aevum sempiternum*, eternal life, immortality (XXV 57).

aliēnus, -a, -um : belonging to another; foreign to; unsuitable; unfavourable (XVII 2).

amoenitas, -atis (*f*) : loveliness, charm (of scenery) (XIV 36).

amplificatio, -onis (*f*) : enlargement, increase, *e.g.* of personal property (XV 9).

amplificator, -oris (*m*) : one who extends, *e.g.* philosophy (II 26).

amplitūdo, -ĭnis (*f*) : vastness, greatness; high rank; (of caves) (XXXII 7).

amplus, -a, -um : spacious; splendid; illustrious.

anfractus, -ūs (*m*) : turning, circuit, revolution (of stars) (XXV 44).

anima, (*f*) : breath; physical life, common to animals and men.

animal, -alis (*n*) : living being, animal (including man).

animans, -antis (*m* or *f*) : living thing.

animus, -i (*m*) : intellect; mind (IV 2); personality; soul, distinct from the body, possessed by man alone (XXVIII 1 Note); defiled by the body (XXV 259); identified with 'God' (XXV 224); immortal (XXV 228 ff.); spirit, energy, courage (XV 3); *magnitudo animi*, greatness of soul (VI 11 Note); inclination (XXXIX 22).

appetitus, -ūs (*m*) : desire, longing for; appetite (XXXIII 14).

appulsus, -ūs (*m*) : impulse; influence; *deorum appulsus*, divine inspiration (XXVIII 15).

aptus, -a, -um : fit, suitable (for), e.g. *pastus*, food (XXXIII 13); *lit.* fastened to, depending on (*abl.*) (V 57).

aquilo, -onis (*m*) : north wind; north; *cingulus subiectus Aquiloni*: zone lying towards the north, the northern temperate zone of the earth (XXV 162 Note).

ars, artis (*f*) : skill; handicraft; profession; art; knowledge; artificial means (opp. *natura*); (pl.) *bonae artes*, liberal arts, cultured studies, education (I 9, and XII 11 Notes).

artifex, -icis (*m*) : craftsman, artist; maker, contriver (XXXI 6).

artificium, -ii (*n*) : skill, art; trade; trick.

artūs (*pl. m*) : limbs, joints.

artūs, -a, -um : tight, close; deep (of sleep) (XXV 19).

astrum, -i (*n*) : star.

auctor, -oris (*m*) : originator; one who sanctions or authorises; adviser, supporter; writer, historian.

auctōritas, -atis (*f*) : authority, influence, dignity, weight; authority of position or personality *e.g.* of the *pater familias* over his household (XXII 5); moral influence (VI 21); warrant, credibility (of a witness) (XII 16); historical authority (XXVI 11).

augur, -ŭris (*m*) : diviner, augur (XXVI 31).

augŭror (1) : foretell (by interpretation of omens).

auspĭcium, -ii (*n*) : auspices, divination from the flight of birds (XXVI 33 Note).

auspĭcor (1) : to take the auspices; *auspicato*, after taking the auspices.

auster, ri (*m*) : south wind (XXV 178), south.

australis, -e : southern; *cingulus australis*, the southern temperate zone (XXV 167).

beatus, -a, -um : happy, fortunate; perfectly happy, blessed (VIII 4); *vita beata*, the blessed life of the Stoic wise man (\ III 20); *beati*, the blessed dead (XXV 57).

beneficium, -ii (*n*) : an act of kindness; service.

benevolentia, -ae (*f*) : goodwill.

bŏnitas, -atis (*f*) : goodness, excellence, virtue; *bonitas naturae*, natural goodness (IV 20).

bŏnus, -a, -um : good; honest, virtuous; noble; loyal, patriotic; *vir bonus*, a man morally good, possessing all the virtues; *boni* (*viri*), sound, loyal citizens (XXV 48 Note), sometimes ironical, *e.g.* 'respectable' citizens, suspicious of philosophers (XXXIX 3); *consentiens laus bonorum*, the unanimous approval of good citizens (XXXVII 23); *bono animo esse*, be of good cheer; be well disposed (towards); (as noun) *bonum -i* (n), physical or moral good, advantage; =*honestum*, virtue (VIII 3); (plur.) *bona*, prosperity; property (XVI 14); good qualities; *in bonis habere*, reckon as 'good' (XXIII 24).

caelestis, -e : of the heavens, heavenly; (pl.) *caelestes*, the gods of the upper world.

caelĭtes, -um (*m pl*) : dwellers in the heavens, stars, gods (XXV 7).

caerimōnia, -ae (*f*) : outward veneration of the gods; sacred rite, religious ceremony.

calămitosus, -a, -um : (of things) ruinous; (of persons) unfortunate (IX 22).

cāritas, -atis (*f*) : esteem; affection, love (XVII 23 Note); *patriae caritas*, patriotism (XX 19).

causa, -ae (*f*) : that which produces an effect, cause; *causae rerum*, the causes of events (III 12); *semen et causa civilium bellorum*, the root cause (*lit.* seed and cause) of civil wars (XVI 29); cause (which one defends); law-suit (XXII 15); *in meliore causa esse*, to have the better cause, to be in a better position (VI 27); *causa indicta*, without a hearing (XX 7); business, commission (VII 8).

censor -oris (*m*) : censor, a Roman magistrate, who, among other powers, had the duty of revising the roll of senators and of expelling unworthy members.

cingŭlus, -i (*m*) : girdle; zone of the earth (XXV 163).

circŭĭtus, -ūs (*m*) : circuit, revolution.

circŭlus, -i (*m*) : circle, orbit.

cīvīlis, -e : belonging to a citizen; *civilis societas*, community, society of citizens, state (XXXVI 24); *bellum civile*, war between citizens, civil war (XVI 29); *ius civile*, law relating to the rights of citizens (VII 40).

cīvitas, -atis (*f*) : state (XXV 60 Note), body of citizens; city; citizenship (XIX 9).

clientēla, -ae (*f*) : relation of client (*cliens*) and patron (*patronus*), see **patrocinium**; (in concrete sense) clients, dependents.

coetus, -ūs (*m*) : assembly, crowd, company (=*concilium*) (XXV 59).

cōgitatio, -onis (*f*) : deliberation, thought, reflection, design (IV 2).

cognatio, -onis (*f*) : blood-relationship, kinship; (of things) natural connection, resemblance.

cognĭtio, -onis (*f*) : learning to know; knowledge.

cognomen, -inis (*n*) : family name; surname; additional title e.g. *Africanus*.

colōnia, -ae (*f*) : colony, settlement in Italy or the provinces, usually of Roman citizens, closely related to Rome, and governed on the Roman model.

commentarius, -ii (*m*) : note-book; notes; (*pl*) memoirs.

commentatio, -onis (*f*) : diligent meditation, careful preparation.

commentor (1 *dep.*) : think over; study; prepare (mentally).

commŏditas, -atis (*f*) : advantage; convenience (abstr.) (XIV 38).

commŏdum, -i (*n*) : an advantage (XXXIV 79).

commūnio, -onis (*f*) : sharing together, mutual participation: *communio litterarum et vocum*, sharing a common literature and language (XXXVIII 5.)

compăro (1) : (from adj. *compar*, equal) to put on a level with, compare.

compăro (1) : (from *parare*, prepare) to prepare, arrange, obtain.

concĭdo, -ĕre, -cĭdi, -īsum : (from *caedo*) cut down, kill.

concĭdo, -ĕre, -cĭdi : (from *cădo*) fall down; be killed; decay, go to ruin (XXV 244).

concretus, -a, -um : grown together, massed, concentrated; *aer concretus in nubes*, air condensed into clouds (XXXII 28).

condĭcio, -onis (*f*) : state, position, circumstances; agreement, condition, terms.

conflo (1) : fuse together; *una ex duabus naturis conflata*, two elements (sea and land) fused into one (XXXII 26); cause, bring about; devise.

conglŏbo (1) : to mass together into a spherical shape.

congruens, -entis : agreeing; harmonious; consistent with (XIII 10).

coniectura, -ae (*f*) : interpretation; of a dream (XXVII 31).

coniunctio, -onis (*f*) : union; relationship (of man with the gods) (XX 25).

consectio, -onis (*f*) : cutting, hewing.

consequens, -entis (*noun n*) : consequence; necessary result; effect (of a cause) (III 12).

constans, -antis : firm, regular, consistent.

constantia, -ae (*f*) : constancy, perseverance, firmness of character, steadfastness, self-possession (VII 31); consistency.

contemplatio, -onis (*f*) : observation; contemplation; disinterested study of the world; philosophy (II 23).

continens, -entis (*adj.*) : continuous, unbroken; (noun f. sc. *terra*) mainland, land frontier.

continentia, -ae (*f*) : restraint of passions or desires, temperance; moderation.

continuatio, -onis (*f*) : unbroken succession.

contractio, -onis (*f*) : contraction (*e.g.* of fingers) (XXXIV 46).

contrarius, -a, -um : contrary, opposed (to); (noun) *contrarium -ii* (*n*), the opposite, the contrary (of) (XXXVI 24).

conversio, -onis (*f*) : revolution (of heavens).

corpus, -ŏris (*n*) : body; as distinct from the soul, see **animus**; moved and controlled by the soul (XXV 229); less beautiful than the soul (VIII 12); prison (*carcer*) of the soul (XXV 66); defiles and contaminates the soul (XXV 259 Note); its wonderful structure (XXXIV); (pl) *corpora*, atoms, according to the Epicureans, an infinite number of indivisible particles falling through infinite space (XXXII 60 Note).

cultus, ūs (*m*) : cultivation; *agrorum cultus*, agriculture; *cultus et victus*, civilised manner of life (III 21); culture, elegance, refinement; civilisation; *cultus deorum*, worship of the gods, religion (XXXVI 6).

curriculum, -i (*n*) : course; race-track; *curricula mentis*, training grounds of the mind (XXII 20).

cursus, -ūs (*m*) : running; course; way; speed; orbit of a heavenly body (XXV 107).

dĕcet (*impers.*) : it is seemly, suitable, fitting, proper (IV 1 Note).

decŏrus, -a, -um : becoming, suitable; *venas ad ornatum decoras*, veins (of metal) for fashioning ornaments (XXXIV 69).

dĕcus, -ŏris (*n*) : 1. ornament; splendour; glory; honour (XXXVI 30). 2. moral dignity, virtue (= *bonum, honestum*).

dēdĕcus, -ŏris (*n*) : dishonour, disgrace; moral dishonour; dishonourable deed.

dēfectio, -onis (*f*) : eclipse of sun or moon.

dērogo (1) : take away, detract from (XII 4); diminish, modify (a law) (XXI 5 Note).

determinatio, -onis (*f*) : boundary (of the universe) (XXXII 35 Note).

dĕus, -i (m) : (sing.) a god; sometimes vaguely used, when the speaker does not care to identify any particular god; (plur.) the gods of ancient polytheism; *ille princeps deus*, the supreme 'God' of philosophy (XXV 58; 224 Note); one divine power or mind ruling the universe, vaguely monotheistic, but scarcely personal (XXX 3 and 33 Note); the immanent god, the principle of life, pervading all things, shared by, and even identified with the individual soul; *scito te deum esse* (XXV 224 Note).

dictator, -oris (m) : dictator, a Roman magistrate (XXV 49 Note).

diffusus, -a, -um : spread abroad; extending over.

dignitas, -atis (f) : distinction, authority, rank (VI 10); excellence, worth.

disceptatio, -onis (f) : discussion (XIX 2).

disceptator, -oris (m) : arbitrator, judge (XXI 13).

discepto (1) : debate, dispute, argue (*de* + abl.).

disciplīna, -ae (f) : teaching, instruction; *disciplina multarum artium*, training in many branches of learning, wide education (XII 11); discipline, *e.g.* parental (IV 21); system *e.g.* of the haruspices (XXVI 35); doctrines, system of philosophy (II 29); way of life (XIV 25); order of the universe (XXX 28).

dīscrībo (3) : to copy, represent, sketch; divide, arrange in order.

dīscriptio, -onis (f) : orderly arrangement, pattern (XXV 195).

dispŭtatio, -onis (f) : argument, debate; logical argument (XXXVI 25 Note). See **subtilis**.

dispŭto (1) : weigh, examine, discuss, argue (with acc. of neut. pron. or *de* + abl.) XI (16).

dissĕro, -ĕre, -ui, -ertum : (lit.) arrange in order; argue, discuss; speak about, treat a subject (*de* + abl. or acc.) (II 2); *disserendi ratio*, the art of rational discussion, logic (XXXVI 22).

distinctio, -onis (f) : difference (in appearance and motion of sun, moon, stars) (XXX 24); arrangement in groups.

distinctus, -a, -um : separate, distinct; set off, adorned (with stars).

diurnus, -a, -um : of the day, daily.

diuturnitas, -atis (f) : long duration, passage of time; permanence.

diuturnus, -a, -um : prolonged, lasting, permanent.

dīvīnatio, -onis (f) : faculty or practice of foretelling the future (XXVI introductory Note).

dīvīno (1) : to foretell, prophecy; conjecture (XIV 48).

dīvīnus, -a, -um : belonging to a god, divine; (of the soul) god-like inspired, prophetic (XXVIII 6); of virtue (VIII 23); (of a poet) inspired (XXVII 18); *res divinae*, religion.

doctrīna, -ae (f); instruction, learning; knowledge, science; study (X 17); education (IX 29); (with *humanitas*), culture and civilisation (V 89).

doctus, -a, -um : learned, experienced, educated (=litteratus).

dominatus, -us (*m*) : rule, dominion, *e.g.* over the earth (XXXIV 80); despotism, tyranny.

dominatio, -onis (*f*) : as above.

domitus, -us (*m*) taming, subduing (XXXIV 62).

effigies, -ei (*f*) : image, imitation, likeness; true likeness; ideal e.g. *virtutis* (XXXVII 21 Note).

eluvio, -onis (*f*) : inundation, flood (XXV 184).

epigramma, -atis (*n*) : inscription (V 82).

eventus, -us (*m*) : event; result (XXVII 32).

exitus, -us (*n*) : way out; end, result.

explanator, -oris (*m*) : interpreter (XXI 8).

expleo, -ere, -evi, -etum : fill; complete; *expletus*, perfect.

explico, -are, -ui, -itum : unfold; explain; set forth an argument; *se explicare*, disentangle oneself (XII 20).

expressus, -a, -um : clear, distinct, sharp (of a drawing, picture, etc.) (XXXVII 23).

exstructio, -onis (*f*) : erection.

extenuatus, -a, -um : rarified (of the atmosphere) (XXXII 27).

exustio, -onis (*f*) : burning up, conflagration (XXV 184).

facilitas, -atis (*f*) : ease; affability; lenience (VII 40).

fas (*noun indecl.*) (*n*) : (with *est*), it is right, lawful; permissible; possible (XXI 5).

fatalis, -e : decreed by destiny, fated (XXV 46).

fatum, -i (*n*) : (often pl. *fata*) fate, destiny; personal destiny (XXV 43); (in philosophical sense) the fixed and unchangeable law of nature, the unbroken chain of cause and effect (XXVI 17 Note); inescapable necessity; (in a bad sense) ruin.

felicitas, -atis (*f*) : happiness, good fortune; happy chance (IV 20).

fetialis, -e : belonging to the fetials (XIX 22 and 24 Notes).

fides, -ei (*f*) : 1. faith, confidence, belief (in a person or thing).
   2. that which creates confidence, trustworthiness, faithfulness (VII 31); *aequitate et fide* (to defend allies) in accordance with law and honour (XVI 7).
   3. assurance, promise, word.
   4. promise of protection; *ad imperatorum fidem confugere*, appeal for protection of a victorious general, surrender unconditionally (XIX 18); *in fidem recipere*, accept the surrender of an enemy, assume obligation to protect him (XIX 21).

figura, -ae (*f*) : figure, shape; design (of human body) (XXXV 13); (pl.) constellations (XXXII 57).

flamma, -ae (*f*) : flame, fire; star.

forensis, -e : of the forum; public; (of oratory) legal or political.

forma, -ae (*f*) : shape, form, appearance; outward appearance of a man; opp. *mores*, character (XII 27); opp. *mens*, intellect (XXV 222); beauty (V 52); *igneae formae*, fiery bodies, stars (XXXII 36).

fortitudo, -inis (*f*) : courage, bravery in facing pain, hardship, or danger (VI 11); one of the four 'cardinal' virtues.

fortuitus, -a, -um : accidental, due to chance (XXX 26).

fortūna, -ae (*f*) : fortune (good or bad); chance, accident (XXXV 14); *potestas et fortuna*, fortunate opportunity (XVIII 25); circumstances; (pl.) property.

fulgor, -oris (*m*) : brightness, splendour; bright star.

furor, -oris (*m*) : madness; ecstatic state, inspiration of a seer; *furoris divinationem*, prophecy through inspiration. (XXVI 40.)

fusus, -a, -um : spread out; (of air) diffused (XXXII 27); *fusa latius oratio*, the more diffuse or unrestricted style of prose (XXXVI 26).

genus, -eris (*n*) : birth; tribe; kind, class; *in hoc genere*, in regard to this class of subject, in this matter.

globus, -i (*m*) : 1. a solid ball or globe, the earth (XXV 77).
2. a hollow sphere, one of the concentric spheres about the earth (XXV 103 Note); (adj.) *globosus*, spherical (XXXII 2).

gloria, -ae (*f*) : fame, renown; of the victor's crown (II 11); *popularis gloria*, popularity, false fame (XXXVII 17); true fame, the praise of good men (XXXVII 23).

grātia, -ae (*f*) : favour; influence (IX 21); gratitude, thanks.

grăvitas, -atis (*f*) : weight (lit.); severity; dignity, seriousness (XIII 8), solidity of character (VII 31 Note).

gymnasium, -ii (*n*) : among the Greeks, a school of physical training; also used by philosophers for their lectures, school of higher education (XI 2). (Hence German 'Gymnasium', Grammar School.)

haruspex, -icis (*m*) : Etruscan diviner (XXVI 35 Note).

honestas, -atis (*f*) : honour, reputation; honesty, integrity, high character; virtue; *vera illa honestas*, the ideal of true virtue (XXXVII 18).

honestus, -a, -um : honourable, respectable; *res honestae*, worthy pursuits (III 40 Note); *mors honesta*, a brave man's death (VII 44); *honesto loco natus*, of distinguished birth (V 12); virtuous, morally good (VIII 3 Note); *honestum* (noun), morality, virtue.

humănitas, -atis (*f*) : human nature; humane conduct, kindness, politeness; education, culture, civilisation (V 88 Note).

ignis, -is (*m*) : (pl.) stars (XXV 79).

ignōmĭnia, -ae (*f*) : loss of good name, dishonour, resulting from civil or military misconduct, or from a censor's stigma.

illīberalis, -e : unworthy of a freeman, ungenerous; (of things) mean, sordid (X 4).

illīteratus, -a, -um : uneducated (XII 9).

imāgo, -ĭnis (*f*) : image, portrait; dream, ghost; sketch, outline (XXXVII 21 Note); echo (XXXVII 24 Note); *imagines maiorum*, busts of ancestors; *imagines mortuorum*, apparitions of the dead (XXVIII 8).

imbŭo, -ĕre, -ŭi, -ūtum : wet, dye, steep in; *variis erroribus imbui*, to be infected with every kind of error (XXXVII 7); impress early, e.g. *parentium praeceptis* (abl.), with parental training (IV 16).

immortalitas, -atis (*f*) : immortality:
    1. of the soul (XXXV 9 Note); proof of (XXV 230 ff. Note); not necessary to the *vita beata* (XXXV 9).
    2. of fame (VII 26).

impĕrium, -ii (*n*) : supreme power; the right to command an army; sovereignty of the Roman state; sphere of rule, empire; *bella de imperio* (XVI 2 Note); contrasted with **patrocinium** (XVI 8 Note).

impĭus, -a, -um : wicked; unpatriotic; (of things) *causa impia* (XVI 17); (of persons) *impii*, disloyal citizens (XVIII 22).

indāgo, (1) : hunt, track, trace, search (for); (adj.) *indagatrix* (f.) (XXXVIII 1).

infīnītus, -a, -um : boundless, endless; *infinita pecuniae cupiditas*, limitless greed of wealth (XV 8); *infinita vetustas*, endless time (XXX 33).

informo (1) : form, shape; conceive (an idea) (XXX 5 Note).

ingĕnero (1) : implant; produce (III 17).

ingĕnium, -ii (*n*) : inborn quality, disposition, nature (XXXVII 1); character; talent, genius; (pl.) men of genius.

ingĕnuus, -a, -um : native; free-born; noble, upright; worthy of a free man = *liberalis* (I 9 Note).

innātus, -a, -um : inborn, innate, natural (XXXVII 1).

institutum, -i (*n*) (*usually pl.*) : arrangement; customs, usages; manner of life, principles; *institutis et artibus exornare*, introduce to the usages and principles of political life (II 28); *instituta populorum* (XX introductory Note).

intĕger, -ra, -rum : untouched; sound; pure; (of a question) undecided, open; *iudicium liberum ac integrum relinquere*, leave the decision unprejudiced (XXIX 20).

interiectus, -ūs (*m*) :   ⎫
interpŏsitus, -ūs (*m*) ;   ⎬ interposition (of the earth between sun and moon, causing an eclipse of the moon) (XXXII 50). ⎭

inventa, -orum (*n pl*) : views, tenets in philosophy (IX 4).

iūs, iūris (*n*) : right, justice, duty; law; *ius civile*, civil law, concerned with relations between citizens (VII 40 Note); *ius augurium, ponti-*

ficum (XXII 16 Note); *ius gentium*, international law (XIX introductory Note); *iuris consultus*, an expert in the interpretation of law (VII 38 Note); *unum ius*, universal law (XX introductory Note).

iūstĭtĭa, -ae (*f*) : justice; the obligation to give every man his due; (in a social sense) respect for the rights and property of others (VII 38 Note); observance of international law (XIX 20); *iustitiam colere et pietatem*, observe righteousness, and duty towards gods and men, *i.e.* the whole duty of man (XXV 86 and XXI, introductory Note); one of the four 'cardinal' virtues.

iūstus, -a, -um : just (of persons and things); *bellum iustum*, a just, regular war (XIX 24 Note); *honor iustus*, due, fitting honour (VII 10).

lābēs, -is (*f*) : 1. fall, landslide; ruin (verb, *lābor*, to fall) (XXX 13).

2. spot, stain; disgrace, dishonour (XXXVI 3).

lĕpōs, -ōris (*m*) : charm; (of speech) wit (XIII 8).

lĕvis, -e : light; unimportant; light-minded, inconstant, unreliable (XII 9).

lex, lēgis (*f*) : law, legal enactment; (pl.) the written laws of particular states (XX 2); condition (XXV 76); *vera lex*, the unwritten law of right and wrong, recognised by all men, the law of nature (XXI 1); see also introductory Notes to XX and XXI.

lĭberalis, -e : belonging to, worthy of a free man; courteous, noble, kind, generous; *artes liberales*, culture, education (I 9 Note).

lĭberalitas, -atis (*f*) : nobility of mind, generosity.

lĭbertas, -atis (*f*) : freedom, liberty; as a political ideal (XVIII introductory Note); as a human right, *ad decus et libertatem nati sumus*, honour and freedom are the birth-right of man (XVIII 18).

lĭcentia, -ae (*f*) : freedom to do as one likes; licence; lawlessness; unrestrained power (XVI 26).

lis lītis (*f*) : law-suit; dispute.

littĕrae, -arum (*f*) : literature; *litteris Graecis uti*, to have a knowledge of Greek literature (XXII 17); learning, education, culture (XII 11).

littĕratus, -a, -um : educated, learned.

lŏcus, -i (*m*) : place; position, rank; opportunity; room for (dat.) (XXXIX 9); subject of discussion; (pl. *loci*) passages in a book.

lubrĭcus, -a, -um : slippery; dangerous; mobile (of the eyes) (XXXIV 20).

lucrum, -i (*n*) : gain, advantage, profit.

lustro (1) : move round or over; traverse; illuminate (of the sun) (XXV 115); review (an army) (XXVII 36).

māchīnātio, -onis (*f*) : contrivance, device; *machinatio atque sollertia*, skill in contrivance (XXXIII 28).

magister, -ri (*m*) : master, chief, leader; *magister populi*, early title of the dictator (VIII 7 Note); *magister et imperator*, general and supreme commander, *e.g.* of God (XXI 12 Note); teacher, instructor; *quasi maximus magister populus*, the people, like some great professor (XXXVII 12); *magister . . . trium vitiorum*, master of three vices (VIII 7 Note).

magnitūdo, -ĭnis (*f*) : size, greatness; *magnitudo animi*, greatness of soul, courage in undertaking great and dangerous enterprises (VI 11).

medicīna, -ae (*f*) : art of healing, medicine; remedy, relief; *animi medicina*, medicine for the mind *i.e.* philosophy (XXXVII 41).

mediōcritas, -ātis (*f*) : moderation; middle state; mean between two extremes (IX 36 Note).

mendax, -ācis (*noun and adj.*) : lying, false.

mendīcus (*noun and adj.*) : beggar; needy, destitute.

mens, mentis (*f*) : (in man) mind, intellect, reason (V 91); (of God) *mens divina*, creative Mind (XXXI 16); *mens mundi*, the divine Reason, immanent in the universe (XXV 114 Note); *mentes divinae*, divine intelligences, the stars, which share in the 'world mind'. (XXV 80 Note).

mŏderatio, -onis (*f*) : guidance, control (XXXIV 76).

moderator, -oris (*m*) : ruler; of the sun as ruler of the heavens (XXV 114).

mŏdus, -i (*m*) : way, manner; (of life) *vitae* (V 90); limit; moderation, (of speech) *in dicendo* (XIII 8).

mōmentum, -i (*m*) : (lit.) movement; weight; amount which turns the scales; short time; influence, importance (IX 21).

mōs, mōris (*m*) : custom, usage; (with *consuetudo*) way of life (of parents) (IV 17); (plur.) character (XIV 24); morals, ethics (II 36).

multitūdo, -ĭnis (*f*) : great number; multitude, crowd; (contemptuous) the masses (XXXVII 13).

mundus, -i (*m*) : the universe, especially the heavens (XXV 114); world; humanity; the universe as the common home of gods and men (XXXV 20).

mūniceps, -cipis (*m*) : citizen of a *municipium*, a self-governing town, especially in Italy.

musĭcă, -orum (*n pl*) : music.

nātīvus, -a, -um : derived from birth; natural, native (opp. artificial); *nativa praesidia*, natural defences (XIV 53); *nativae testae*, native shells (XXXII 24).

nātūra, -ae (*f*) : 1. nature; natural constitution, essential nature (XXV 248 Note).

2. human nature: *bonitas naturae*, natural goodness (IV 20); see also XXXVII 2 Note.

3. the universe itself (XXV 244); *rerum natura*, the nature of things, the universe (II 20); *cognitio naturae*, investigation of the natural world, physical science (XXIX 15); *secundum naturam*, according to nature, the natural order of things (XXIII 24); see Introduction II 7 (iv).

4. personified, more or less, as an active, living power: *natura fert ut* . . ., nature ordains that . . . (XXV 129); *est a natura tributum*, it has been granted by Nature (III 1).

5. as the bond of society: *natura hominem conciliat homini*, nature unites men with each other (III 16).

6. as the source of law: *est vera lex recta ratio naturae congruens*, the true law is right reason in conformity with nature, natural law (XXI 1); see also XX and XXI introductory Notes.

7. of the gods: *de natura deorum*, on the being of the gods (XXIX 5); *praestans aliqua aeternaque natura*, supreme and immortal being, God (XXIX 10); *naturae ratio intellegentis*, the design of a rational being, God (XXXIII 2); *naturae providentia*, divine foresight (as a benevolent power) (XXXIV 1).

8. element, substance: *una ex duabus naturis conflata*, fused together out of two elements (land and sea) into one (XXXII 25).

9. nature opp. to training: *non a natura, verum a magistro*, not from natural inclination, but from his teacher (IX 3).

nāturalis, -e : natural, according to nature: *circuitus naturalis*, appointed course (XXV 46).

necessitas, -atis (*f*) : necessity, rigid succession of cause and effect, fate, destiny (XXXI 15).

nŏta, -ae (*f*) : sign, mark, trace (XIV 21): *veritatis notae*, marks of the truth (XXVIII 19); censure.

nōtio, -onis (*f*) : idea, conception; *notiones deorum*, the idea of 'gods' (XXX 5).

nŏto (1) : mark, record, indicate; *animo notare*, observe (XIV 54).

nūmen, -inis (*n*) : (lit.) nod; divine power or will of the gods; a deity, a god.

nŭmerus, -i (*m*) : number; (pl.) mathematics, astronomy (II 31); harmony, rhythm, metre.

nūtus, -us (*m*) : nod; beck and call (V 52); downward pull, gravity (XXV 122); (pl.) see XXXII 2 Note.

obĭtus, -ūs (*m*) : setting (of sun).

occĭdens, -entis (*m*) : the setting sun, the west (XXXII 38 Note).

ŏpifex, -icis (*m*) : workman, labourer (X 9).

ōratio, -onis (*f*) : faculty of speech (III 17); language; style; oration; *perpetua oratio*, continuous speech of oratorical prose (XXXVI 26).

orbis, -is (*m*) : circle; rotation; orbit; *lacteus orbis*, the Milky Way (XXV 92 Note); *orbis terrarum*, the world.

orbus, -a, -um : deprived, destitute (of); *orbus ac debilitatus*, deserted and weakened (VII 9).

ordo, -inis (*m*) : arrangement, regular order, orderly succession (of events); of heavenly bodies (XXIX 13).

ŏriens, -ientis (*m*) : the rising sun; the East (XXXII 38 Note).

pārio, -ĕre, pĕpĕri, partum : (lit.) give birth to; produce, create; bring about, accomplish; *urbes parere*, found cities (XXXVIII 3); *cognomen parere*, win a title (XXV 33). *N.B.* Do not confuse with *părāre* (prepare), and *pārēre* (obey).

parricīdium, -ii (*n*) : murder of parent, relative, or fellow-citizen; treason (against one's own country, the common parent).

patrōcinium, -ii (*n*) : patronage, relation of patron to client (dependent); the obligation of a patron (*fides*) to protect his client, whether individual or province; the Roman power as a world protectorate in contrast with **imperium** (XVI 8 Note).

patrōnus, -i (*m*) : guardian or legal protector (XIX 21 Note).

peccatum, -i (*n*) : fault, offence, sin, *e.g.* violence towards parents, treason, temple-robbery, excessive fear, grief, passion, etc.; *omnia peccata sunt paria*, all sins are equal (IX 13) (the third Stoic Paradox; see Introduction II 7 iv).

perennis, -e : lasting, continual; everlasting; of *sermo*, talk, rumour (XXV 214); of *amnis*, river (XIV 43).

perpetuus, -a, -um : continuous, unbroken; constant, lasting; see **oratio**.

persōna, -ae (*f*) : actor's mask; character in a play; character of Stoic Wise Man (VIII 2); type of person.

philosŏphia, -ae (*f*) : philosophy; the love of wisdom; the knowledge of all things human and divine, and of the causes from which they spring (XXXIX 35); the medicine of the soul (XXXVII 41); the guide of life (XXXVIII 1); the creator of civilisation and builder of cities (XXXVIII 3-4).

philosŏphus, -i (*m*) : philosopher; a student of wisdom (*sapientiae studiosus* II 21).

piĕtas, -atis (*f*) : sense of duty, dutiful conduct towards
 1. the gods; religion (XXXV 7).
 2. parents, children, relatives; affection (XXV 86).
 3. native land; patriotism (XXV 87 Note).
 Adj. *pius*, with corresponding meanings.

pŏpularis, -e : (adj.) popular, vulgar; counterfeit; *popularis gloria, fama*, false fame; contrasted with true fame (XXXVII 17, 22 and Notes); (noun) citizen; *e.g. alicuius definiti loci*, of one fixed place (XXXVI 15).

pŏtentia, -ae (*f*) : might, power; political power (XIV 51).

pŏtestas, -atis (*f*) : power; official power; (with *fortuna*) power of doing something, opportunity (XVIII 25–26).

praeceptum, -i (*n*) : advice; command; rule; (pl.) teaching; *e.g.* of parents (IV 17); of Zeno (IX 6).

princeps, -ĭpis (*m*) : (noun) leader, ruler, head, chief; *principes orbis terrarum*, leaders of the world, the Senate (XVIII 15); *principes*, the most eminent men of the senatorial party (XV 5 Note). (adj.) = *primus*, first, chief, supreme; *princeps ille deus*, the supreme God (XXV 58).

principatus, -ūs (*m*) : pre-eminence; dominion = **dominatus**, tyranny (XV 16).

principium, -ii (*n*) : beginning; first cause of things; *principii nulla est origo*, the beginning cannot have a 'beginning' (XXV 236); *principio*, in the first place, first of all (III 1).

prŏpāgo, (1) : propagate a plant by slip; enlarge; extend; of religion (XXIX 14).

prŏpitius, -a, -um : favourable, well-disposed (of the gods).

prŏprius, -a, -um : peculiar to, proper to (genit.) (III 25); (noun) *proprium*, essential property of, characteristic.

prōvidentia, -ae (*f*) : foresight; human (XIV 9); of nature (XXXIV 1).

prudentia, -ae (*f*) : good sense, intelligence, judgement; the power to distinguish good from evil; practical wisdom (VII 32, XXXIX 37 Note).

pulcher, -ra, -rum : beautiful; (in a moral sense) fine, noble, excellent (IV 19).

pulchritudo, -inis (*f*) : beauty, excellence; of **honestas** (XXXVII 30).

quaestio, -onis (*f*) : question; enquiry; investigation; examination; *quaestionem adhibere*, to interrogate an accused person (XXVII 23).

quaestor, -oris (*m*) : quaestor, official of the treasury.

quaestus, -ūs (*m*) : gain, profit; business (X 1).

rădius, -ii (*m*) : pointer; measuring rod; beam of light.

rătio, -onis (*f*) : reckoning, account; way, manner, method; principle, system, rule; reason, power of reasoning (III introductory Note); *ratio et mens divina*, the divine reason, designer of the universe (XXXI 16); *ratio disserendi*, logical argument (XXXVI 22 Note); *N.B. ratio* with the genit. of the gerund often thus serves for an abstract noun; *recta ratio*, see XX, XXI introductory Notes; *rationem habere* (genit.), have regard to . . .

rătus, -a, -um : fixed, established; *pro rata parte*, in proportion (XXV 126).

rector, -oris (*m*) : governor, controller (XXV 60 Note).

rectus, -a, -um : straight, upright; right, honest, virtuous, good; *recta via vitae*, the true way of life, the good life (IV 21); *recta ratio*, see **ratio**.

religio, -onis (*f*) : 1. reverence for the gods; religion; system of worship; piety; (distinguished from superstition XXIX 9).
    2. religious scruple; awe of the divine; *religioni habere*, to treat as a matter of religion or conscience (XXVII 39).
    3. religious obligation; *testimoniorum religio et fides*, moral obligation of a witness (XII 14).
    4. holiness, inviolability of a religious object, *e.g.* a temple.
    5. (plur.) religious matters, religious worship (XX 24).

religiosus, -a, -um : pious, scrupulous; (of things) sacred; *affirmatio religiosa*, a declaration morally binding, an oath (VI 29).

remissio, -onis (*f*) : relaxation.

res rei (*f*) : thing; affair; event; circumstance; fact; reality; (plur.) business affairs, interests; *res publica*, the public interest, the state, etc. (see XXXIX 18 Note); *res divinae*, religion; *res repetĕre*, to demand restitution (XIX 24).

reversio, -onis (*f*) : a turning back; return course of the sun between its extreme points of rising and setting (XXXII 40; see Note on 38).

saeculum, -i (*n*) : lifetime; generation (33 years) (XXV 197); century; age (without limit).

sagacitas, -atis : keenness of perception (XXXIV 66).

sanctus, -a, -um : inviolable (of things or persons dedicated to a god); venerable, sacred, holy; (of the dead) *Pater sanctissime*, O most blessed Father (XXV 71).

sapientia, -ae (*f*) : 1. = **prudentia**, practical wisdom.
    2. wisdom, knowledge for its own sake; (one of the four 'cardinal' virtues, XXXV 8); *studium sapientiae*, philosophy, the highest intellectual virtue; see **philosophia**.

schŏla, -ae (*f*) : (Gk.σχολή) leisure for learning; place of learning, school; philosophical school or system.

scientia, -ae (*f*) : knowledge; skill; science.

secta, -ae (*f*) : party; school of thought.

semen, -inis (*n*) : seed; element; (plur.) elements; *semina innata virtutum*, inborn germs of virtue (XXXVII 1); see **causa**.

sempiternus, -a, -um : everlasting, lasting as long as time (less emphatic than **aeternus**).

sensus, -ūs (*m*) : power of perceiving, sense, feeling, sensation; *sensus audiendi*, the sense of hearing (XXV 145); physical perception, as opposed to reason (III 9).

sermo, -onis (*m*) : talk; rumour; idle talk (XXV 208).

sidus, -ĕris (*n*) : group of stars, constellation; star.

signum, -i (*n*) : 1. sign; token; 2. military standard; 3. statue; 4. constellation, star.

similitudo, -inis (*f*) : likeness; comparison; analogy (III 13 Note).

situs, -ūs (*m*) : situation, site; *situs membrorum*, arrangement of the human body (XXXV 13).

situs, -a, -um : situated; *situs esse in* (abl.), to rest on, depend on.

sŏciĕtas, -atis (*f*) : human society, union of persons bound by a common law (XX 9); *societas vitae*, community of life (III 17); *societas et contagio corporis*, defiling association (of soul) with the body (XXVIII 1-2); political alliance.

sōlarium, -ii (*n*) : sun-dial (XXXI 4 Note).

solidus, -a, -um : massive, compact; of the earth (XXXII 2); substantial, real, true; of *gloria*, (XXXVII 22 Note).

sollertia, -ae (*f*) : skill, cleverness, cunning.

sŏlum, -i (*n*) : earth, ground.

somnium, -ii (*n*) : dream.

somnus, -i (*m*) : sleep.

spătium, -ii (*n*) : room, extent; space; distance; interval; open space; space of time; course, track (of stars) (XXXII 45 Note); (plur.) walk, promenade (XI 9).

spĕciĕs, -ei (*f*) : look; appearance; sight; view (of the sea) (XXXII 20); mere appearance, opposed to reality; *utilitatis species*, a false appearance of expediency (VI 6).

sphaera, -ae (*f*) : (= Gk.σφαῖρα, Lat. *globus*); ball, sphere, globe; a device for showing the motions of the stars, planetarium (XXXI 9).

spiritus, -ūs (*m*) : air; breath; breath of life; *extremus spiritus*, the last breath (VII 17).

stătus, -ūs (*m*) : state, condition; position; condition of public affairs (XXXIX 13); form of constitution, government.

stŭdium, -ii (*n*) : eagerness, enthusiasm, desire; study; (plur.) learning, research, scientific and literary pursuits (I 9 Note).

subiectus, -a, -um : lying under, near; adjacent to; *subiectus Aquiloni*, close to the North (lit. North wind); *luna soli subiecta*, the moon in conjunction with the sun (XXXII 48 Note).

subtīlis, -e : precise, accurate; keen, subtle; *illa subtilis disputatio*, exactness of language, logical argument (XXXVI 25).

summa, -ae (*f*) : sum, total; main point of an argument (XXX 1).

superstitio, -onis (*f*) : superstition, excessive or irrational fear of the gods, opp. **religio** (XXIX 2 and 7 Notes).

temĕritas, -atis (*f*) : rashness, want of consideration, foolhardiness (XV 14).

temperantia, -ae (*f*) : due regulation of impulses, self-control; abstinence from pleasure; sobriety; one of the four 'cardinal' virtues (XXXV 8 Note).

temperatio, -onis (*f*) : due proportion, proper regulation; **of the** climate (*caeli*) (XXX 8–9); principle of order.

templum, -i (*n*) : sacred enclosure, temple; area of the sky mapped out for the purpose of augury; heavens (XXV 74).

tempus, -ŏris (*n*) : time; opportunity; circumstances; (plur.) dangerous times, emergency.

trāiectio, -onis (*f*) : passage, transit (of a star).

tyrannicus, -a, -um : tyrannical; *leges tyrannicae*, tyrannous laws (XX 5).

universitas, -atis (*f*) : the whole; *universitas rerum*, the universe.

ūsus, -ūs (*m*) : use; experience (XIII 6); need; *usu venit*, it happens, befalls.

utilitas, -atis (*f*) : usefulness; advantage, gain; useful purpose (X 17); expediency (XX 17).

văgus, -a, -um : wandering (stars), *i.e.* planets.

vānitas, -atis (*f*) : emptiness; deception, falsehood; **opp. veritas** (XXXVII 8).

vēritas, -atis (*f*) : truth; the real, reality (see above).

versor (1 *dep.*) : turn about (intr.); be in; be engaged, involved in; be occupied with; be in the midst of; *in summa inanitate versari*, be completely frustrated (XXXVII 20).

vertex, -icis (*m*) : pole (of heavens) (XXV 164).

vetustas, -atis (*f*) : long existence, long duration; ancient times; *immensa et infinita vetustas*, the vast and limitless ages of the past (XXX 33); posterity, remote future; *vetustati condere*, to store up for future use (XXXIV 60).

vicissitudo, -inis (*f*) : change, change of fortune, alternation; often plur: *in tantis motionibus tantisque vicissitudinibus*, amid all these motions (of the heavens) and their complicated alternations (XXX 30–31).

victus, -ūs (*m*) : means of living, food; way of life; *victus cultusque*, civilised life (XIV 46).

virtūs, -ūtis (*f*) : 1. the quality that makes a man (*vir*); manliness, courage, fortitude; strength; capacity.

2. virtue, moral excellence, right living; the perfection of human nature; the *summum bonum* of the Stoics, a disposition of the soul possessed only by the wise; *virtutes*, particular virtues, esp. the four 'cardinal' virtues: *sapientia, fortitudo, temperantia, iustitia* (XXXV 8 Note).

3. according to Aristotle, the 'mean' between two extremes, *mediocritas* (IX 36 Note).

vis, vim, vi (*f*) : force; violence; power; *eloquendi vis*, power of speech, oratory (XXXIV 29–30); meaning, essence, essential nature; *vis naturae*, true meaning of the nature of things (XXXVII 15); quantity, abundance; *infinita vi smarmoris*, inexhaustible supplies of marble (XXXII 10); *vis lacrimarum*, flood of tears (XXV 68); capacity of remaining true to species (XXXIII 11); (plur.) *vires*, strength (XXXIII 27).

vitium, -ii (*n*) : fault, defect; *duo vitia vitanda sunt*, two errors are to be avoided (III 33 Note); moral fault; crime, vice.

voluntas, -atis (*f*) : will, purpose; *non tam voluntate quam cursus errore falluntur*, they err not so much by intention as by a mistaken choice of policy (XXXVII 34); will to do good (XX 20); good-will.

voluptas, -atis (*f*) : pleasure (esp. sensual) (XXXVI 2).